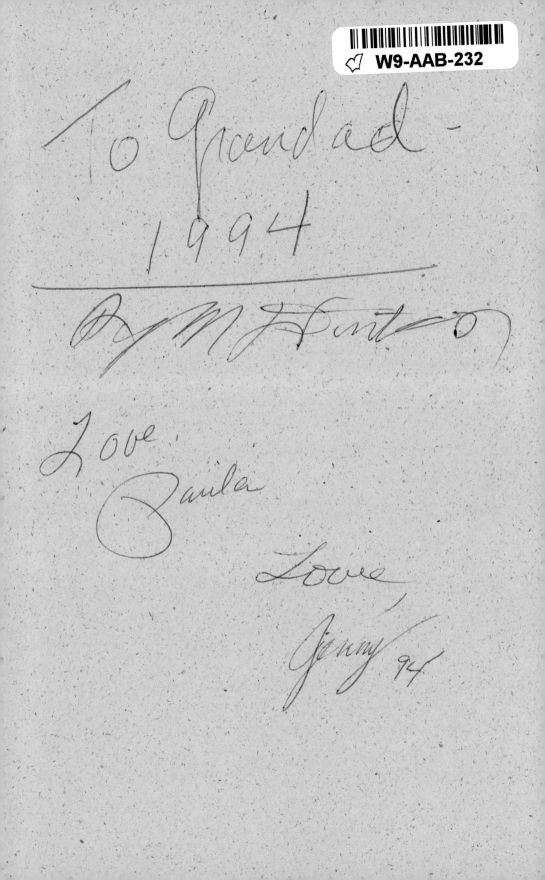

To Grandad -
1994

Love
Paula

Love

Jenny 94

Bury Me
in a
Pot Bunker

Bury Me
in a
Pot Bunker

Golf through the Eyes of
the Game's Most Challenging
Course Designer

Pete Dye
with Mark Shaw

Addison-Wesley Publishing Company

Reading, Massachusetts   Menlo Park, California   New York
Don Mills, Ontario   Wokingham, England   Amsterdam   Bonn
Sydney   Singapore   Tokyo   Madrid   San Juan
Paris   Seoul   Milan   Mexico City   Taipei

Library of Congress Cataloging-in-Publication Data

Dye, Pete.
  Bury me in a pot bunker : golf through the eyes of the game's most challenging course designer / Pete Dye with Mark Shaw ; foreword by Greg Norman.
     p.   cm.
   ISBN 0-201-40769-8
   1. Dye, Pete.   2. Golf course architects—United States—
Biography.   I. Shaw, Mark, 1945–   .   II. Title.
GV964.D94A3   1995
796.352′06′8092—dc20
[B]   94–18252
                                                                                            CIP

Jacket design by Jean Seal
Jacket photograph by Ken May
Text design by Deborah Clark
Set in 11-point New Caledonia by Weimer Graphics, Inc.

1 2 3 4 5 6 7 8 9 10-MA-9897969594
First printing, September 1994

Contents

Foreword

by
Greg Norman

Reading *Bury Me in a Pot Bunker* will change forever the way you look at the game of golf. That's because Pete Dye has an incredibly unique relationship with the game I love, and his words will inspire you to have a better understanding of how golf should be played.

And who should know better than Pete, whose ability to mold innovative courses out of nondescript land is legendary? Fortunately he has now chronicled his more than thirty years of building championship golf courses, providing great insight into the man golfers love to hate.

I have known Pete Dye for more than seven years, but it was during our collaboration on the design and construction of my new course at the Medalist Club in Hobe Sound, Florida, in 1994, that I realized more than ever that he is a true genius.

Little wonder then that a number of the most highly acclaimed courses built in the last quarter century or so bear the stamp of Pete Dye.

I know because I've had the opportunity to play many of the

courses Pete discusses in this book, including Crooked Stick, Oak Tree, the Stadium Courses at the TPC and PGA West, Old Marsh, The Golf Club, Brickyard Crossing, the Mountain Course at La Quinta, and Harbour Town Golf Links.

Pete provides a behind-the-scenes view of the design and construction of these courses, but his account of the evolution of Harbour Town is especially fascinating for me since it was the first Pete Dye course I ever played. Even though it is more than twenty-five years old, it's a beautiful course that tests the skills of the professionals who compete in the Heritage Classic as much today as it did in 1969 when Arnold Palmer was the winner. And, I mean, it tests *all* your skills.

While Harbour Town is demanding for the professionals, you'll learn as I have why Pete's courses are playable for every level of golfer.

With the technology so far advanced these days in the area of golf balls and equipment, it's increasingly more difficult to present a strong but fair challenge. Pete tells you how he does this by requiring golfers to not only execute demanding shots but also to think their way around his bedeviling courses.

As you read about this man who takes imagination and turns it into reality, you'll find that Pete's designs don't let players lackadaisically hit to point A and then to point B. Instead, golfers must carefully position shots so that they can manipulate the ball onto Pete's well-defended greens.

I first respected Pete from the viewpoint of a professional golfer and have now developed a great admiration for him as a fellow architect. This book further enlightened me about design principles that will surely influence the courses I build in the future.

The amazing thing you will discover about Pete Dye is that he does not work from any plans. It's noteworthy that many legendary architects never used plans, but they had an uncommon feel for the lay of the land and what was required for a well-balanced, strategic golf course.

Pete will tell you that he has a rough conceptual idea for the layout of a course in his head and that's it. From that point on, it's like he's painting a masterpiece without having any directions to follow! He sketched the original routing for the Stadium Course at TPC on the back of a placemat, and it wasn't much different when we started the Medalist Club.

One of Pete's design concepts he discusses in this book that I admire most is the way he gives golfers a wonderful sight line. Players know exactly what's ahead of them and where the trouble is. I've seen that feature at every one of the courses he has designed and it's even more dramatically evident at the Stadium Course at TPC, where I was fortunate to win the 1994 Tournament Players Championship.

Despite his vast experience and success, Pete Dye gives ample credit to those who have influenced as well as collaborated with him on his creations. He points out how he welcomes input, and I have seen firsthand how that works. Contrary to what many might think, Pete *will* listen. Like him, I'm a traditionalist when it comes to golf course design, and so Pete welcomed my ideas at the Medalist Club.

A good example of his open-mindedness occurred on the 290-yard, par-four fourteenth hole. Like Pete, I intend to have intriguing short par-fours on my courses. To catch those golfers who lay up, I positioned a sand bunker thirty yards short of the green.

When I came back the next day, Pete had changed the location for the bunker. We discussed it and ended up placing the bunker in the same general area, but altering the style and design to make it more formidable.

In my opinion, Pete Dye is one of the true visionaries of our time. During the award ceremonies at the Brickyard Crossing Invitational in Indianapolis in the spring of 1994, I called him a great ambassador for the game of golf. His dedication to make the game a better one is unparalleled, and Pete and his wife, Alice, also a talented designer, will stand alongside the great designers in the history of the profession.

Bury Me in a Pot Bunker, which reads as if you are having a conversation with the man himself, is a very exciting book that will offer you vivid insight into Pete and his course design magic. I'm proud that he asked me to write the foreword, and very honored to call him my friend.

Greg Norman

Introduction

by
Mark Shaw

In 1969, longtime friend Wayne Timberman invited me to play with Pete and Alice Dye at Crooked Stick Golf Club in Indianapolis.

A scratch player, Wayne set up the match ostensibly to introduce me to the up-and-coming golf course designers and really to see whether I was interested in membership in the club.

Any local sports fan unaware of the Dyes' success as golf competitors hadn't read a newspaper in years. Alice had won the Indiana State Amateur nine times, the North and South Amateur, the Eastern Amateur, and competed in several United States Women's Open Championships. Pete, an Indianapolis District and Indiana State Amateur Champion, had reached the third round of the British Amateur and qualified for five United States Amateur Championships.

Those impressive credentials didn't faze me a bit when I met Pete and Alice on the tee of the 458-yard tenth hole. I had been a member of a Big Ten Championship team at Purdue and was ready to take on anyone, anytime, anyplace.

Besides, what I saw that morning was the slightly built Pete dressed in khaki pants, a white "no-logo" golf shirt that had not seen an iron, black socks, unlaced work boots, and a dumpy pork-pie hat that seemed a size too small.

Standing next to him was Alice, who looked more like my kindly mother than the razor-edged, tenacious championship golfer I had heard about.

When the subject of wagering came up, I quickly accepted a twenty-five-cent bet with both Dyes. While my betting dead-even with a woman over forty seemed a bit unfair, who was I to take pity on the overmatched Alice?

Pete began the match by hitting one of his patented hooks that started across a large lake and somehow made it back into the dead center of the fairway. I was next. Full of confidence, I came off both feet and ripped my Spalding Dot 260 yards straight down the pike. I then tossed my Tony Penna driver to my be-spectacled young caddie and turned around to hear the first of many Pete Dye witticisms that has driven me to rib-cracking laughter over the years.

"Well," Pete calmly told Wayne as he began the "Pete Dye trot" toward the women's tee, "Shaw must not be able to chip and putt or I would have heard of him!"

My huge ego deflated, I headed for the women's tee, where for the first time I witnessed Alice's textbook-perfect, rhythmic swing. The result was a beautifully positioned drive that cata-pulted by mine on the fly!

Undaunted, I hit a crisp four-iron shot to within twenty-five feet of the pin. Satisfied, I watched Alice address the ball, waggle those gifted hands of hers, and then begin that sure-shot arc that had produced so many championships.

My recollection of what happened next is so clear I can still see the dimples on the ball as it flew away. Alice's fluid swing propelled the spherical object up, up, and away toward the green, where it hit ever so gently and then rolled, rolled, rolled until it abruptly disappeared into the hole for an eagle two!

The big-time college boy never won a hole from the "over-matched" Alice that sunny afternoon. Her feat, however, com-bined with Pete's whimsical "I would have heard of him" comment, served to initiate me into a twenty-five-year, fun-filled relationship that continues to this day.

That enduring friendship with Pete and Alice led to my being selected to collaborate with them on this book. Since many more experienced and talented writers than I have approached the Dyes, I am very flattered that they chose me.

Attempting to include in the following pages all that Pete and Alice want to say has been most difficult. They are both multi-dimensional characters whose larger-than-life experiences could fill ten volumes.

Alice Dye, who has a heart the size of a washtub, may be the most generous lady I have ever met. Despite a fierce competitive spirit and a tough edge that appears only when she becomes frustrated with unprofessionalism, she is a loyal person who can be counted on by people in need.

Throughout my research for this book, I have heard the words "wonderful," "the best," and "quite a lady" used to describe Alice. Even those competitors who have witnessed first-hand Alice's deadly golf game come away with more respect than sorrow.

Several times Pete has told me that the straight-shooting Alice is "the most honest woman on the face of the earth." Others have echoed that thought and related countless stories in which Alice has corrected a wrong that disturbed her deep-rooted sense of fair play.

In the early 1950s a first-time competitor entered the Indianapolis Women's City Amateur Championship at Hillcrest Country Club. A very pregnant Alice was not competing but headed the rules committee. She was advised that while the teenager had shot 76, she had inadvertently broken three of the two-stroke-penalty rules of golf on every hole.

Realizing the devastating impact a 108-stroke penalty might have on the future aspirations of this talented player, Alice balanced the inequities by assessing two strokes for each infraction, making a six-stroke penalty. That ruling was fair not only to the young golfer but also to the rest of the competitors, since it kept the player in the championship flight and not in a higher one, where she would have soundly defeated any opponent.

Over the years, that golfer has told this story countless times. She is LPGA Tour veteran Sandy Spuzich, who won the United States Women's Open Championship in 1966.

Alice Dye's alter ego is Pete, an unpretentious character whose down-home folksy ways are a fooler. With a twinkle in his eye, Pete Dye will charm you with his wit and storytelling, but he's a focused, intense visionary who is still twenty-five years ahead of his time.

Pete's protégés will tell you he's the most energetic man they have ever known. Alice says Pete could outwork the Energizer Bunny, and exhausted workers many years younger than Pete are amazed that he is always the first one on the job site and the last one to go home.

Pete Dye is a humble, give-the-credit-to-someone-else gentleman whose sense of humor and optimism are legendary. He's a creative artist and a wave-his-arms barker salesman rolled into one, and his imagination permits him to visualize a completed golf course when a normal person sees vast acres of nothing.

Pete is also the only person who accepts an invitation to dine with Robert Redford but has no idea who he is! Until recently, the last movie he had seen was *The Sound of Music,* and Pete would be shocked to learn that ten cents won't buy a postage stamp.

Pete Dye is available twenty-four hours a day, seven days a week except for Thursday nights, when "Matlock" is on television. Like his idol, Pete is a simple man who will choose Motel 6 over a fancy hotel room.

In 1993 Pete became world-famous through the "Do you know me?" American Express commercial. Shortly after the commercial aired, I had dinner with him and was amazed when he took out a crumpled, Scotch-taped, barely functional American Express card. "I've got to get a new one of these," he told me. I'm sure he never has.

In a sport filled with nice people, Pete and Alice Dye, who genuinely love the game of golf, are at the top of the list. History will record their contribution to playing the game, but their positive impact on countless members of golf's family outweighs that contribution many times over.

Collaborating with them on this book has been a once-in-a-lifetime experience, and my heartfelt thanks go to my highly respected literary agent, Richard Pine, without whose guidance this book would not have been possible. I also want to thank a special lady, Elizabeth Perle McKenna, and her colleagues at Addison-Wesley Publishing Company for their enthusiasm, friendship, and belief in this book.

I'm indebted as well to my lovely wife, Chris Roark Shaw, whom I dearly love, for her contribution not only to the book's physical preparation but also to its content. My talented associate Donna Stouder deserves thanks for taking what I write and always making it better.

I also appreciate the love and support of my band of teenagers, Kimberly, Kevin, Kent, and Kyle, who keep me young, and the affection of canine buddies Bach, Duffy, Snickers, White Sox, Peanut Butter, Shadow, and Reggie, whose companionship at five a.m. is most comforting.

Numerous other people, including respected golf writer Ron Whitten, great friends Wayne Timberman and Jack Leer, former PGA commissioner Deane Beman, Pete's sister and brother-in-law Ann and Tom Doss, and Jack Nicklaus, who took time to spend a never-to-be-forgotten lunch with Pete and me, deserve special thanks as well.

Above all, I thank Pete and Alice Dye for permitting me to share a lifetime of memories with them. The intent of this book is to shed light on where two of God's most special children came from, how they got started as course designers, and by what means they have designed and built many of the finest golf courses in the world. More than that, I'm hopeful it captures the never-give-up, zest-for-life spirit that is the true essence of Pete and Alice.

Mark Shaw

The Road to Pinehurst

The strategy of a golf course is the soul of the game.

George Thomas, Jr.
Golf Architecture in America
1927

My first official experience with golf course supervision involved one hundred disoriented Italian prisoners of war. Instead of jumping out of airplanes in combat during World War II as I'd hoped, I'd ended up at Fort Benning, Georgia, in 1945, trying to explain that a bunker wasn't something you dove into to avoid getting shot!

Since that unorthodox beginning, my wife Alice and I have personally designed and built more than seventy championship golf courses around the world. This still astonishes me, since I never intended to become a golf course designer.

When I'm asked how I got started in the profession and where my unusual and frequently controversial design ideas originate, I must admit that the journey has been an amazing one. It is only now, after thirty years of designing golf courses, that I can reflect on the significant people, places, and things that led me to where I am today.

Over the years, I have been blessed to experience the unique camaraderie of those special people who share my devotion to golf. Their heartfelt commitment to the game has reinforced mine and served as a constant reminder that my golf courses should perpetuate the integrity of the game.

In addition to my interaction with what I call the family of golf, I have experienced the joy of playing the greatest courses ever created. Exposure to the creative images of those legendary courses has influenced my own design ideas, for they require golf to be played in its purest form.

Since 1960 I have also witnessed whirlwind changes in the game, in both the equipment and the strategy with which the sport is played. Besides improvements in golf course irrigation, grass mixes, maintenance, and environmental protections, there have been tremendous technological advances in the design of golf clubs and golf balls.

All of these factors have influenced my evolution as a golf course designer. My main purpose has been to provide golfers with an exciting challenge. The incredible love I have for the game can be traced back to my introduction to the sport before I reached the age of six.

While I am often portrayed today as a wicked designer from hell, I am in fact from the quiet midwestern town of Urbana, Ohio.

My mother and father were born and raised there. No two finer people ever graced this earth, and I will always be thankful for their love and support. My father, Paul Francis Dye, was a slightly built, effervescent man originally from Liberty, a small town in east central Indiana. A full crop of red hair in his younger days earned him the nickname "Pink," and while I never called him anything but Dad, business associates, friends, and family knew him by no other name.

My beloved mother, Elizabeth Johnson Dye, was a strikingly beautiful, petite woman. Her father was a member of the Johnson Manufacturing family, the makers of long-spouted oilcans and round-bottom water buckets shaped to hang on trains; her mother's family owned Marvin Manufacturing Company, famous for developing the innovative process that took the pits out of dates.

My father was a hardworking man who held positions as a politician, bar owner, insurance agent, and postmaster of Urbana.

Although he lost a battle for Congress in 1932, Dad became chairman of the state Democratic party. When Franklin Roosevelt ran for president, I was given the privilege of introducing him from the back platform of the presidential train.

The saloon Dad owned was called the Brass Rail, and while my mother didn't approve of that venture, Dad told us that his profit there put my younger brother Andy and me through school. I don't remember much about the bar, but I know Dad later joined my grandfather's insurance agency and became a successful insurance agent who, like me twenty-five years later, would turn to golf course design as a sideline.

Dad's lively personality made him a popular man with everyone in Urbana, a town with a population of just under six thousand. Dad never knew the word quit, and my determination and tenacity come directly from him.

By the time I was five years old, my father had me out in the backyard swinging an old Spalding golf club. The game was born and bred into me by my dad, and I've always been grateful for his choice of sport.

I often caddied for my mother, who played social golf every Tuesday, but it was Dad who was obsessed with the game. He played to a five or six handicap and won the Urbana Country Club Championship in 1931 and 1932.

Dad had a fluid, orthodox swing that reminded me of Bobby Jones's. Like Jones, he had a tendency to break his left arm just slightly on his backswing.

More than Dad's golf swing, I remember his putting prowess. He had an old hickory-shaft putter with a four-inch steel blade and putted the ball off the extreme toe of the club. He would aim the ball way outside the hole and, like the great South African Bobby Locke, hook it back to the hole.

Neither my older sister Anne, our younger brother Andy, nor I had any choice as to whether we would become involved with golf. From her earliest days, Anne remembers Dad, who was a good teacher, yelling at her to "follow through, follow through," while my Urbana friend and Anne's future husband, Tom Doss, recalls Dad reminding him to "chop down, chop down."

Dad's love for golf led him to join a committee that persuaded the great Scottish architect Donald Ross to design the nearby

Springfield Country Club. That golf course was completed in 1921, and I remember seeing it for the first time when I was about ten. Little did I know that Mr. Ross's creative genius would influence my future course design.

Frustrated with the fact that he and the other golfers in the area had to drive twelve miles to Springfield to play, Dad persuaded my grandmother to donate some of her farm acreage just outside Urbana so that he could start a local golf club. Dad tried to engage Donald Ross and other architects of note to design the course, but nine holes in a small town like Urbana was apparently not of interest to them.

Even though he had no formal training in golf course design or construction, my father finally decided to take matters into his own hands. In 1922, three years before I was born, he and his compatriots broke ground for what is known as the Urbana Country Club. Using old Ford tractors with wide steel spikes, it took almost a full year for Dad and his construction crew to rough out six holes in the sixty acres.

After those six holes were completed, three more were added one year later in 1923. My younger son, P.B., built nine more for the club in 1993, and in an emotional ceremony that fall, the members dedicated the full eighteen holes to the memory of my father and mother.

My interest in alternative means of designing and building golf courses apparently came from my dad, who was never one to accept the status quo. Benefiting from his exposure to the great courses in the area such as Scioto and Inverness and from his study of the new developments in golf course design, he somehow learned enough to oversee construction of the Urbana course.

Dad was always trying something new, and I recall him taking my sister Anne, who is the kindest, gentlest lady you'll ever meet, and me along when he went to nearby Marysville, Ohio, to meet with the Scott Seed Company experts. Scott was developing new hybrid bent-grass formulas and Dad attempted to convince them to allow him to use a new seed mix at the Urbana Country Club.

Even today, I remember his passionate plea, to the effect that Urbana was the perfect course for Scott's experiments with the new grasses. Based on his efforts, the Urbana Country Club had some of the earliest Washington fine-bladed bent greens in Ohio. They were called "velvet" in those days, and Dad was very proud of his achievement.

The Urbana Country Club was built on hilly acreage—no great long steep areas, just small wavy hills. My introduction to the lure of the short-but-risky par-four was based on my love for Dad's opening hole, which plays just 320 yards. The drive may be played to a wide landing area, but then the golfer is confronted with a huge maple tree that hovers over the putting surface just to the right side of the small green. Unless the drive is positioned to the left, there is the risk of hitting that looming maple on the approach shot.

I never asked him, but I suspect Dad patterned the first hole and the small greens from Donald Ross. Just as Ross influenced my courses in later years, my father's respect for Mr. Ross and his work must have inspired the nine holes he built at Urbana.

The Urbana Country Club was widely praised and accepted by locals as well as the fine amateurs and professionals of that era who toured the course. Ironically, that acclaim was given to a type of design that is fiercely criticized today, since the Urbana course featured blind uphill shots, side-hill stances, and severely contoured greens, all unacceptable in the modern design world.

Despite what are considered antiquated concepts today, Dad's design of the quaint nine holes was emblematic of such great championship golf courses as Olympic in San Francisco, Oakmont, and Oakland Hills, all of which are hilly layouts with severe contours. The professionals who played at Urbana accepted these characteristics as the norm, and its original design makes it a unique course today.

Three great golf courses were within driving distance of our white two-story, wood-frame, porch-wrapped house located on Scioto Street in Urbana. From my earliest days, Dad took me with him to first visit and later play such fine courses as Camargo in Cincinnati, Inverness in Toledo, and Scioto, in Columbus.

Without realizing it at the time, I began to salt away design concepts from these wonderful old courses. What a valuable education I was getting from my father, who I'm sure never anticipated my future profession.

• • •

Despite all his business responsibilities, my father took a hands-on approach in watching over the new nine holes at Urbana in the summer months. In the winter, our family had always visited Delray Beach, Florida, for several weeks. But when I began experiencing serious attacks of asthma at age seven, my parents decided we should stay in Florida for all the winter months.

In Delray, our family lived in two different rented houses before building a small home at the corner of Nassau Street and Ocean Boulevard (now Highway AIA), just across the street from the Atlantic Ocean. Dad took the train back and forth to Ohio to tend to his business affairs. Meanwhile my mother became friends with many of the elite "snowbirds" in the Palm Beach area, including the Vanderbilts and Phippses.

While I have met many affluent people in my life, I first encountered real wealth when I had dinner at Seward Vanderbilt Webb's house. My sister's friend "Punchy" Webb had asked us over, and when I came home I told my mother that the food was good but that the teaspoons were too heavy.

My mother was one of the founders of the prestigious Bath and Tennis Club, a short distance from the grand old Gulf Stream Golf Club. Our current home in Delray is less than a mile from both of these landmarks, and memories of my early days in Florida recur when I drive by them.

During those winter months in Florida, I began to play golf in earnest and was allowed to play Delray Beach Municipal and two courses designed by Donald Ross, Gulf Stream Golf Club and the legendary Seminole Golf Club. In between trips to Ohio, my father frequently played with Dick Wilson, a golf professional at Delray Beach Municipal. Wilson was associated with the architectural firm of Toomey and Flynn and later became a nationally known architect who designed such great courses as the West Palm Beach Country Club, Doral Country Club, Bay Hill Country Club, and Cog Hill #4 in Chicago.

During one of our last winters in Florida, I remember my father taking me over to the golf course at the famous Boca Raton Hotel where Tommy Armour taught. He was the head professional at the Boca South Course, which was one of the best of its day. Although I merely shook hands with the silver-haired Scotsman, I still remember how impressed I was to meet a man

who had won both the United States and British Open Championships.

My given name is Paul, but since that was my dad's name as well,
I was called P.D. Somehow that turned from P.D. to Pede to
Pete, which has stuck to this day.

I attended grades one through nine during our months in
Florida, but when the weather cleared up north, Dad would pack
up the family and transport us back to Ohio. During the summer,
Dad continued to tinker with the Urbana course in his spare
time, and I worked there and played as much golf as possible.

By the time I was eight or nine, I was in charge of turning the
water sprinklers on and off. Later I was permitted to drive one of
the gang mowers we used on the fairways but I had to mow the
tees and greens with an old Worthington push mower.

Since I was small in stature, pushing that heavy Worthington
around was really tough. Dad's greens were severely sloped from
back to front and he demanded we mow up the slopes and then
back down to reduce the direction of the grain.

Most of the time, I followed his orders, but after six or seven
greens, my arms and legs were worn out. I then mowed side to
side when Dad wasn't watching, but I'm sure he knew what I was
up to!

Just before World War II broke out, Dad brought home a
spanking new bright-red Fordson tractor. Even though I was responsible, I let my brother Andy take a whirl at driving it, and our
childhood buddy Chuck Marvin rode on the cycle bar that was
hitched to the tractor.

Unfortunately, Andy got sideways in the deep ravine in front of
the par-three ninth green and turned the Fordson over. While I
should have been concerned about Andy and Chuck, who fortunately were not hurt, I was relieved when we were able to put
that tractor back on all fours before Dad found out.

When World War II broke out, I was given more responsibility
at the course, since all of the eligible men went off to fight for
our country. At fifteen years old, I assumed the duties of greenskeeper. For the most part my work at the Urbana Country Club
succeeded in pleasing my dad, but there were times when I'm
sure he wondered whether I might destroy his prized golf course.

Ernie Wilson, a typical Ohio farmer, complete with overalls and a big straw hat, was the original greenskeeper. The wily ex-farmer taught me everything from how to repair equipment with baling wire to the primitive ways to spread the few chemicals employed on the golf course.

His direction came in handy one summer when the greens faded to a dull brown. Even though I didn't know much about such things, I decided to try a mixture of sulfate of ammonia and water, which would inject a hot dose of nitrogen into the putting surfaces. Along with Andy, we paddled up batch after batch in an old fifty-gallon wooden drum and then waved a sprinkling can full of the liquid fertilizer over all of the putting surfaces.

I was amazed when the greens began to turn pale green, and based on that success, I decided I'd just keep adding the nitrogen mixture every day until I had a beautiful green luster. Unfortunately, I went a bit too far and the putting surfaces went from being light green to medium green to dark green to black and then to a yellow straw that spelled disaster for me and the course.

The heroes of my early years were golfers such as Bobby Jones, Horton Smith, Gene Sarazen, Byron Nelson, Craig Wood, and the illustrious Walter Hagen.

The golf professionals in those days couldn't make a living on their meager prize money, so many of them traveled around to towns like Urbana, where they played exhibition matches.

It was not uncommon in the 1930s for me to come home and find such famous golfers as Walter Hagen, Gene Sarazen, and Johnny Farrell sitting on our front porch. I would listen for hours to their stories about the game. I remember Walter Hagen specifically because of an incident where Dad tried to teach him a lesson in manners.

At that time the professionals were paid a fee—five hundred dollars or so—to compete in the exhibition. It was the custom to give them a small bonus as well, but Dad wouldn't give one to Walter Hagen because the great golfer didn't stand up when my mother came into the room!

That episode with Hagen epitomized Dad's belief in courtesy, and more than once he knocked me down to size when I failed to show respect or appeared discourteous.

My father taught me a lesson I would never forget when I was fourteen or fifteen, competing in a pro-am in Piqua, Ohio, along with professional Al Marshy.

My putting touch was awful that day, and in disgust I heaved the wooden-shaft putter high into a poplar tree. I yelled to my caddie "Go get it!" only to hear the stern words "You get it!" from my father. After I shimmied up the tree and retrieved the putter, I returned to find that not only had my dad disappeared from the gallery but my clubs were gone as well!

Friends and family would probably say I was a bit of a scoundrel in my teenage days, but I never caused serious problems. My boyhood friend Tom Doss does remember some wild escapades in those days, including our being falsely accused of robbing a local jewelry store and my accidentally burning down the barn in back of our house!

I was fifteen years old when Pearl Harbor was attacked. I felt ashamed that I wasn't dodging bullets overseas, but I was exempt from service because I was still in high school. World War II gas rationing and the blackouts along the east coast of Florida caused us to stay in Urbana, where I entered Urbana High School to begin my junior year.

During this time I played some of the best golf of my life. Besides high-school competition, there were frequent interclub tournaments, and even though I was only fifteen, my skill earned me the chance to compete against the older and more experienced players from Scioto, Inverness, and Springfield Country Club.

I was shooting in the seventies then, but my first big title was the Ohio High School Championship in 1942, when I was seventeen years old. Dad's encouragement of junior golf through his organization of club tournaments and pro-ams created a hotbed for young golfers in Urbana. In fact, at one time, four of the six players on the Ohio State University golf team were from our town.

Many people have asked me if I ever considered a career as a golf professional or golf course architect in my teenage years, but I never thought it was an option. In the 1930s and 1940s, those professions were usually either hobbies or secondary to more traditional lines of work such as business, politics, and farming.

My sister Anne remembers that none of my family ever thought I'd amount to anything. My carefree attitude about life in general and academics in particular prompted my dad to send me to a prep school in Asheville, North Carolina, to complete my final year of high school.

Much to my father's displeasure, all I did at Asheville was play golf and have fun. A change of scenery hadn't triggered my concern about the future much, and my grade performance was mediocre at best.

I finally left school in the spring of my senior year, signed up with the army, and spent basic training at Camp Blanding in Florida. For the remaining three years, I was stationed at both Fort Benning in Georgia and Fort Bragg in North Carolina.

I desperately wanted to be sent to the fighting front, but every time those orders seemed imminent, something came up. I even joined the parachute infantry since they usually ended up on the front lines; instead, my unit was sent around the country to stage exhibition parachute jumps to raise money for war bonds.

After we trained in Georgia for an invasion of Korea, it looked as though our unit—incorporated after the war into the famous 82nd Airborne—would see some action. A bunch of us younger guys began training with sixty-five-pound radio units strapped to our backs just outside Asheville, where the mountainous terrain duplicated that found in Korea. Before our unit was sent, President Truman's use of the atomic bomb ended the war.

Jumping from airplanes was for the most part an exhilarating experience. But once in the middle of the night my parachute got caught in a bunch of tree limbs and I had no idea how far off the ground I was hanging. I kept dropping various pieces of equipment, trying to estimate the distance I might fall; I spent many dark, uneasy hours wondering what fate was in store for me as the parachute continued to slip slowly through the branches. At daybreak, I found myself less than ten feet from the mushy terrain, and it was only then that my heart stopped pounding.

While training at Fort Benning, I won the base golf tournament and met a couple of golf-crazy captains who learned about my background in golf course maintenance in Urbana. Together we played a great deal of golf around the area, and eventually I was asked to assume the superintendent's position at the base golf course.

The next thing I knew I was in charge of those Italian POWs. Since all of them were anxious to make a good impression so they could remain in the United States after the war, the men kept the golf course in immaculate condition.

I did make a suggestion here and there as to what work was needed to maintain the course, but I must admit my attention to the job at hand was secondary to playing golf as much as possible. I met with the prisoners early each day, went over their duties with one of the men who was fairly adept at understanding my "Urbanaese" dialect, and then left to play at a nearby course.

I tended the base golf course for about three months before I was transferred to Fort Bragg, which is just about forty miles from Pinehurst. As luck would have it, two different captains learned of my golf skill, and soon the three of us were making daily trips to play Pinehurst No. 2.

I was still stationed at Fort Bragg, almost ready for discharge as a tech sergeant, when my father called me with the news that Andy was graduating with honors from Asheville School. My dad insisted that I be there to celebrate Andy's achievement, but I had no leave time so I falsified a pass to exit the base.

After the graduation ceremony, I made the mistake of telling Dad what I'd done. Being the practical joker that he was, he told a military policeman on duty at the club where the reception was being held. Dad thought my fake pass hilarious, but the M.P. arrested me on the spot, and I spent the last sixty days of my military career in the brig with a big blue "P" on the back of my uniform.

The exposure to Pinehurst No. 2 during my military years greatly affected me in the decades to come. I've returned there to play many times over the years and have come to appreciate the rich history of Pinehurst, how Donald Ross first arrived there, and the source of the creativity that led to his design.

Pinehurst originated when James Walker Tufts, who made his fortune from the invention of the marble soda fountain, first purchased 5,500 acres in 1895. For some time the area was known as Tuftstown. Finally, Mr. Tufts chose the name Pinehurst: *pine* for the beautiful trees of the area and *hurst,* which means a wooded plot of rising ground.

James Tufts commissioned Frederick Law Olmsted, designer of New York's Central Park, as the landscape architect for the area. Under Mr. Tufts' direction, Olmsted planted more than two hundred thousand seedlings and shrubs.

In its early days, golf was not the center of attention at Pinehurst. Hunting, polo, riding, archery, lawn bowling, and bicycling were the more popular recreations of the day.

While Mr. Tufts was completing plans for his resort around the turn of the century, Donald Ross was gaining an education in golf course design in his native Scotland. The son of a stonemason, Mr. Ross was from the picturesque north coast village of Dornoch.

In addition to being a fine player as a youngster, Donald Ross also exhibited an early interest in golf course design. Mr. Ross's mentor was John Sutherland, the secretary at Royal Dornoch Golf Club, who convinced young Ross to study at St. Andrews under Old Tom Morris, the legendary player and golf course designer.

After apprenticing under Morris, Mr. Ross returned to his native village, where Sutherland persuaded him at age twenty to take over as head professional as well as greenskeeper. That experience at Dornoch, now recognized as one of the finest seaside courses in the world, prepared him for his trek to the United States at the turn of the twentieth century.

By this time, James Tufts' grandson Richard had built a nine-hole golf course at Pinehurst to appease the guests who were hitting golf balls into the herd of dairy cows that grazed next to the Holly Inn. Realizing the need for a new eighteen-hole course, Mr. Tufts learned of Mr. Ross's background and soon retained his services. After redesigning the No. 1 course, Mr. Ross crafted the famous No. 2, which hosted the PGA Championship as early as 1936.

While many courses have a noble aura about them, starting with the clubhouse entrance and locker room facilities, when I first played Pinehurst in the 1940s, it had none. Undeveloped dirt roads led to the old barren clubhouse and an unsightly caddie bin outside.

All was forgotten, however, when I stood on the first tee at the famed No. 2. Even today I can remember my eagerness to play Pinehurst, and while I appreciated the course simply as a player, I will never forget my jubilation as I walked the pine-tree-lined fairways and putted on the severely contoured greens.

Donald Ross's masterpiece was the prototype for the "parkland" (not on the sea) golf courses that would be built in the United States through the mid-1940s. Pinehurst No. 2 can be stretched out to more than 7,000 yards. Mr. Ross shaped severe undulations into the natural terrain, lined the holes with pine trees to give it symmetry, shaped medium-size greens, employed no water hazards, and strategically placed sand bunkers, requiring golfers to use every club in their bag.

While bunkers at Pinehurst No. 2 caught the off-line approach shots, I was also quite aware of the severe penalty imposed on the player who missed the fairways. The course played firm, and only the fairways were mowed, leaving the pine needles and bare sandy-soil rough to capture a misdirected shot.

Even though I wasn't looking at the course through designer's eyes, Pinehurst No. 2 impressed me more than any other golf course I had ever seen. The medium-size, offset greens with sharp drop-offs are vivid in my mind, and I learned that one had to carefully manipulate the ball around and through the dips and swales in order to, as Mr. Ross put it, "invent short shots that no other form of hazard can call for."

Donald Ross was the unrivaled master of melding putting surfaces into the existing terrain. In 1958 I was so enthralled with Mr. Ross's design that I convinced my fun-loving friend Jack Leer to drive thirteen hours in an old Ford with me to Pinehurst to play in the North and South Amateur. Jack, whose recent habit of sleeping in a pen with his beloved pack of seventeen gray eastern timberwolves has prompted questions regarding his sanity, thought I was the crazy one when I made him stand and hold a measuring rod so I could look through a transit and record the contours on Mr. Ross's greens.

Donald Ross called the course "the fairest test of championship golf I have ever designed," and the legendary Sam Snead anointed it by saying, "You have to be alert and sharp for eighteen consecutive holes; otherwise it will jump up and bite you." Ben Hogan won his first professional tournament there, the 1940 North and South Open, and as a tribute to its longevity as a heralded course, the United States Open will be played there in 1999.

I held Pinehurst No. 2 in great esteem even in 1945, for I was aware of Hogan's victory there. I never knew until years later that Mr. Ross actually built the course first, and then thousands of pine trees were planted on top of the sandy soil, providing an illusion that the greens were below ground level.

The wonderful contour of the greens and the strategic manner in which the holes were designed elevates Pinehurst No. 2 to the top of my list, but I disagree with those who say that subtlety is No. 2's finest asset.

When Mr. Ross designed the course, he planned on the professional golfer hitting a four or five iron to the upside-down saucer-shaped green at the 396-yard first hole. If Mr. Ross were to crawl out of his grave and watch Tour players hit nine irons to the first green, he would immediately move the tee back fifty yards into the parking lot.

When he finished the course, Donald Ross had no idea it would be labeled subtle. The subtleties have come after his death, owing to the advances in golf ball and club technology.

Despite the undeniable artistic talent Mr. Ross displayed at Pinehurst, the diversity of the more than six hundred courses he designed indicates that he was the most innovative in sandy soil, where he was able to create various undulations and gradual rolls. At Oakland Hills, Scioto, Inverness, and many other courses with clay-based soil, the spectacular land chosen required less sculpting. Those courses became more renowned for their magnificent setting than for Mr. Ross's dips and hollows.

Pinehurst No. 2 is a one-of-a-kind miracle though, and I was able to play it more than the law should allow. My first loves had been Scioto, Inverness, Camargo, and Seminole, but I was smitten forever when I discovered Mr. Ross's North Carolina creation.

Years later, Donald Ross was introduced to me by the department-store tycoon J. C. Penney. After Mr. Ross's death, I often saw Mr. Penney at the North and South Tournament, and when a competitor hit a ball past the sandy rough and into the pines, Mr. Penney would say, "Well, Donald's got 'em!"

The experience of playing Pinehurst No. 2 added valuable knowledge to lessons learned during the eight summers by my dad's side at the Urbana Country Club. Nearly fifteen years would pass before I was given the chance to build a golf course, and only then would I appreciate the significance of my early experiences.

The Country Club of Indianapolis

Golf architecture is an art closely allied to that of the artist or the sculptor, but also necessitating a scientific knowledge of many other subjects.

Dr. Alister Mackenzie
Golf Architecture
1920

In July 1955 I came home from my job as a Connecticut Mutual Life Insurance salesman and announced to my wife, Alice, that I didn't want to sell insurance anymore; I wanted to build golf courses.

This proclamation was based on my continuing enthusiasm for golf course design and maintenance. Years of part-time work assisting the greens superintendent at the Indianapolis Country Club resulted in my desire to design and build golf courses on my own.

While it certainly wasn't obvious at the time, this decision to join the ranks of the innovative golf course designers who turn commonplace land into lavish fairways and greens turned out to be a fortuitous one. Despite much frustration and disappointment, I would discover a profession receptive to creative ideas that were reminiscent of the golf course architects of old.

My intention to switch careers was seconded by Alice, whose love and understanding have been the one constant factor in my life.

While I receive most of the headlines these days for our courses, it is Alice O'Neal Dye who deserves equal credit for any success we've had. There would be no Pete Dye golf courses today if Alice hadn't been by my side. In addition, I knew that once I married her I'd be the second-best golfer in the family.

I was attracted to my future wife from the moment I met her at Rollins College, in Winter Park, Florida, in 1946, but I almost blew any chance I had when I caddied for her in an intersorority match against Roseanne Shafer. Alice was favored that day, and to show my faith in her, I bet my educational GI Bill check that she would win.

Unfortunately, Alice had stayed out late with another boyfriend the night before, and she was off her game. At the end of eighteen holes the match was even.

Both players hit good drives on the first extra hole, and then Roseanne hit her second shot into a greenside bunker, opening the way for Alice. I was all ready to count my winnings when Alice topped her second into a narrow ditch some seventy yards ahead! Panicky about my investment, I raced up the fairway to see if by any chance the ball was playable, but found it nestled in green, slimy muck.

Furious, I glared back at Alice and then tossed her bag full of clubs into the muck and stomped off, leaving her to fend for herself. Needless to say, Alice was a bit cold for several weeks, but thank goodness she finally forgave me.

Anybody who knows me will flat out tell you that Alice is the reason I'm still on the face of this earth. I love her dearly, and while I may be the one who receives the credit for designing the championship golf courses, our success is largely attributable to Alice's organization and common sense.

The daughter of avid golfer and successful corporate attorney Perry O'Neal and Lucy Holliday O'Neal, Alice possessed a rhythmic textbook swing that was developed at Woodstock Country Club in a junior swing class. Alice became the club champion at Woodstock at age sixteen, and she was a regular competitor in the prestigious Women's Western Amateur. In the summer, on break from Shortridge High School in Indianapolis, Alice began to build a reputation as an up-and-coming amateur not only in Indiana but in national events as well.

Alice's longtime friend and competitor Carolyn Lautner believes that while Alice's golf swing was always a classic one, 85 percent of her success was due to dogged determination and ability to outthink her opponents. "I wouldn't say Alice was out to kill," Carolyn says, "but she never, ever believed she couldn't beat someone no matter how talented she might be."

A golf reporter for more than twenty years, Carolyn remembers being asked one day to help a young amateur with her putting stroke, and when the kid played Alice and gave her a tough match that afternoon, Alice wouldn't speak to Carolyn for weeks!

Alice entered Rollins College in 1944 and dominated play there except for the unfortunate match against Roseanne Shafer. In the mid-1940s there was no Ladies' Professional Golf Tour or an organized NCAA, so Alice competed in the national amateur tournaments and local ones in Indiana during the summer. Like me, Alice was exposed to many of the great courses in our country, including Pinehurst, Pebble Beach, the Olympic Club, Winged Foot, and Knollwood Country Club in Chicago.

Being the second-best player in the family isn't all bad when you consider Alice's achievements. She's won nine Indiana Women's Amateur titles, eleven Indianapolis City Championships, the Women's Eastern, the 1968 North and South at Pinehurst, and back-to-back USGA Senior Amateur Championships in 1978 and 1979. Alice also was a member of the victorious Curtis Cup Team in 1970 and captained the 1992 United States Women's World Amateur Team that competed in Vancouver, Canada.

Someone asked me recently if I feel bad about getting most of the headlines in the family these days. I just told him "hell no"— I played second fiddle to Alice for so many years in Indianapolis that it's finally my turn!

Alice was starting her third year at Rollins when my mother and I drove down to Winter Park to see if I could enter. While Mom made inquiries at the admissions office, I headed for Dubsdread, a well-known course near the school.

On the practice tee, I ran into a man named Pete Schnoonmaker, the coach of the Rollins golf team. I told him I wanted to attend school there, and after some discussion he informed me that a semi-scholarship might be possible. That combined with my GI Bill check allowed me to enter college in 1946.

Alice says she first spotted me at the school commissary and thought I was "cute." Then she saw me out at the golf course. What drew her to me I don't know, but her perky smile and a great pair of legs certainly caught my attention.

We were never what you call romantically involved at Rollins. A true friendship and a mutual love for the game of golf bound us together, although Alice's college friend Lee Hilkenee will tell you Alice had matrimony on her mind when she graduated in 1948.

Scholastics were never of primary importance to me, and I did not stay to graduate from Rollins. To supplement my scholarship and GI Bill check, I picked up trays at the Beanery, our school commissary, and since that job didn't end until 8:30 a.m., I always missed the first half hour of a class where we studied some sort of medieval history. After history came accounting, and since it took a half hour to get to the golf course, I was usually on the first tee by 11:00.

I also bartended a bit, so with my government check, cafeteria pay, bar tips, and a few shekels from golf wagers, I managed a pretty good income. Alice was always broke in those days, but she had a car and that made up for it!

The partial scholarship I got at Rollins was funded by a fellow named Tom Jamison out of Pittsburgh, who also played golf at Dubsdread. Rollins was trying to upgrade its athletic program and Jamison was an enthusiastic booster.

Dubsdread was an old golf course first designed by Tom Bendelow in 1923, and all the great players of the day gathered there. Another course named Dubsdread was later built up in Chicago, and designed by Joe Lee and owned by Joe Jemsek, a wonderful gentleman whom I first met at the original Dubsdread.

While at Rollins, I met many fine players: Carl Dann, the Florida State Amateur Champion; "Lozie" Langford of the Langford Hotel chain out of Chicago, who used to "back" me in big-stakes golf wagers; and Jim Fones, whose uncle started Oakmont.

All my teammates on the golf team—Stockton Rogers, Herman Goodwin, Bill O'Hara—and I found stiff competition at

Dubsdread. Good competition there prepared us for the team matches against the University of Miami, Florida, Florida State, Duke, Florida Southern, University of Georgia, and the University of North Carolina.

I captained the golf team in 1947, and my college competitors were such players as Al Besselink (Miami), Harvey Ward and Mike Souchak (North Carolina), Art Wall and Jim McNair (Duke), and some guy named A. Palmer who played for Wake Forest. At that time, many collegiate players beat Arnold, and even though he hit the ball long, he rarely saw the fairway. Nobody was that impressed, but years later he certainly fooled us.

Of that group, Al Besselink was the real character. He had a natural flair for the game and was almost as sharp a dresser as Jimmy Demaret. Al used to get as mad as hell when I'd wear an old T-shirt that had a rusty crease across the front. He didn't know I had deliberately dried it on a wire line, and he would kid me about wearing such an awful-looking shirt when we played together.

Al Besselink was a darn good player, and he could talk a blue streak, especially when he thought he might lose a couple of bucks. One time I was doing pretty well and Al asked me whether I always favored playing the ball down the left side of the fairway near the out-of-bounds. With that thought planted in my mind, I proceeded to hit the next four drives out-of-bounds right!

At the time, I was ranked probably fourth or fifth in the Intercollegiate, which included teams from all the southern schools. Jim McNair, who never played the tour, beat all of us.

I played in my first United States Amateur in 1946, at Baltusrol. What a privilege it was to play that wonderful old course in Springfield, New Jersey, designed and built in 1922 by A. W. Tillinghast.

I remember that first Amateur very well because I birdied the eighteenth hole to tie thirteen others for the sixty-fourth and last spot. Only eight of us would make the first round of match play.

The first playoff hole was a short par-five, and I reached the green with two perfect wood shots. Unfortunately, my eagle attempt not only missed the cup but sailed clear off the green. Luckily, I chipped back close for a par, avoiding a three putt. When five other players faltered, I won a spot in the tournament.

I began match play the following day, but was beaten in the first round by Ted Bishop, who beat Smiley Quick one-up for the championship. I also qualified for the 1948 tournament, but my old pal Al Besselink beat me at the Memphis Country Club, and in 1949 at Oakland Hills, local favorite Sam Rosetta ousted me.

Professionals such as Ben Hogan, Ed Furgol, Henry Picard (one of the longest hitters I ever saw), Clayton Heffner, Dale Douglas, Joe Ezar, Dave Ragen, and Ky Laffoon all came to Dubsdread. Owner Carl Dann let them all play for free, and they hung around there every winter for three or four weeks prior to the Florida tour.

The craziest guy of the lot had to be Ky Laffoon, a professional from St. Louis, who actually carried a .22-caliber rifle in his bag so he could shoot rabbits between golf shots!

One time he convinced me that I wouldn't hook the ball so much if I bent the shaft on my driver. Like an idiot I let him bend my MacGregor Tommy Armour driver with Ben Hogan's name on the sole plate until it looked like one of those Australian boomerangs.

The experiment was a failure and my favorite college driver never quite recovered from the abuse. In December 1993 I ran across it in a closet along with other discarded clubs, and the shaft, terminally injured by Laffoon's alteration, promptly snapped in two when I held it up to show a friend.

Joe Ezar, whose claim to fame came during the Italian Open in the late 1940s, was also a character. Apparently Joe boasted to an Italian dignitary that in the third round he would not only shoot 66, but do so with a hole-by-hole score that he wrote down on a scorecard.

Based on the enormous odds involved, a rather high wager was made, and the next day Joe not only shot 66 but duplicated the exact score as promised. Legend says that Ezar, who was second only to Joe Kirkwood as the best trick-shot artist of the day, simply collected his winnings on the bet and left town without completing the fourth round even though he led the tournament.

Alice's rivals in the 1940s were amateurs Peggy Kirk Bell, Louise Suggs, Betsy Rawls, Jackie Pung, Babe Didrikson Zaharias, and professional golfer Patty Berg.

While all of these women were terrific players, Babe Zaharias was equally as fascinating as Ky Laffoon or Joe Ezar. Long honored as the greatest woman athlete ever, the Babe excelled at virtually every sport she tried.

In golf, Babe Zaharias won both the United States Amateur and the United States Women's Open in 1946, and she would win two more United States Opens and also the British Amateur in 1947. A gallery's delight, the Babe would many times electrify an exhibition gallery by placing a kitchen match behind the ball so there was a loud crack when she hit it.

I first met Babe at the old Haig and Haig Tournament in Florida, when Alice and I paired up against men and women professionals and amateurs. Babe played with "Offbase" Walker, the erstwhile second baseman for the Chicago Cubs, who was a pretty fair golfer.

In the late 1940s, I thought I could really hit the ball long, but the Babe could knock it right by me at times. She was a great competitor and had an unequaled short game, but I know firsthand how strong that lady was.

The grill at Dubsdread near Rollins was a gathering spot for all of the golfers, and everyone enjoyed the after-golf frivolities. Oftentimes I'd find myself right in the thick of things, and somehow I ended up being one of those who took Babe Zaharias up on her boast that she could beat anyone in the place at Indian arm wrestling.

Just out of the parachute infantry, I figured I was tough enough to easily beat the Babe. Time and time again she proved me wrong by somehow manipulating me down low toward the floor, where she used her powerful arms to flip me upside-down!

During her first year at Rollins, Alice began to take golf instructions from a broad-shouldered, red-faced Irishman named Tom Carney, who had been a fine player in the mid-1930s. Famed writer Grantland Rice labeled Tom the "next Bobby Jones," but a terrible automobile accident put an end to his career.

Tom was a wonderful teacher, and he worked with Ben Hogan after his disastrous automobile accident in 1949. Although he was the head professional at St. Clairsville Country Club in

West Virginia, Tom was one of the winter golf instructors at Dubsdread, where he worked with many of the top touring professionals.

Tom Carney became Alice's teacher, and she thought my golf game might benefit from seeing him as well. I had my short Urbana-born golf swing working pretty well in those days, but Alice lauded Tom so much that I finally went to see him.

The crusty old professional watched me hit a bundle of drivers straight down the middle so close together you could cover them with a tablecloth. Undaunted, Tom picked up my driver and proceeded to smack one just as straight and a few yards past all of mine.

Without hesitation, he gently handed me the driver. "Pete," he said, "if I was a guy who'd just come back from the parachute infantry and couldn't out-hit a broken-down old golf pro, I'd quit the game."

It took me months to convince Tom to work with me. Unfortunately his coaching got me to a point where I almost couldn't break a hundred. His idea of lengthening my swing helped me hit the ball a lot farther, but I had no idea where it was going.

Tom Carney was a real character. I recall watching him hit a golf ball from the top of an inverted martini glass well over two hundred yards. Alice tried it one time and sprayed glass all over herself!

Tom was the finest bunker player I ever saw. Professionals like Gary Player and Fred Couples may lay claim to that title, but Tom Carney could get up and down from below sea level.

Many gamblers left Dubsdread in the 1940s with a little less weight in their pockets after they'd taken one of Tom's wagers. His favorite was to allow his adversary to throw ten balls in a sand bunker and bet that he could get down in less than twenty shots. I never saw him lose.

At that time the Florida circuit played by the golf professionals included tournaments at Hollywood, Miami Lakes, Orlando, and Tampa. First place paid $10,000, and best of all, they let amateurs play. One time Lloyd Mangram and Jimmy Demaret were leading the field, and since I was low amateur, I got to play with those two great players in the final round.

During the summer breaks at Rollins I returned to Urbana and played a great deal of golf. I was a medalist in the Ohio Amateur and also played the Northern PGA Tour as an amateur.

That circuit stopped at the Motor City Open in Detroit, Columbus, Ohio, and then Hershey, Pennsylvania. Once again I competed against many of the professionals, but my goal at that time was to beat amateur Frank Stranahan, who was winning everything in sight.

I often played golf with Frank, a fellow Buckeye who was three or four years older than I. Frank, Willie Turnesa, and Charlie Coe from Oklahoma were the best amateurs of the day, and Frank came up just one hole shy of winning the 1950 United States Amateur.

In the spring of 1949, I was asked to play with Jim Turnesa in a pro-am held at the Palmetto Country Club in Aiken, South Carolina. The Tour professionals used the tournament to warm up for the Masters.

A friend named Jimmy Johnson took me up to Aiken, and I stayed in a house with Byron Nelson, Jimmy Demaret, and Lloyd Mangrum, among others. Talk about being nervous. I just sat at dinner barely able to speak, and when I did I just said "Pass the salt" so I wouldn't embarrass myself!

I played in tournaments that included professionals Ben Hogan, Jimmy Demaret, Sam Snead, Byron Nelson, Cary Middlecoff, and Lloyd Mangrum. I always thought Hogan was the greatest even in his early years, but he really came into greater prominence after his accident. He won everything—including the United States Open in 1950 and 1951, and the United States Open, the Masters, and the British Open in 1953.

I can't say that being a touring professional didn't interest me, but I was never a player of the caliber of Snead or Hogan. My long-iron game didn't measure up, and if a player couldn't consistently finish in the top five or six, there was little chance to make a living on the Tour.

By taking only one or two classes a semester at Rollins, where I majored in economics, I didn't accumulate enough credits to leave the "lower division," so after three years, one interested professor suggested I might find my niche at another institution. The field of law had always fascinated me, so I moved up north of Orlando to Stetson University and enrolled there.

Back in the 1940s, you didn't have to have a college degree to be accepted at law school, but once again I put the golf game before the classroom and never made much headway toward a degree. I dropped out after less than a year, and I now had unceremoniously assembled an academic record that did not include graduation from elementary school, high school, prep school, college, or law school.

Unlike me, Alice graduated, and in the spring of 1949, I called her and told her that I was coming over to Indianapolis to *talk* about marriage. She shared that discussion with her parents and they all prepared for my proposal.

While my intentions were good, when I reached Indianapolis I started playing great golf with Alice and many of the finest players of the day, including Indiana State Amateur Champion and future professional Fred Wampler. Scores in the high sixties quickly sidetracked my thoughts of marriage.

As we sat in her kitchen eating sandwiches on the final evening of my visit, while her anxious parents waited in the living room, a perplexed Alice finally inquired as to what happened to the idea of "talking about marriage." Straight-faced, I simply said, "Well, *not* in golf season." Luckily, I came to my senses the following winter, and Alice and I were married in a snowstorm on Groundhog Day in 1950.

Alice would admit to having little experience as a homemaker. Accustomed to domestic help handling household chores, Alice had a rude awakening when we were first married.

In fact, I remember the very day when she walked into the bathroom, got a puzzled look on her face, and then called her mother, saying, "Mother, the bathroom floor is dirty, what do I do?" Fortunately, we survived the trauma of those days, including one when I came home to find that she'd fixed a *Betty Crocker Cook Book* special, "Baked Oranges," for dinner!

Before we were married, Alice was employed selling life insurance, and she was very successful. In her short time as an agent with the Connecticut Mutual Life Insurance Company, she sold nearly a quarter of a million dollars of insurance, which was quite an achievement for a woman in those days.

Since I was familiar with the insurance business through my dad's agency, I never considered any other profession. Connecticut Mutual offered me a position, and I began to sell life insurance around the Indianapolis area.

Through her championship play in Indiana, Alice was very well known, but I needed to establish myself, and so I scoured the city looking for potential clients. Somehow I came up with the idea of searching out young doctors, and I remember spending endless hours and many late nights at the Indiana University Medical Center talking insurance with resident physicians.

Selling life insurance proved successful for me, but I sold my fair share of corporate business insurance as well. My numbers were impressive even in that first year, and during the second one, I became a member of the Million Dollar Round Table.

My golf ability was a real advantage, since I sold a ton of insurance on the golf course. Both Alice and I received a lot of exposure in the media through our golf achievements, and I didn't hesitate to use that publicity to my advantage.

While I've never been known as much of a businessman, I made several speeches for Connecticut Mutual explaining my successful selling techniques. I kept accurate records of every call, how I approached the potential clients, and what the response was.

I even put together a booklet and had several sample letters in it that I could use with a particular type of client. Connecticut Mutual liked the idea so well they used it in their training materials.

Of course, today everybody has the impression that I'm a dunderhead who can't find his car keys. These people are always surprised to learn that I was very organized back then, and I was even asked to take over the agency.

During this time, I never considered golf course design as a career because it never occurred to me that I could make a living that way. All I wanted to do was dabble in it as a hobby and continue to establish myself in the insurance industry.

While selling insurance was priority one, Wayne Fuson, the respected sports columnist for the *Indianapolis News,* reminded me recently about my enthusiasm for golf course maintenance and design during this time. "Pete was selling insurance, but he was thinking golf," Wayne said, and he knew that my initial interest in those fields came through my membership at the Country Club of Indianapolis in the early 1950s.

Their golf course had been through some rough times, and when I asked to be placed on the greens committee, the members acquiesced. That was a decision they would deeply regret, but it took a while for them to realize how much of a disaster it would be.

The best thing about my initial efforts was that nobody at the Country Club of Indianapolis gave a damn about what I wanted to do. There was little interest in the design of the course at that time, and I had free reign to do as I saw fit.

Since a devastating disease had killed most of the stately Dutch elms, my initial work with the course began when I planted thousands of new trees to replace the nearly four thousand elms that died. Alice's mother's farm had plenty of saplings, which we dug out, along with some huge trees. We froze the large trees in winter so they'd be easier to transport, and then carted them to the Country Club of Indianapolis on huge Holliday Steel Company flatbed trucks.

Even though I was very inexperienced at the time, I had great success with the new trees. We even transferred two twelve-inch-diameter white oaks to our neighbor Jack Appel's home, and when those trees and the ones at the Country Club of Indianapolis survived, Fred Hobbs, an established nursery owner, told everyone I was the luckiest guy he'd ever known.

Besides being a tree mover, I also relocated a few bunkers on the course, and attempted to provide some curvature to many of the holes by altering the mowing patterns for the fairways. In all, I would labor with the Country Club of Indianapolis for nearly ten years, but the tree replacement, bunker relocation, and new tees were mild compared to my bold experiments with the grass on the fairways.

My venture into golf course maintenance and design in the 1950s was a complete disaster. In fact, there are those at the Country Club of Indianapolis, which sported the finest players of the day, who remember me as the man who single-handedly annihilated their golf course.

My downfall came when I decided to assist greens superintendent Mel Warneke with his mixture of grasses on the course. Believing I needed to become more knowledgeable on the subject, I sought experts who could guide me along.

My insurance office was on North Meridian Street in Indianapolis and there was a Purdue University extension nearby that held classes on turf management. I also drove sixty miles up to Lafayette, Indiana, to take classes at Purdue University, and while there I met Dr. William Daniels, head of the agronomy school.

Dr. Daniels and Dr. Marvin Furgeson, a professor at Texas A&M who was also the executive director of the USGA Greens Section, conducted seminars on turf and golf course maintenance around the country. I attended those meetings and learned about different grasses, turf, pesticides, fungicides, and turf roots. I also went to golf course superintendents' meetings in the area to learn what techniques were used in maintaining various courses.

With the information I gleaned from the seminars and meetings, I began to experiment with different chemical mixes on the fairways at the Country Club of Indianapolis. Unfortunately, my ratios were way off. As a result, I assaulted that unsuspecting course with my ill-founded theories, causing it to lose the little grass it once possessed.

In fact, things got so bad that when I asked if I could test a new theory on the first hole, the members insisted that I only attack half of the fairway. Within a month, the members could play only their half, for the "Dye Half," as it became known, was dark brown, devoid of any turf whatsoever.

By this time, Alice and I had moved into a small house on Kenwood Avenue in Indianapolis. The Country Club was on the other side of town, and I remember getting up at the crack of dawn to drive out to see if even one blade of grass had come up. It hadn't!

My naiveté in the area of golf course maintenance reared its ugly head again when I failed miserably with another experiment involving the building of what I called "lifetime bridges." At the time, the Country Club of Indianapolis had wooden bridges that were very shaky. I decided to improve the situation by constructing a concrete bridge over the creek on the second hole that would be there for eternity.

After a fair amount of research on the subject, my first attempt at a lifetime bridge was built of cement and stone. I was so proud that I inscribed the date and my initials in the cement.

The next spring, while Alice and I were vacationing in Florida, heavy showers blasted the Indianapolis area. Early one morning I got a frantic call from the course superintendent, telling me my "lifetime bridge" hadn't even made it through the first spring rainstorm.

Unfortunately I'd placed the bridge right on top of quicksand, and when the rains came, the whole bridge, abutment, and everything disappeared.

When I returned, I saw that my eternal bridge was buried and that the only thing going over the bridge was the water itself. Needless to say, I became leery of conventional bridges right then and there, and perhaps that led me to use old railroad cars later on.

Despite my dubious track record, the greens committee at the Country Club of Indianapolis asked me if I would recontour their greens in 1993. God only knows why, but since I'd decimated their course so badly in the 1950s, I thought the least I could do was help them out.

Longtime Country Club of Indianapolis professional Larry Bianco is correct when he says I charged the course "a dollar, a bucket of balls, and lunch" for my services. In June 1994 they held a special "day" honoring Alice and me, quite a switch from the 1960s, when I was afraid to answer the door for fear the membership was there to lynch me.

El Dorado

Really good golf holes are full of surprises, each one a bit better than the last.

Robert Hunter
The Links
1926

When Alice and I were finally given the opportunity to design and build El Dorado Golf Club in Indianapolis during the fall of 1959, we both wanted to pour everything we knew about great golf courses into those nine holes. Alice drew up the first routings, and we were so excited we decided to feature the sketch on the front of our Christmas card.

The layout may have been a bit too challenging, for we received a nice note from Richard Tufts, past president of the USGA, that said, "I certainly enjoyed looking at your routing, but don't you think crossing the creek *thirteen* times in nine holes is a bit much?"

Building El Dorado was the culmination of a long struggle to become recognized as a golf course designer, a title I give myself since I have no formal degree in architecture.

The phrase *golf course architect* was coined by Charles Blair Macdonald, a fiery Canadian who later became the first recognized United States Amateur Champion. His design in 1894 of the 5,877-yard Chicago Golf Club, one of the original five founding members of the United States Golf Association, resulted in the first eighteen-hole layout in the United States.

The popularity of golf spread rapidly, and by 1896 there were eighty golf courses in the United States. Four years later, almost one thousand courses had been built, outnumbering the total in the British Isles.

With a few noted exceptions such as Shinnecock, the Garden City Golf Club, and Oakmont, golf course design in those days could be described as functional. By and large, most of the courses were primitive and unimaginative, since there usually wasn't enough money or equipment available for the architect to stray from the norm.

Fortunately, from 1900 until the early 1930s, gifted architects such as Donald Ross, A. W. Tillinghast, George Crump, Alister Mackenzie, Seth Raynor, George Thomas, Jr., Hugh Wilson, and Charles Blair Macdonald would leave their mark in the United States. Many of the greatest courses in the world would be built during this period, and the new designs were characterized by creativity, imagination, and a striking similarity to the wonderful courses in the British Isles.

When I'm asked to name the finest examples of golf-course design in the United States other than mine, I always include Pinehurst No. 2, Pine Valley, Seminole, Merion, and Camargo. All of these treasured jewels were built before 1933, and together with the courses mentioned earlier, they match up well against anything in the British Isles.

In fact, the 1920s were labeled the Golden Age of Architecture. With land plentiful and financing readily available, golf courses were being built at an incredible rate, and by 1930 almost six thousand courses existed in the United States.

Unfortunately, golf course construction in the United States during the next two decades would come almost to a halt due to the stock market crash in 1929, bank failures in the 1930s, World War II in the 1940s, and the continuing seizure of golf course property for interstate highways and housing developments.

It is difficult to believe, but records indicate that from 1932 until the beginning of 1955, the exact year Alice and I began to consider the golf course design profession, only *two hundred* courses opened, while a total of *six hundred* disappeared forever.

That means that an average of only ten new courses was built each year, and golf course architects were forced to seek alternative income sources by remodeling courses and designing commercial landscape projects.

During this same period, the golf course architecture profession, which continued its up-and-down pattern, lost many of its pioneers. The 1930s saw the passing of such great creative geniuses as Devereux Emmet (Garden City Golf Course), Charles Blair Macdonald (the National Golf Links, Lido Golf Course), Alister Mackenzie (Cypress Point, Augusta National), and George Thomas, Jr. (Los Angeles Country Club, Riviera Country Club). Gifted architect A. W. Tillinghast (Winged Foot, Baltusrol) died during World War II, Donald Ross (Pinehurst No. 2, Seminole) passed away in 1948, and H. S. Colt (Knollwood, Pine Valley), C. H. Alison (North Shore Country Club), Perry Maxwell (Prairie Dunes), and Canadian Stanley Thompson (Banff) all died in the early 1950s.

By the time Alice and I considered entering the profession in the mid-1950s, Robert Trent Jones, Dick Wilson, and Ellis Maples were essentially the only designers I knew. While all these gentlemen built fine courses, Mr. Jones was already emerging as the future superstar of golf architecture, having designed and built such prestigious courses as Coral Ridge, Peachtree, and the Point of Woods Golf and Country Club. Little did I realize that if Alice and I could somehow get started, the opportunity existed to join these three men in filling the void left by the departure of the old masters.

In spite of my disasters at the Country Club of Indianapolis, Alice and I started to alert everyone about our intention to design and build golf courses. We placed advertisements in *Golf World* and other publications, but getting the word around wasn't a problem, since we both were still receiving enormous publicity for our golf achievements.

In the mid-1950s, amateur sports were in their heyday and were covered more thoroughly by the news media than they are today. In Indianapolis for instance, amateur golf tournament results made front page in the daily *Star, News,* and the *Times.*

Alice was winning everything locally, and rarely did a week go by when her picture wasn't featured. Many times there were stories about both of us, since I went to the finals of the State Amateur two out of three years before winning the championship in 1958.

Through a friendship Alice had with Virginia Denehey, a member of the USGA Women's Committee, she was invited to become a member of that select group in February 1955. Alice assisted them in obtaining Meridian Hills as the substitute host for the 1956 Women's United States Amateur, and her relationship with Mrs. Denehey allowed us to make a very important trip to Chicago.

There we played Shore Acres, designed by Seth Raynor; Knollwood, by C. H. Alison and H. S. Colt; Glenview, by H. J. Tweedie; Onwensia, by James and Robert Foulis; North Shore, by C. S. Alison and H. S. Colt; and Oak Park, Evanston, and Beverly, all designed by Donald Ross. Exposure to these courses, which were built by both noted professional architects and rank amateurs, permitted us to witness firsthand a variety of design concepts.

During this time, I also became involved with the USGA and a short time later was appointed their Sectional Affairs chairman. With the advertisements in golf magazines, the media exposure of our playing achievements, and the USGA work, Alice and I were trying as hard as possible to attract someone who would hire us to build a golf course.

Despite our passion, no one would give us a chance, apparently believing that we were too inexperienced. Most everyone thought I was nuts, including my boss at the insurance company, who upon hearing of my intent to pursue the profession, sent me a note suggesting I seek psychiatric help.

Desperate to learn and to become involved in design at any level, Alice and I went to see Robert Trent Jones, hoping he might employ us as designers. To our disappointment, Mr. Jones would offer only management positions, which did not interest us.

Even though Mr. Jones turned us down, we thought so much of his work that we ventured down to Coral Ridge in Ft. Lauderdale in 1956 to see firsthand his new design, which featured big rolling greens, huge oval sand bunkers, and long tees. Both Alice and I were intrigued with his tee concept, and when spring came I immediately lengthened the one on the first hole at the Country Club of Indianapolis—only to discover that the player couldn't see the fairway below from the back of the tee!

To obtain what we felt would be a valued opinion as to our prospects, we went to see Bill Diddel, the straight-shooting architect from Carmel, Indiana, who lived to be a hundred. Besides building several well-designed courses around the country such as the Kenwood Country Club in Cincinnati, the Country Club of Naples, and the Denver Country Club, Bill won the Indiana State Amateur on five occasions and was recognized for having shot his age more than one thousand times.

When Alice and I visited Bill in his log cabin at Woodland Country Club, he was less than encouraging, pointing out that golf course architecture was a risky profession. Mr. Diddel was concerned that I was a young man with two children to support, and that the golf course design business was at best economically unpredictable.

After the discouraging meetings with Robert Trent Jones and Bill Diddel, Alice and I could have easily abandoned our plans. Months went by with no takers. We were especially disheartened when Indiana University in Bloomington hired their greens-keeper to build the university course without even considering us.

Fortunately I had my percentage of life insurance renewal premiums to keep us afloat, and Alice's parents also helped us out from time to time.

Despite our burning desire to build golf courses, nobody contacted us. We might have been pretty good golfers and damn good at selling life insurance, but we couldn't find anyone who believed we could build a course.

In effect, Alice and I were all dressed up with nowhere to go.

Our frustration continued when two separate opportunities south of Indianapolis fell through. The first one involved an apple orchard, and we went so far as to draw up our very first routing. A fancy brochure was then printed, but the owners could never raise the capital.

The second one involved a farmer who sold his land so he could use the million dollars to provide his wife with indoor plumbing. Unfortunately, the developers who bought it couldn't secure financing, and so that deal never materialized either.

In spite of our efforts to make something happen, nothing did until Bill and Henry Nordsiek, two experienced Indianapolis contractors, called us in the summer of 1959 and asked if we'd design a golf course for them on a plot of land just south of Indianapolis. To this day, I can't remember whether there was much of a fee involved—I would have paid the Nordsieks for the opportunity.

Finally, we were going to design and build a golf course! After the handshakes and celebrations, we were ready to go in spite of the fact that we had almost no practical knowledge of what golf course design was all about. There were no golf course architectural schools, and we were so naive that we weren't even aware of the excellent books on the subject by some of the great golf course architects.

We were the proverbial babes in the woods in a profession that was mostly nonexistent at the time. There really wasn't anyone we could talk to about our ideas, and except for a few courses on agronomy, I had no formal training as to how to design or build a golf course.

In some ways, Alice and I were throwbacks to men like Donald Ross, Alister Mackenzie, Charles Blair Macdonald, and Seth Raynor, who did not learn their craft from books or formal training. Instead, their ability as good golfers permitted them to study many of the designs created by predecessors such as Old Tom Morris and Allan Robertson at such wonderful Scottish courses as St. Andrews, Muirfield, Prestwick, and Dornoch.

Much like those legendary designers, Alice and I would design a course based on the thoughts, images, and memories of the many great courses we had played across the United States. We were aware of the finest features of those courses, and we thought we could rely on our abilities as good players to implement their most outstanding design features into our first course.

Alice drew the routings for El Dorado, and I sketched an "E" for eyeball on one section of the topography map to indicate the benchmark from where I "eyed" the holes!

Once we finalized the proposed site for the holes, I began to make construction plans. When it was time to build the greens, my limited knowledge of green substructures made me curious as to whether I could implement new concepts into my first course. Drs. Marvin Furgeson and William Daniels had filled my head with ideas, and so I sent samples of sand, peat, and dirt down to Texas A&M for analysis.

Their advice was to follow the new USGA specifications, using a ratio of eight parts sand to one part peat and one part soil. I was very excited with all the scientific work I was doing and eagerly calculated how much of each material it would take to build the greens for the first nine holes.

Based on my numbers, 2,500 cubic yards of sand and 300 cubic yards each of peat and soil were ordered. While my addition was correct, I didn't realize that more than 3,000 cubic yards of material would take up so much space and that multiple truckloads would fill up an old Indiana barn with a pile that was one hundred feet long, sixty feet wide, and thirty feet high!

The day those trucks came rolling down the narrow highway is still fresh in my mind. There must have been twenty of them, and the traffic jam was tremendous. I tried my best to calm everyone down and figure out a way to pile the material in one place so that truckloads didn't spot the countryside all the way to downtown Indianapolis.

I discussed my new mountains of greens mix with the folks at Texas A&M, and they told me that they'd only worked with very small amounts of the material. They also informed me that they hadn't considered how to go about homogenizing the correct mix for nine greens, and I recall the panic Alice and I felt at the overwhelming situation.

There was no large machinery to handle the mix, and so we had no alternative but to do it by hand. Stringing up lights in the barn, we worked day and night. Using four farm tractors with end loaders and an old Royer soil shredder, we fed in each material by eyeballing the correct amount. I'm not positive we hit the suggested ratio right on the mark, but I'll bet we weren't far off.

Once the mix was completed, we trucked the proper amount to each green, and then set up a wheelbarrow brigade to scatter the material on the green. By September we had finished planting the greens and we anxiously waited for the results.

Besides working with the new USGA greens specs, we also experimented with the use of plastic pipe for irrigation. Paul O'Kane, with whom Alice would later be playing when she had her first hole in one, approached her at a barber shop in Indianapolis regarding the potential use of plastic pipe at El Dorado.

Always open to new ideas, Alice listened to Paul's thoughts on the matter while our sons got their haircuts and then directed Paul to me. He repeated his sales pitch, and I agreed to try plastic pipe instead of the bulky cast iron.

Water flows more easily through plastic pipe because its interior walls have less friction than those of iron pipe. The Crescent Pipe people brought their experts up from Evansville to assist us, and we cut and glued the pipe into place all over the course.

Plastic pipe had always been an option, but the pipe had to be sized down to be competitive in price. The fittings didn't work too well—two-inch pipe to fit six-inch to fit four-inch—but we "Rube Goldberged" them together and buried them underground.

We spent so much money on these connecting fittings that we considered constructing a see-through glass covering over one of the joint connections to show everyone our handiwork, but we never had the nerve to do it.

El Dorado ended up with the very first nine USGA-specification greens in the country. We grew all of the bent grass for those greens in the front yard of our home on 79th Street in Indianapolis.

We bought a sod cutter, lifted up the sod, and separated the dirt from the roots. We then wrapped the sod in burlap bags and stacked them in the trunk of our Oldsmobile. Neighbors used to kid Alice that they could tell when she had a load of bent in the trunk because the front end was raised so high the car looked like a motorboat!

Our biggest mistake in building El Dorado stemmed from our overall approach in designing it specifically for good players like us. Requiring high-handicap golfers to cross a diagonally positioned creek thirteen times in nine holes was in retrospect absurd. I also penalized the great percentage of players by locating the out-of-bounds to the right, which was disastrous since most golfers slice the ball more than they hook it.

In addition, my attempt to build USGA-specification greens

resulted in too-severe contouring, as I made the base layer too severe and each additional layer increased the contour. We didn't have a great source of water, so I pumped from the stream onto the greens, not realizing that we needed to use clean water. The silt in the creek settled on the greens and sealed them off, causing future maintenance problems.

Overall, though, Alice and I managed to build a respectable nine-hole course. I'm not sure what we expected when we began, since there wasn't any one particular architect or course we tried to copy.

While El Dorado, which is now known as Royal Oak Country Club, was under construction, Tour professionals Mike Souchak and Mason Rudolph inspected the layout when they came to Indianapolis for the "500" Festival Golf Tournament. Photos show Mike hitting a driver from a dirt fairway, and their comments regarding the potential for the course were politely generous.

Shortly after completion of the nine holes at El Dorado, I received a telephone call from an Indianapolis developer, Tommy Perine, who told me he was going to build an eighteen-hole golf course on the east side of Indianapolis. After all the lean years of frustration and disappointment, Alice and I were really excited to have the opportunity to build a second course so soon.

The first eighteen-hole layout Alice and I ever designed and built was meant to be a nice family course. Only eighty acres were available. Alice finished drawing our design plans during the first week of August 1961.

Measuring slightly over 6,000 yards, and playing to a par of 71, Heather Hills was described in an *Indianapolis Star* article as having "forty-two traps and more than 100 grass mounds that are strategically placed to add character to the layout."

The swiftness and ease with which we built Heather Hills made me wonder why I hadn't entered the golf course design and construction business sooner. Unlike our difficult experiences at El Dorado, everything that could go right went right, and I was convinced that building golf courses was pretty easy.

The soil at Heather Hills was quite tillable, and Cliff Compton and a gentleman named Horace operated a scraper and a bulldozer. At El Dorado, the Nordsiek brothers knew all about construction and we simply told them what to do, but at Heather Hills we served as the contractors as well.

Trial and error was the only way to proceed, and we made many mistakes along the way. Attempting to build some of the first Pete Dye mounds out of discarded corncobs was one of them, and it nearly resulted in a visit from the fire department.

We needed to dispose of thousands of corncobs that were scattered across the course site, so I had Cliff Compton pile them all together. We then covered them with dirt, creating a pointed mound that made a background for one of the holes.

Unfortunately, 95-degree temperatures in the summer started those corncobs decomposing. Pretty soon the mound began to look like a fifteen-foot-high smoking tepee and gradually sank to ground level.

During construction very little rain fell, and we were able to work every day to complete building the course. By the middle of September, we were planting. Once the seed was sown, gentle rains pushed it down, and five days later grass was greening the fairways.

Miraculously, by the end of November, Heather Hills was playable. The president of the club, all the new members, and Tommy Perine joined a proud Alice and me for an inspection walk around the course, and everyone seemed pleased with what we had created.

In spite of all the accolades, one anxious moment occurred when a kindly lady member whispered to us, "I've been all over the golf course, and I can only find seventeen holes." At first we laughed to ourselves, but that evening my night's sleep was repeatedly interrupted by a persistent nightmare that somehow the lady was right.

The next morning I raced to the course and quickly counted the holes myself. Fortunately, one par-three was so short the lady had missed it. Our first eighteen-hole course actually included eighteen holes!

The number eight was significant to Heather Hills because my fee was $8,000, we built the course on 80 acres, and our cost to construct the entire course was $80,000. We were our own worst enemies by building the course so quickly, because Tommy Perine decided that the $8,000 design fee for only ten weeks of work was not warranted. Luckily, Alice's father's law firm convinced him otherwise, and we were paid our modest fee.

Heather Hills was completed and open for play in 1962. I was then asked to build nine holes west of Indianapolis for the Elks Lodge in Plainfield.

Assignments continued to come our way: we spread our efforts between designing nine holes at Brazil, Indiana; eighteen for a par-three course in Yorktown, Illinois; eighteen for the Tippecanoe Country Club in Monticello, Indiana; eighteen for the William S. Sahm Municipal Course in Indianapolis; and eighteen at Oakwood Country Club in Moline, Illinois, where they play the PGA Tour's Hardee's Classic.

Except for the Moline job, there was no competition, since nobody pursued those jobs but me. I traveled all over Indiana, Illinois, and Ohio in search of work; our fees never matched the mounting expenses.

My work for the USGA greens committee resulted in the assignment at Oakwood when their agronomist, Jim Holmes, recommended me for the course. Slowly I was shedding the businessman/golfer image that Alice believed was holding me back.

Balancing the construction of all of these courses wasn't difficult since they were not too far apart. Unlike today, we were responsible for the entire operation, and we had an office and secretary to assist us with employment, payroll, purchasing, and paying the bills.

Being selected to design and build the Sahm Municipal Course was significant. We bid for the job, and when the City of Indianapolis awarded it to us, it meant they recognized two of their own as legitimate designers.

Alice actually designed the course, which .featured a "star" configuration, bringing the holes back to the clubhouse. The total budget for our fee and construction costs was $180,000: the city didn't want the course to have any bunkers, which would need raking, or additional trees, which would create leaf problems in the fall.

All the people I worked with were patient, none more so than a man named Karl Dickerson in Brazil, Indiana. Nine holes were already in existence in that city when Karl called to inform me that a clause in the town code prevented building nine more. It would take three years to overcome all the red tape, but Karl never gave up even when the town was forced to raise the money for the course through sewer bonds!

During my work on these courses, Dr. Harlan Hansen, the president of the University of Michigan, played our nine-hole course at El Dorado. Apparently impressed with the layout, he asked us to consider designing the new eighteen-hole Radrick Farms course in Ann Arbor.

The original eighteen at the University of Michigan was designed by Alister Mackenzie and Perry Maxwell in 1931. Originally from Yorkshire, England, Dr. Mackenzie would be best known for his design of Cypress Point and Augusta National.

When Dr. Hansen chose Alice and me to design the University of Michigan course, we were ecstatic; but I understood his selection raised a few eyebrows, since this was quite a prestigious assignment. I made several trips to Ann Arbor, and we spent considerable time formulating routings that incorporated lessons learned from all our other courses.

While we had been in charge of both design and construction at our previous courses, Radrick Farms was built by a contractor who was unable to implement many of the creative ideas I envisioned.

That experience made us question where we were headed. We had now completed ten golf courses, and while I prepared to join Alice as she played in the 1962 Women's North and South Amateur at Pinehurst that spring, I felt we needed to focus on what type of Pete and Alice Dye golf course we wanted to design in the years ahead.

While I was building El Dorado, I also became concerned about what impact my being a golf course designer might have on my amateur standing. To check that status, I wrote to Joe Dey (pronounced Dye), then executive director of the United States Golf Association and later commissioner of the PGA Tour.

Alice and I have wonderful memories of Mr. Dey. I first met him in 1946, when I played in the United States Amateur at Baltusrol. I was there on a shoestring, and even though I was given a locker in the fabled locker room, I changed my shoes and shirt in the car.

After I lost my first-round match, I was leaving the course when a friend asked me if I received my favor from the tournament committee. Never one to turn down a gift, I went to my locker, but when I opened it, out burst reams of papers and forms that Mr. Dey had been frantically looking for to run the tournament.

Sometime later Alice and I arrived at the 1955 United States Women's Amateur in Charlotte, North Carolina, and were given an air-conditioned suite with a sitting room that was meant for Joe Dey. I told Alice how pleased I was that the USGA treated us so well, not realizing that Mr. Dey spent the tournament days sweltering in a tiny no-view room without air conditioning.

Despite these mix-ups—and one where Joe instead of me was called off the Memphis Country Club course in 100-degree heat only to hear Alice tell him, "Honey I won! I won!" after a successful match in the Western Amateur—Joe Dey became one of our best friends. His impeccable reputation and dedication to preserving the integrity of the game are unequaled.

My letter to Mr. Dey at USGA headquarters questioned whether Alice and I would lose our amateur golfer standings since we were now golf course designers. The answer was of great interest to us since we wanted to continue competing in national tournaments such as the United States Amateur, the North and South, and the Western, as well as in local events in Indiana.

Joe Dey wrote back a wonderful letter that said: "Believe me, it won't make any difference." Years later, I understood what Mr. Dey had meant, since the sixteen-hours-a-day, seven-days-a-week, down-in-the-trenches profession I'd chosen seldom allowed me to play in any national tournaments again.

Despite the time and hard work involved, Alice and I had realized a dream by successfully designing and building our first few golf courses. We weren't certain what the future held, but as fate would have it, our return to Donald Ross' famous Pinehurst course would trigger a visit to the ancient courses of Scotland. After that trip, our vision of golf course design would come clearly into focus.

St. Andrews and the Magic of Scotland

The more I studied the Old Course at St. Andrews, the more I loved it, and the more I loved it, the more I studied it.

Robert Tyre (Bobby) Jones, Jr.

After my first qualifying round in the 1963 British Amateur Championship, I brashly told an astonished Scottish reporter that the Old Course at St. Andrews was a goat ranch, and if I played it a thousand times, it would still be a goat ranch! Three days and seven rounds later, I realized it was one of the greatest golf courses in the world.

Standing on the first tee at the Old Course day after day marked the turning point in my golf course design career. Making the overseas trip to the British Isles at age thirty-eight had come at the urging of former USGA executive Richard Tufts, and I'm eternally grateful to Mr. Tufts for his suggestion.

Aware of our budding career as golf course designers, Mr. Tufts believed Alice and I could "broaden our scope" through exposure to the legendary courses. He knew of our love for the game and wanted us to experience firsthand the mystical essence that surrounds the ancient courses of Scotland.

Neither Alice nor I had ever been to the British Isles, but we both knew of the age-old tradition associated with the English and Scottish courses and the fact that almost all of the great American courses we'd played were fashioned by architects born in the British Isles.

On the airplane to Scotland, I sat with Mr. Tufts, an austere man who loved golf more than life itself. Armed with a keen sense of tradition, he provided me with an abbreviated history lesson of the legendary courses there.

Since I greatly respected Mr. Tufts' opinion, I listened with strong interest. He vividly described intriguing courses that I had only seen in pictures, and his colorful stories heightened my interest in visiting the home of golf course architecture.

My introduction to Scotland, however, was not exactly what I had imagined. Moments after landing at Prestwick Airport, I was unexpectedly detained by the authorities and taken to an inquisition room. There the bobbies questioned me about why my suitcase was full of women's underwear and toiletries. I began to wonder whether they thought I was a cross-dresser, and unfortunately my explanations didn't seem to satisfy their curiosity. It wasn't until Alice's plane arrived and she corroborated my story—we'd traveled separately because we had two young sons at home—that they released me.

That introduction to Scotland preceded our whirlwind tour of more than thirty courses in the British Isles. Thirsty for new concepts, Alice and I studied and photographed as we played and began a library of ideas and concepts for future course designs.

While all of the Scottish courses provided us with imaginative ideas, five of them presented spectacular images that would substantially influence the design of every single golf course we would build in the future.

Of all of the great Scottish links, I believe Turnberry, where Nick Price won the 1994 British Open, may be the most imposing. Laid out overlooking the golden sweep of the sands of Turnberry Bay, the course is set along the rockbound coast in the shadows of the stately Edwardian Hotel that is perched on a hilltop.

Designed by Willie Fernie in 1909, the championship Ailsa Course features innovative holes with such intimidating names as

"Woe-be-tide" (watch out or the lurking waters of the firth can be your downfall), "Risk-an-hope" (self-explanatory), and "Ca' Canny" (take care, for heavy punishment lurks all around).

The first championship held at Turnberry was the 1912 Women's British Open Amateur, and the course remained intact until it was utilized as an airfield during World War II. Observant British reporters wrote that "instead of pitch marks and divots, Turnberry was strewn with skid marks, runways, wind socks, and hangars."

Restoration by architects Frank Hole and Mackenzie Ross after the war was difficult and time-consuming, especially in the flat areas where the runway foundations had been constructed. More than 30,000 cubic yards of topsoil were transported to the course from nearby fields, and by 1951 the course was restored to its original beauty.

Turnberry's most famous hole is the ninth, aptly called Bruce's Castle after Robert the Bruce, the Scottish king who ruled from 1306 to 1329. The remains of his castle overlook the precipice of Turnberry Bay and lie between the eighth green and the ninth tee, which is perched high on a promontory rock.

While many great championships have been played at Turnberry, the confrontation between Jack Nicklaus and Tom Watson in the 1977 British Open is still vivid in my mind. With Watson leading by a single shot, the two great champions came to the "Ailsa Hame" (home hole), where Watson hit an incredible seven iron within two feet of the hole to win the old Claret Jug that serves as the championship trophy.

Coming as I did from the Midwest, I was dazzled to see the beautiful vistas of the sea, the rolling sand dunes, the vast open areas where the holes were built, and the incredible rock formations that bordered the seaside holes at Turnberry.

Alice and I were also struck by the different grasses that enveloped the countryside. Multiple shades of green dotted the fairways, roughs, and approaches to the greens, causing the course to appear even more undulating than it really was.

Seeing Turnberry was quite an eye-opener. I've always said Turnberry and a similar course called Royal Port Rush (in Ireland) may be the two greatest courses in the world when you combine beauty and strategic play.

I was so enthralled with Turnberry that I had the audacity to even jot down notes regarding a few design modifications that I believed to be in order. I wanted to send them to the owners of the course, but I figured they would think a young upstart like me was full of beans!

After we left Turnberry, Alice and I moved up the coast twenty miles to play fabled Prestwick, where the original twelve holes were laid out by Old Tom Morris. Now eighteen holes, Prestwick is aptly billed as the "Home of the Open Championship" since the first British Open was held there in 1860.

Set just across the road from Prestwick Airport, the ancient course is most famous for the "sleepers," or railroad ties, that are used to bulkhead the bunkers. Many other features at Prestwick stood out as well, including the narrow first hole (Railway) with the railroad track out-of-bounds to the right and a pot bunker placed strategically along the left, demanding the golfer pay attention from the very first tee.

Prestwick was built along the railroad route so players could take the train to the course. When the old railroad ties were replaced, the discarded ones were thrown onto the course, where they were ultimately used to hold back the erosion of the hillside bunkers.

The Scots accepted the use of railroad ties as just part of the golf course, and my round at Prestwick marked the very first time I had ever seen them. I was fascinated by their ability to add a striking, demanding dimension to the course by not only providing a means to control erosion but also presenting the golfer with a highly visible obstacle.

Prestwick features a golf hole unlike any in the world—the 206-yard par-three fifth hole, aptly named "Himalayas." The tee shot is completely blind, with the only aid being the caddie and a small marker set on top of the mini mountain to suggest the recommended flight of the ball.

Prestwick is a delightful test that features its famous railroad ties, pot bunkers, multicolored heather, seaside bent grass, cavernous bunkers, blind holes, narrow sloping fairways, and the menacing Pow Burn (a winding, weaving creek). Adding to the challenge is a prevailing wind that one day may be a zephyr and the next a tempest.

Despite its difficulty, Prestwick plays to just 6,544 yards, and I was amazed that this short golf course could present such a formidable challenge. Alice and I had now added Prestwick's sleepers and Turnberry's vastness to our design notes as we continued our trek across Scotland.

Carnoustie is located just across the estuary from St. Andrews on the central Scottish coast and is played around the edges of a hollow square. Since most of the holes head off in a different direction, judgment of the seaside wind is critical to playing well at the famed links course.

First designed as a ten-hole layout by Allan Robertson in 1850 and then completed over the next twenty years, Carnoustie's length is a determining factor, but the placement of the drive is more crucial. The Barry Burn, a twisting, narrow, three-foot strip of water, winds in and around the course and must be reckoned with on nearly every tee shot.

Very few trees interrupt the Carnoustie landscape, but the prickly gorse impedes a player more than any tree ever could. The abrupt mounds and uneven terrain make the golfer's stance inconsistent, and many shots need to be bounced in to Carnoustie's firm, undulating greens.

As I walked the fabled links, Ben Hogan's miraculous win ten years earlier was still fresh in my mind. Coming as it did shortly after his near-fatal car crash, the "Wee Ice Man's" score of 282 was good enough to give him the championship.

Even now, I can remember standing in "Hogan's Alley," a narrow strip of fairway that stretches between the dangerous bunkers in the middle of the fairway and the out-of-bounds to the left of the par-five, 575-yard sixth hole. On his way to the championship, Hogan amazed the spectators when he successfully hit his drive way left of the boundary line and then curved it back forty yards to the right onto the fairway landing area.

Set next to the sea among the flatlands, Carnoustie may not be as scenic as other Scottish courses, but there is no doubt that it is one of the world's most demanding courses.

Jack Nicklaus found out firsthand about the resistance of Carnoustie's governing body to his suggestions that they soften the course. At the "Railway" ninth, a 474-yard par-four with out-of-bounds to the left side, Nicklaus apparently told officials he was upset that his drive to the right side of the fairway always seemed to end up on a downhill incline.

Those officials listened very carefully to Nicklaus's words, and when he left, Jack was certain the situation would be remedied next time he played there. Sure enough, when Jack returned, Carnoustie's finest had replaced the downhill incline with a steep pot bunker that they aptly named "Jack Nicklaus"!

When Alice and I played Carnoustie, we not only played a course that is rich in British Open history but also gained an adopted son. Part of the magic of playing in Scotland is to bond with a proud, wily veteran caddie who knows the course as well as his Scottish ancestry. At Carnoustie, however, we were assigned two fourteen-year-old caddies, Joe Soutar and Andy Coogan, Jr. These two boys shepherded us around the course, and I could tell Alice had taken an instant liking to Andy because of his courteous manner.

Toward the end of our round, Alice surprised me by suggesting that "maybe we should take this boy home with us." At first I thought she was kidding, but once the round was over, I realized Alice was serious. I went to the starter, a man named Lardlaw, and told him we wanted to talk to Andy's parents about his coming to the United States to visit us.

Mr. Coogan turned out to be a chisel-boned, rosy-cheeked, lively gent who thirty years later would be awarded the Queen's medal for his work in coaching young Scottish distance runners. He recalls Alice's first words to him being, "I want to take your son home with us." After some discussion of the particulars, he agreed to allow the boy to fly to America a few weeks later.

Andy Jr. joined us in Indianapolis in the fall of 1963, and with his great dimples and Scottish brogue, he was a big success with all the teenage girls. He continued his education in Indianapolis, and our friend Wayne Timberman, Sr., found him a job in the pro shop at Meridian Hills Country Club.

Andy stayed with us for eighteen months and then returned to Scotland, where he finished his education. Today he lives in Australia, where he is a very successful timepiece distributor and a member of the prestigious Victoria Golf Club.

Andy's charm and wit permitted Alice and me to see Carnoustie from every angle. In contrast to Turnberry and Prestwick, the nearly 150-year-old course plays long, and I often hit woods for the second shot to the par-four greens.

That's because Carnoustie features seven par-fours of more than 450 yards. Most of them are played either into or across the wind, and I hit my snappy little hook so the ball would run far enough to give me a fighting chance to reach those par-fours in two.

Above all, Carnoustie struck me as a fooler. Alice and I may have adopted a son at Carnoustie, but we'd also had imprinted on our minds a type of design that was straightforward and honest while still being difficult as hell.

My first experience playing Royal Dornoch, which is set along the extreme north coast of Scotland, came after a long, laborious motor trip up the Scottish countryside. Even though I was exhausted from the drive, I still wanted to play, but I saw two women in long pleated skirts heading for the first tee.

I begged Alice to hurry, but she had learned that Donald Ross's brother Alec was on the nearby practice green, and she wanted to take a picture of him. By the time she finished, the two women had teed off and were headed down the first fairway.

I was intent on going through the women, so I hurried every shot on the first two holes. Finally, Alice stopped my fast-paced play by pointing out that the twosome was now on number *seven*!

Our caddies told us the two women, a librarian and a schoolteacher, played every evening at five-thirty and finished eighteen holes a little after seven! That was my introduction to how quickly the Scots played the game. That evening, while we inserted quarters in the room heater to keep warm, Alice was still laughing at my male chauvinist behavior.

Donald Ross's hometown of Dornoch is located just fifty miles north of Loch Ness. It's situated just four degrees below the Arctic Circle, and I remember Alice waking up and getting dressed when light came through the window, only to discover the time was two a.m.!

For many years, Royal Dornoch, which plays to just 6,500 yards in length, was a little-known jewel. Slowly its reputation grew, and it's now listed by many experts as one of the top ten courses in the world.

In a letter to the members at the club, Tom Watson called playing Royal Dornoch "the most fun I ever had playing golf." Herbert Warren Wind has described Royal Dornoch as the "most natural course in the world." Both are right.

Royal Dornoch has an open feeling and such incredible beauty that even a golfer who can't post a score will love to play there. Royal Dornoch is a most forgiving golf course with generous landing areas, and no matter what tee is played, golfers can experience approach shots that offer bail-out areas conducive to recovery.

Alice and I also noticed that the sea was visible from nearly every location on the golf course. I was in awe of how Old Tom Morris and Mr. Sutherland had blended eighteen holes into the seaside hills.

Most distinctive at Royal Dornoch, which features yellow gorse and purple-heather-lined fairways (there are no trees), were the pint-size greens on the par-three holes. We saw how effective this design feature could be in demanding a precision shot, and in making recovery ones difficult from the severe slopes just off the collar of the green.

I also noted that while many of the greens appeared to be elevated, they were not. Instead, the earth in front of these putting surfaces had been excavated, making the ground-level greens look elevated.

Turnberry. Prestwick. Carnoustie. Royal Dornoch. Four different visions of Scottish course majesty had come our way as we headed to St. Andrews, the mecca of golf.

Winning two matches to reach the third round of the 1963 British Amateur at St. Andrews was more than I ever expected, and it permitted me to play the Old Course enough times (I played seven rounds in all—two in practice, two qualifying, and three in the tournament) to truly appreciate Old Tom Morris's strategy of design.

My new thoughts about the course coincided with the perceptions Alice had as she watched me and the other Walker Cup players compete in the British Amateur. Alice thought St. Andrews' simple beauty with clean lines and wonderful vegetation enhanced a sense of spaciousness, since none of the holes were hemmed in by trees.

Alice also talked a great deal about the lack of definition and the vastness of the course. Definition came with the straight side of a pot bunker or when the gorse provided framing for the holes, far different from the lines of U.S. courses that relied on trees to outline the holes.

We both discussed the fact that none of the slopes at St. Andrews were gradual. Instead, the natural terrain lent itself to steep, sharp mounds and cutoffs that demanded innovative play.

At St. Andrews, we witnessed golf course design in its purest form. Fortunately, Allan Robertson and Old Tom Morris, true pioneers of golf course architecture, respected what God provided and molded it carefully into a golf course. Sometimes less is better, and fortunately the designers of the Old Course used great care not to significantly alter the wonderful natural look of the terrain.

The double-size greens at St. Andrews are especially unique and are so huge the player can have a sixty-yard putt! Even at that early stage of my design career, I noticed that those double greens were shaped so that there is one long matching contour to join them.

Since the holes parallel one another in one long back-and-forth loop, a player on one side of the green who is playing an outward hole could possibly be struck by a ball hit by a golfer heading in the opposite direction. Fortunately, this rarely occurs, since the greens are so large that one foursome is seldom aware of the other.

The wide fairways and roughs are somewhat indistinguishable from one another at St. Andrews, but the straying shot disappears in the gorse, a prickly, dense, sometimes seasonally colorful bush. The wind bellows across the sandy hills stronger than any Texas sidewinder, and it's not unusual for it to change direction three times in ten minutes.

There may be no greater feeling a golfer can have than to stand on the first tee at St. Andrews and hear the starter yell,

"Play ahead." Even with a forty-mile-an-hour wind and sleet gusting sideways, the ardent golfers stand their ground and try to strike a drive down the first fairway toward the wee burn 260 yards away.

While there are many outstanding holes at the Old Course, I will never forget playing the seventeenth, which may very well be the best par-four in the world. Whether that's true or not, the legend of the Road Hole befits its image, for in my opinion the design is textbook perfect.

Every time I played the seventeenth, I appreciated the strategy for the hole more. The hole measures 461 yards, and when the wind blows off the sea, it howls dead straight into the golfer's teeth. The tee shot was played from a tee positioned next to the out-of-bounds, left to right around an old coal yard, where the new hotel is now. The green then opens right to left, with a severe pot bunker guarding the left side of the green and the road and wall protecting the right.

I was so impressed with the design of the green at seventeen that Alice and I rented a tripod in the city to measure the dimensions. We were amazed to see that the green was in fact a perfect rectangular shape even though it appears oval from the fairway.

The distinctiveness of the Road Hole comes from the positioning of the pot bunker, the severe slope of the green down into the swale, and the close proximity of the stone wall. I once suggested to Walt Disney that we attempt to duplicate the hole, complete with the old coal yard steam engine, on a course he wanted to design, but he died before we could follow through.

Quite apart from the ancient ambience of St. Andrews, the course impressed Alice and me with its ability to require golfers to play every variety of shot. We felt the course, whose sandy-soil terrain reminded me of Pinehurst No. 2, demanded great skill, with both the physical and mental aspects of the game.

That impression is not apparent until the golfer is able to appreciate the uniqueness of the design, since it is difficult at first to distinguish one hole from another. The first few times I played, I felt as if the caddie just pointed in some direction and I shot into a vast area with nothing to guide me.

After a few rounds, something suddenly clicked in my mind

and I unconsciously began to visualize the holes as if I were in a helicopter. Even though I was playing blind at ground level, my mind could visualize the course. I could "see" all the mounds, swales, and bunkers and appreciate the great strategy of a course designed like no other in the world today.

By playing at least thirty-six holes a day, Alice and I also toured Muirfield, Western Gales, Ayr, Troon, Nairn, Gullane, and North Berwick, among others. Each course was distinctive, and I've returned several times to play these courses again, and to visit Ireland and England as well.

Any unexpected hopes of winning the 1963 British Amateur were squelched in the third round by a gentleman whose day job was professional roller skating! That loss barely diminished my wonderful week at St. Andrews.

I again qualified for the British Amateur in 1973, but I was defeated when my opponent holed his approach shot on the sixteenth hole for an eagle two.

My son P.B. and I traveled to Ireland after that British Amateur and toured Royal Portmarnock for the first time. We were able to play this wonderful old course, which is set on a long tongue of links land by the Irish Sea, with the great Irish amateur Joe Carr. Bobby Locke called Portmarnock his favorite course, but when we finished, one of the caddies told P.B., "Too bad, laddie, that ya haven't seen our best."

The caddie was referring to Royal Portrush, near Belfast in Northern Ireland. Despite P.B.'s assurances, I was reluctant to make the trip to that war-torn zone, since trouble brews there daily.

Somehow P.B. talked me into going, but my apprehension grew when we landed at the airport square in the middle of Belfast. Army troops greeted us with a strip-search and they even rattled our golf clubs to make certain we weren't hiding any bullets.

Before I could relax, P.B. and I were speeding out of the airport in our rental car. Despite my pleas to the contrary, he almost gave me a heart attack when he became a daredevil on the highways, passing convoys of heavily armored cars and tanks.

Playing very few courses in the world would be worth that type of danger. Royal Portrush is the exception though, and it remains one of the most dramatic courses in the world.

During that initial trip to Scotland, Alice and I found out that most of the time the designer of the great Scottish courses was also involved in the building. This reinforced our feeling that it was difficult for a contractor to take a set of our plans and implement the vision that we had for the details of the course.

Based on these impressions, we knew the only way to build the specific type of greens, fairways, tees, and hazards we had in mind was for us to be intimately involved in the construction of our courses. That way, we would always have the opportunity to improvise and change things while the shaping was in progress.

This discovery would trigger another revelation. With so much hands-on attention needed for each course, we would have to dedicate ourselves to designing a select few.

The new direction I intended to take would incorporate many of the design features Alice and I collected during our exploratory trip to Scotland. Not all would prove successful, but my new understanding of the use of small greens, wide fairways, the impression that ground-level greens were elevated, contrasting grass mixes, severe undulations in the fairways, pot bunkers, railroad ties, blind holes and inclusion of gorse-like vegetation to frame holes would affect all our future designs.

Based on these impressions, Alice and I knew that if we were going to make our livelihood from golf course design, we needed to establish a link between our future courses and those of the past. The Good Lord through Richard Tufts had led us to Scotland to discover what beats in the heart of the game of golf, and when we returned to the United States to build Crooked Stick, we were ready to pursue our new vision.

Crooked Stick

A round of golf should permit eighteen inspirations.

A. W. Tillinghast
1929

When Mark O'Meara first stepped onto the thirteenth tee during the practice round for the 1991 PGA Championship at Crooked Stick, he took one look at the pin placement and yelled over at me, "Oh, I see, Pete, a dogleg par-three!"

If I don't hear those kinds of comments about my courses, I'm not a happy man. Silence may be golden and accolades cherished, but unless a few golf professionals are bellyaching about my course design, I wonder whether I've done enough to challenge them.

I call Crooked Stick our firstborn because, unlike our previous courses, Alice and I were involved with every aspect of the course development. We located the land, a 400-acre cornfield, purchased the option, raised the money, drew the routings, began construction of the back nine holes, raised more money, and then built the front nine.

Thoughts regarding the planning of this course started prior to our trip to Scotland in 1963, when Alice and I discussed the potential for building a new golf course on the north side of

Indianapolis. While the city could lay claim to such fine country club courses as Meridian Hills, the Country Club of Indianapolis, Broadmoor, Highland, and Hillcrest, we felt the Indianapolis area could use a bold new golf club to seriously challenge the better players of the day.

We envisioned a golf club modeled after Camargo in Cincinnati, with a small clubhouse and a tented area for parties and weddings. A swimming crib in the lake and tennis courts would be located somewhere on the property away from the main clubhouse.

The property finally optioned was near the corner of 116th Street and Ditch Road fifteen miles north of downtown Indianapolis. A cagey old lady named Mae Kerns owned the land. I remember sipping elderberry wine with her glass for glass one afternoon until my lack of sobriety permitted her to influence me to sign an option agreement to purchase the farmland for $1,200 an acre, which was double the market value!

Four businessmen, including Eugene Pulliam, owner of the *Indianapolis Star* and uncle of former vice president Dan Quayle, shared my vision for the course, and 106th Ditch Corporation was formed. Two hundred invitations for dinner were sent to a variety of people, all of whom were either family members or personal friends who were golf enthusiasts.

At 1964 dollar values, we would need two hundred members at $6,000 each or a total of $1,200,000 to buy the land and build the course. As soon as fifty-eight men and two women responded positively, we decided to proceed with the initial nine holes and hope that future financial matters would somehow be resolved. Eventually residential lots were sold along the borders of the course, and based on the success of those sales and our progress in constructing Crooked Stick, Merchants Bank in Indianapolis loaned the corporation the money to finish all eighteen holes.

For some time, the golf club had no name. "Spring Run Golf Club," "Old Farms Country Club," and my favorite, "Muir of Ord," a tribute to an out-of-the-way course in Scotland, were rejected. It wasn't until 1966, when the first nine holes were opened, that the name Crooked Stick was selected. When I picked up a knobby, crooked stick one day while walking the course, and used it to swat at a stone, charter member Bill Wick suggested the name.

Before starting construction on Crooked Stick, I purchased a used Caterpillar D-2 bulldozer with money earmarked for a fur coat for Alice. Several truckloads of fill dirt were ordered and dumped in our front yard.

For weeks the bulldozer, nicknamed "Mother's Mink," and a John Deere tractor moved the dirt around to see what sort of Scottish-type configurations I could create. People who drove by thought I was crazy, but I loved maneuvering the dirt into oblong mounds and odd-shaped slopes. The Scottish flavor was now in my blood, and I was determined to bring old-world ideas into the modern age.

Even though Crooked Stick has now hosted two major championships, the 1991 PGA and the 1993 USGA Women's Open, Alice and I never intended it to be anything but a challenging golf course playable by male and female golfers of every skill level. While Crooked Stick has become famous, our initial purpose was just to build a demanding course with the same sort of creative design characteristics we had seen in our travels.

Although golfers believe Alice and I build demonically difficult courses, that is true only when they are played from the back tees. We hope golfers will select the proper tees that fit their skill level, and be challenged with our intended design from those yardages.

A standard golf course will usually have a par of 72, and if that is true the course will generally consist of four par-threes, four par-fives, and ten par-fours. The length of the course will depend on available land and the goal of the owners, but it will usually measure somewhere in the range of 6,600 to 7,000-plus yards.

Between 150 and 200 acres are needed to build eighteen holes. There usually is a clubhouse, and so the architect normally loops the holes out and back so that the ninth and for certain the eighteenth green will be close to the clubhouse.

If the par-threes' total yardage approximates 700 yards (4 × 175 average) and the par-fives total nearly 2,000 yards (4 × 500 average), that means the ten par-fours will total some 4,000 yards (10 × 400 average) in length.

The setup on the back nine, which was the first nine built at Crooked Stick, looked as follows: two par-threes, one short, the other of considerable length; two par-fives, both lengthy, but reachable in two; and five par-fours, three of considerable length and two of average distance.

The holes were deliberately separated by the degree of difficulty. The demanding 440-yard par-four tenth was followed by the easier par-five eleventh. The medium-length par-four twelfth was followed by the exacting par-three thirteenth. The long par-four dogleg fourteenth, which many feel is the toughest hole on the course, is next, followed by the breather par-five fifteenth.

The last three holes should and do require great shots. Water comes into play on the approach shot at the par-four sixteenth, a severe bunker awaits the golfer on the devilish par-three seventeenth, and water hazards confront the player on both the drive and the approach shot at eighteen. My intention is to force golfers to think about the difficult finishing holes early in the round, so that pressure builds as they anticipate playing the final, demanding holes.

In order to present the golfer with into-the-wind, crosswind, and with-the-wind shots, the directions of the holes were balanced by heading the fourteenth to the west and south into the prevailing wind, the fifteenth to the west, the sixteenth back east, and the seventeenth north, with the eighteenth moving northeast. The holes themselves also bend at different angles. The par-four fourteenth plays right to left, the sixteenth left to right, the seventeenth right to left, and the eighteenth once again left to right, providing different tee-shot angles.

My main purpose in routing all of the holes in an alternating right-to-left and left-to-right sequence is to ask the player to implement a variety of shot techniques. I also like to follow a right-to-left tee shot with a green opening left to right.

Starting at the par-three thirteenth, Crooked Stick has some of the most natural holes I've ever built. Except for the par-four eighteenth, which had to be manufactured to get back to the clubhouse, holes thirteen through seventeen contain suitable elevated areas for tees and sloping downhill terrain blending into level ground for landing areas or greens.

Positioning the hazards on the back nine (built first) in alternating sequence was a priority, especially on the par-threes. A small winding creek was set to the right of the thirteenth green, while the sand bunker (*trap* is a word reserved for mice) on the seventeenth was positioned to the left.

The same sort of hole scheme would later be implemented when the front side was built. A short, narrow par-four opened the nine, followed by a tough dogleg-left par-four and the long but straightforward par-three third hole. The lengthy par-four fourth is followed by the long-but-lenient 591-yard par-five fifth. The short but dangerous across-the-water par-three sixth hole is followed by the medium-length par-four seventh, the treacherous around-the-lake dogleg eighth, and then the gambling short, reachable in two, par-five ninth.

Alternate placement of the hazards at the par-threes on the front side is notable, for the pot bunkers at three are placed to the left of the green while the pond at number six lies in front of and to the right of the green.

By 1964 we had built ten courses and made revisions on a dozen others. At El Dorado, the Nordsiek brothers built the course based on our instruction, but beginning with Heather Hills, where we rented the scraper and bulldozer, we began to take charge of all facets of the operation.

We had continued to increase our knowledge about construction as we built the early courses. Budgets varied, and we increased the amount of innovative design features as we learned.

Throughout the construction of Crooked Stick, we took note of lessons learned from the first courses we designed. At El Dorado, Alice and I put our heart and soul into the course, but we were just rank amateurs trying to build a dream course.

Fortunately, our opportunity to gain valuable experience at those early courses permitted us to be more ingenious working at Crooked Stick. There we would incorporate all of our visual experience, playing experience, and construction experience. Added to our exposure to the great courses in the United States were the old-world design ideas we learned during our trip to Scotland. Combined with our construction experience, we felt qualified to build a distinctive golf course.

Unlike golf courses such as Scioto and Inverness, where the rolling hills present the opportunity for natural elevation changes, Crooked Stick was a major challenge, since we started with mostly flat farmland. To create mounds and undulations as well as two large lakes, a great deal of earth had to be moved.

Fortunately, John Geupel, a partner in the Indianapolis construction firm of Geupel-DeMars, loaned us large earth-moving equipment. Although John thought I kept it a bit longer than he intended, the equipment allowed us to move an enormous amount of earth.

People have asked me whether I ever operate equipment. I do from time to time, but my main task is to direct the operation.

Five-a.m.-to-nine-p.m. workdays seven days a week were common as we gradually configured the land at Crooked Stick into a golf course. Hands-on participation allowed for improvisation, and the holes painstakingly began to appear.

While our work at the early courses was rewarding, I loved the day-to-day thrill of carving out the eighteen holes at Crooked Stick, since we were in charge of all aspects of construction. Trial and error was the method, but amazingly enough the course evolved with a look close to our original vision.

I experimented with using small, more versatile machinery that could produce pockets, dips, swales, hollows, undulations, and odd shapes reminiscent of the courses I'd seen in Scotland and such American courses as Pinehurst No. 2, Shore Acres, Seminole, and Camargo.

At Pinehurst, Donald Ross used "drag pans" drawn by mules to sculpt his mounds and hollows. Richard Tufts described these pans as resembling the blade of a broad, flat sugar scoop with two handles attached to the rear.

According to Mr. Tufts, when the operator lifted the handles, the front edge of the pan scooped up a slice of earth. Several runs were made before the desired amount of soil was then dumped in another location. Many mounds were configured at a time, and the operator moved around in a circular fashion to create the unusual knobs and ridges so unique to Pinehurst.

To emulate this look, we used small equipment like the D-2 bulldozer, a Caterpillar 955 loader, and a wheel tractor that pulled an old broken-down farm disc. Undulating mounds were created that looked worn and eroded. Instead of the dome shape created by larger bulldozers, the mounds and swales roughed out were ragged and uneven, just as I had practiced doing in our lot at home.

Inexperienced dozer operators were perfect for this kind of shaping. A beautiful lawn around a bank building was not the object, and so I stayed away from any operator who had experience with landscape design.

To this day, there is nothing else on the face of this earth that I'd rather do than climb up on a tractor and shape some dirt. I don't have any preconceived notion about what I'm going to build, but my scrambled-egg vision somehow works itself around to something meaningful as construction continues.

That is especially true regarding the undulations I shape. They just happen, and I suppose I'd compare myself to an artist working and reworking his clay.

That method was used when we experimented with the configurations for the greenside bunkers at Crooked Stick. Using a Caterpillar 955 loader, I found that I could dump various loads of dirt where I wanted the back of the bunkers, and then take the Ford wheel tractor with a mat attached on the back and drag it across the piles to create a windswept look.

In an effort to duplicate the grassy swales and hollows that are found at Pinehurst No. 2 and in the sandy seaside courses that drained naturally, an artificial internal drainage system had to be devised at Crooked Stick.

While I admit to being influenced by Donald Ross' strategic style of designing holes, Charles Blair Macdonald, Seth Raynor, and Alister Mackenzie's creations have had an even greater impact on my work.

I admired Mr. Macdonald's imagination and his sense for the dramatic. Besides his design of deep bunkers and severe sloping mounds near his greens, he believed in building fall-away angle greens reminiscent of Scotland. When Mr. Macdonald died, Seth Raynor continued that pattern, and those two creative men are responsible for a select group of courses that are among the best in the world.

Alister Mackenzie on the other hand was clearly a stylist who intended that the roll which began with the approach should continue on through the putting surface. The greens at number ten and number fourteen at Crooked Stick represent Dr. Mackenzie's influence.

While the bunker at the par-five eleventh was reminiscent of Henry Fownes's "church-pew" bunker at Oakmont, number fourteen was originally intended to be a copy of Alister Mackenzie's picturesque par-five thirteenth at Augusta National. There wasn't enough yardage available, and so it became a sharp dogleg par-four over a creek that cut the fairway at a severe angle. The par-five fifteenth features a large horseshoe green with a deep sand bunker in the middle, copying Mackenzie's hole at the University of Michigan.

Donald Ross's style at Pinehurst No. 2 is apparent in several features on the course. Besides the Ross crowned green at number two, I emulated his concept of providing wide landing areas off the tee with a preferred position for playing to the opening of tightly guarded greens.

The object here was to keep the driver in the player's hands and cut back on the number of times when a long iron or four wood is used for accuracy. The roughs were planned to be medium length so that even if golfers missed the fairways they would attempt to hit the risky approach shot to the green instead of pitching out with a wedge.

Like Mr. Ross's design at Pinehurst, this begs the golfer to play aggressively. Narrow fairway landing areas and deep rough make for caution, since the intelligent golfer plays more conservatively by leaving the driver in the bag on many of the holes.

The seventh green reflects Charles Blair Macdonald's work, and the green at the par-three thirteenth with its severe reverse-slope angles was patterned after Dr. Mackenzie's design at the University of Michigan. The large, rolling look of the greens on the third, eighth, tenth, and thirteenth through fifteenth holes were also influenced by Mackenzie.

The greens at Crooked Stick have always been its calling card. My improved skill with the USGA specifications formula on the original greens, along with the modifications I made in 1985, personally lead me to believe the putting surfaces are among the best I've ever built.

Crooked Stick is for the most part a straightforward golf course where golfers appear to be playing down toward an illusionary elevated green. Most of the greens are really at ground level, but with so much earth removed in front, they appear elevated in the mind's eye.

In several situations at Crooked Stick, the player is deceived with optical illusions. What you see may not be what you get at my courses, and the setup by the green at number ten is a prime example.

Success at this hole requires the tee shot to avoid the lake on the right and find a preferred position on the left side of the fairway, since the green opens from that angle. First glance indicates that the safest approach shot is to the left side of the green, since there is a series of rugged sand bunkers stacked to the right.

Closer inspection discloses just the opposite to be true. Since the green is sloped severely left to right, if the ball misses the green to the left, the pitch shot to the pin will land on a downhill slope. On the other hand, the bunkers to the right are shallow and the shot is played into the upslope of the green, making it much easier to stop the ball near the flagstick.

Because Crooked Stick needed to have its own look, different-colored grasses were used to give the course contrast. The greens were planted with an apple Cohansey bent and the fairways with a dark purplish-green Penncross bent. These different shades of green were bordered with short rough of tannish-green fescue.

Crooked Stick was finished and all eighteen holes opened for play in 1967. It's not a course that has one overwhelmingly difficult hole, but there's a saying among the members that sooner or later "The Stick will get ya."

Since our youngsters Perry and Paul Burke (P.B.) helped Alice and me, Crooked Stick was a real family affair. Both boys raked bunkers, hauled water, and drove small tractors to spread green mix.

Our white German shepherd Otto also influenced the play of the course by moving one of the marking stakes. His exploits got me into hot water later with one of the finest amateur golfers the sport has ever seen. Who would have thought our beloved Otto's playfulness would cause the great Ed Tutwiler, winner of numerous amateur championships and runner-up in the 1964 United States Amateur, to lose an important match at Crooked Stick?

During construction, a crew member was asked to haul large rocks found along the lake bordering the hole to a place marked by a stake three hundred yards off the tee, out of play in the rough on the right side of the eighth hole. Unbeknownst to me, Otto had used those strong teeth of his to yank the stake out of the ground, and he moved it sixty yards closer, just off the fairway.

Following my instructions, the worker piled the rocks near the stake, and I never saw the need to move them. Unfortunately, one day Ed's straight-arrow tee shot hit those rocks dead center and careened to the left forty yards into the lake. Ed's penalty shot was not taken lightly, and he arranged to have Otto's rocks removed the next day.

Experiences such as these made building Crooked Stick even more special to me, and when the course was completed I felt we had achieved our goal by building a demanding golf course for Indianapolis. When our low-handicap members competed in national events and extolled its virtues, the course began to gain a national reputation.

Most of the comments about Crooked Stick were complimentary, but I really never believed the course was finished. Time and money originally prevented me from positioning bunkers on the fairways, and it wasn't until the late 1970s that I was able to build bunkers on the left sides of numbers two and fifteen and on the right side of the sixteenth hole. Over the next few years, I continued to attempt to finish the course, oftentimes to the disgruntlement of the members, who got tired of hearing the *beep, beep, beep* of a bulldozer in their backswing.

In 1983 the USGA Senior Amateur Championship was held at Crooked Stick, but the experience turned out to be a disaster for me. Officials at the club and the USGA let the roughs grow too high, and the greens were made so lightning fast that my fellow senior competitors were taking three, four, and even five putts on some greens.

In addition, the tournament was played in October, and the cool weather added to the seniors' misery. I had qualified for match play, but the brash criticism, with which I agreed, made me want to withdraw and throw all the green mowers into the lake.

This experience made it apparent that if Crooked Stick were ever to hold any major championships, modifications of the greens would be necessary. Increased green speeds made my twenty-year-old greens almost unplayable. I knew that since Crooked Stick might very well be looked upon as a potential host for a major championship there were modifications to be considered.

The contour of the original greens was simply too severe for the new speeds. The rolls in those greens were playable at slower speeds, but when the greens were cut shorter, the golf ball simply exploded down the slopes.

That revelation at the USGA Senior Amateur Championship started me thinking about remodeling the greens, but my chance to do so came quite by accident two years later. In 1985, a blight struck the greens, and that unfortunate event, in combination with our being notified that the 1991 PGA Championship could be awarded to the course, presented the opportunity to recontour all eighteen greens.

By this time I had built the Stadium Course at the Tournament Players Club and was aware of the need for spectator mounds at Crooked Stick. Besides slowing the green rolls, I spent a considerable amount of time on eighteen, replacing the long hourglass green with a spherical one that had a huge spectator mound directly behind it.

The recontouring of the greens was in line with green speeds demanded by PGA tournament officials. Penncross bent replaced Cohansey, and I slowed the greens down by adding counter-rolls to even out the contours.

Later, I positioned the new tenth tee on a portion of the mound behind number eighteen, causing the hole to play more at a left-to-right angle off the tee. Dirt for building the mound came when I increased the size of the lake that bordered the right edge of the eighteenth green.

The par-three seventeenth was also revamped when I replaced the original "committee" green—built based on suggestions by too many friends—with a long, narrow, curved one guarded by a deep sand bunker twelve feet below the putting surface.

At its distance of nearly 7,000 yards in the mid-1960s, Crooked Stick could handle even the longest of drivers. To protect the course from being overpowered by long hitters, I had built slight inclines in the landing areas, which slowed the ball from rolling forward. Recent changes in ball and club technology permitted most golfers to hit the ball farther, and many of them could now drive over the inclines that had been built to retain them. Players would then catch the downhill slopes and pick up a great deal of extra yardage.

To counteract this, I moved back almost every championship tee at Crooked Stick, adding nearly four hundred yards to the length of the course. *Most* of the PGA contestants, save eventual champion John Daly, were unable to fly the ball over the original landing area and they hit into the uphill inclines.

The length of the rough in a major championship is always of considerable interest. Because the playing professionals had complained about the length of the Bermuda rough at Shoal Creek the year before, the PGA was especially sensitive to this issue.

Crooked Stick was set up for the 1991 PGA Championship along the lines of the traditional courses that had been selected in the past. I felt the risk/reward ratio was in balance, the green speed moderate but challenging, and that a score around ten under par would win the championship.

Crooked Stick's selection to host the PGA meant even more to me because the twenty-five-year-old course had been successfully improved to the point where it was worthy of hosting such a prestigious event.

The man most responsible for bringing the tournament to the course was professional golfer Mickey Powell. Alice and I knew Mickey from our days at the Country Club of Indianapolis, where he caddied for us from the time he was thirteen.

Mickey used to walk six or seven miles along a railroad track to the Country Club from his home in Clermont. The fact that he would caddie double and then have to walk those miles back was impressive, and when it came time for him to go to college, we helped him out financially.

Several years later, Mickey, who would go on to become a top club professional and owner of the Golf Club of Indiana as well as president of the PGA of America, appeared on our doorstep ready to pay us back. I told him to use the funds to help some other young man, but I can remember Mickey saying, "No Pete, *you* take the money and *you* help somebody."

That is characteristic of the type of man Mickey is. More than thirty years later, he would spearhead efforts for Crooked Stick to host the PGA, and his determination paid off when the announcement was made on March 17, 1986.

Just as the victory by the legendary Arnold Palmer in the very first Heritage Classic in 1969 brought recognition to Harbour Town, the miracle win by unheralded John Daly in the PGA brought immense publicity to Crooked Stick. No one could have written a more perfect Hollywood script, and when long-driving John walked off with the crown, it was a great moment for the game and Crooked Stick.

Over four days John demolished my golf course! He drove the ball where no man had ever driven it, and sometimes his golf ball seemed to just start rising as it cleared those fairway inclines of mine.

Daly's blasting of the ball brought Crooked Stick to its knees, since most of the hazardous areas never came into play for him. At the dogleg-left fourteenth, a brute across a creek with out-of-bounds on the left, John crushed the ball over the out-of-bounds, the trees, and the creek onto the fairway just seventy-five yards short of the green!

This feat shocked me, since before the tournament I was obsessed with guaranteeing that none of the professionals could cut the dogleg. I wanted to make certain they were forced to drive the ball out to the right side of the fairway and then have a long iron into the green.

I took the longest-hitting Crooked Stick members to the proposed area for the new fourteenth tee and had them drive dozens of golf balls out over the creek. Based on my observations, the final position for the tee required the golfer to *carry* the ball 265 yards if he took the shortcut. That is exactly what long John did all *four* days!

Adding to the Cinderella story was the fact that if it hadn't been for Nick Price's last-minute withdrawal due to the impending arrival of his baby, John Daly would have never played in the tournament. Four days later he was a sure-fire, larger-than-life superman with the world at his fingertips.

While Daly may have been a brash twenty-five-year-old from Memphis, his play reminded me of the way young Jack Nicklaus used to overwhelm the competition. John's length was awesome, but as the tournament continued, it was more the way the other players *watched* Daly, as if they knew the new kid on the block was taking over.

"He might be a one-week phenomenon," second-place finisher Bruce Lietzke told the press after the tournament, "but I'm leaning toward this kid being for real."

Bruce was an eyewitness regarding that incredible length of Daly's. One of the most vivid television moments of the tournament occurred when Bruce stopped and turned back toward the fourteenth tee just as Daly's three-hundred-yard-plus drive was bouncing past him.

"I can't remember when I've hit my driver this straight," Daly told the awestruck press. "All four days, I didn't think. I just said 'hit it.' Squeaky [his caddie] said 'kill' and I killed it . . . I had no fear out there."

Remember how I moved the tees? Lengthened the holes? Remodeled the bunkers? Rebuilt the greens? For what?

All for naught, as evidenced by John's play in the second round at the 495-yard par-five ninth hole. Disregarding the water and bunkers protecting the left side, Mr. Daly simply drove up and over everything and then cradled a short iron to within three feet of the hole for an eagle three. During the week, he played the four par-fives in *twelve* under par.

I could offer the excuse that the heavy rains before the tournament and the lack of any stiff wind aided his efforts, but I'm not sure that would have made any difference with Daly. He beat me and ol' Crooked Stick fair and square, and his fairy tale story captured the fancy of golfers around the world.

Two years later, the 1994 USGA Women's Open Golf Championship was played at Crooked Stick. Indiana supported the tournament with the largest galleries ever to see the event.

Play of the final round was in jeopardy when a torrential rain and wind storm hit the area. Because of tremendous efforts by golf course superintendent Chris Hague and his crew, club members, and volunteers to hose off muddy greens, pump out bunkers, and remove downed tree limbs, the tournament was completed on schedule.

Crooked Stick played to a distance of just under 6,000 yards, causing some members of the media to criticize the course as too

short. This proved to be inaccurate, since the women professionals hit approximately the same irons to the greens as the PGA
players did.

Alice and I were pleased that chipper thirty-two-year-old Laurie Merten won the championship, but it was a comment by
David Eger, the USGA's senior director of rules and competitions
and a former Mid-Amateur Champion, that warmed my heart.
When asked by reporters to compare Crooked Stick with other
great courses, David said, "Mr. Dye's ability to require the player
to strategically place the ball in the wide fairways so as to permit
the proper angle to the pin on the second shot reminds me a
great deal of Pinehurst No. 2."

Having hosted the USGA Junior, USGA Senior, and USGA
Mid-Amateur championships, the PGA, and the USGA Women's
Open, Crooked Stick has achieved more acclaim than I ever
thought possible. I would still like to modify two of the holes to
permit play of two great short par-fours, but in total the course
has proven worthy of its demanding reputation.

Recently Alice and I built a home on the eighteenth hole at
Crooked Stick, where we can look out and see our firstborn. The
great courses in Scotland may have the magic, but Crooked Stick
has our hearts.

Crooked Stick Golf Club Carmel, Indiana Par 72		
	Men	Women
Yardage:	7159, 6620, 5964	5964, 5207
Rating/ Slope:	75.3/141, 72.3/129, 69.3/123	74/129, 69.7/118

Resolution Presented to Pete Dye
at Crooked Stick, December 1969

WHEREAS, there was once a time when CROOKED STICK GOLF CLUB was merely a gleam in the eye of PETE DYE, a life insurance huckster, who could do a thing or two with a crooked stick and who dreamed of becoming a golf course architect;

WHEREAS, there was another time when PETE DYE's negotiating skills (and ability to consume vast quantities of elderberry wine) enabled him to cozen the owners of about 400 hundred acres of Hamilton County farm land out of their fields and streams, which they let him steal from them at not more than twice what the ground was worth;

WHEREAS, there was still another time when PETE DYE's irresistible salesmanship conned a group of assorted golf nuts, with more enthusiasm than good sense, into putting up the funds (somewhat less than was actually needed, but somewhat more than they could comfortably afford) to pay for the land and build thereon a golf course:

WHEREAS, there was still another time, during a walk in the woods near the clubhouse site, when PETE DYE is reputed to have picked up the gnarled old stick which gave CROOKED STICK GOLF CLUB its name;

WHEREAS, there was still a later time (interminable, so it seemed) when flatlands became rolling hills, and creek beds became lakes, and little swales became bottomless pits, and open glades appeared on the edge of the forest, and, overlooking it all in his old rubber boots, stood its creator, PETE DYE, surveying the scene with baleful eye, like a condor on a dead limb;

WHEREAS, one season followed another, and still another, until one day the wild land, so suitable for falconry, turned green and suddenly there was a golf course unlike any seen before or likely ever to be seen again;

WHEREAS, there were field holes without fairways; there were water holes without land; there were holes with streams so fiendishly criss-crossed that a ball missing the first criss would surely catch the second cross, or (if exceptionally well struck) the third criss; there were some great sand traps like the Gobi Desert and many small ones scattered about like buckshot; there were some greens so large as to require putting with a full back swing; others so small as to leave no room for the hole; one green, requiring a wedge shot over a trap at its mid-point; some greens so contoured as to roll in two directions at once, and still other greens so buried in the woods as to be invisible from any direction;

WHEREAS, there were tees marked with sections of railroad track, which gave golfers the sensation of driving from a grade crossing with a train coming; there were banks lined with utility poles which gave golfers an electric shock as they watched their drives strike the poles and ricochet thirty feet into the water; and there were fairways so hard to find that they were marked with piles of stones evidently stolen from the graves of lost golfers;

WHEREAS, there were shots to be played from beneath the feet and other shots from over the head and the eighth hole from the back tee could best be played by a golfer on his knees; and

WHEREAS, there has come a time at last when the man responsible for this green monster, the first CLUB president and a charter member of the Board of Directors, must step down from his throne;

NOW, THEREFORE, BE IT RESOLVED by the Board of Directors of CROOKED STICK GOLF CLUB, speaking for itself and for all of the members, without a dissenting vote or a dry eye, that words are inadequate to describe our gratitude to our founder, PETE DYE, who has done so much to so few with so little provocation.

The Golf Club

The spice of golf, as of life, lies in variety.

Robert Hunter
The Links
1982

In early 1965 Fred Jones, the one-man force behind the creation of The Golf Club in New Albany, Ohio, asked Alice to give him her unbiased opinion of his brand-new course. Seldom subtle, Alice told Fred that, while she believed I had done a better job than she ever thought possible, the first hole was, to use her exact words, "undoubtedly the worst starting hole in golf!"

Much to my chagrin, Alice was right. Her perceptions continue to influence my designs profoundly, and while I may come up with peculiar ideas about how to design a certain hole, it is Alice who helps make them more playable.

My wife has won more than forty tournaments in her life and played with or watched all of the great players of our era. I trust her sixth-sense knowledge of the game, and when she speaks, I listen.

In fact, golf writer Ron Whitten said recently, "Alice Dye understands the game better than Pete does," and he's right. Alice "thinks" her way around a golf course better than anybody, and that talent allows her to help mold my design philosophies. Alice is quick to spot a design flaw that inhibits the good shot. I've seen her studying the touring professionals as they play our courses to decipher whether a shot is feasible or too demanding.

Above all, Alice Dye speaks her mind. When I try to make excuses or back away from criticism, she'll say: "Don't give me the excuse that you weren't standing there when the hole was built. You were there, and you approved it. I don't want to listen to your alibis, let's just fix the hole."

Alice, who is a member of the Advisory Committee of the LPGA, was the very first woman elected to the prestigious American Society of Golf Course Architects and is in line to become president in 1997. She may have taken a backseat to whatever publicity I've had over the last thirty years, but everyone in the golf industry knows how important her contributions have been, since she has such an intuition for what makes a golf course challenging but playable.

Nowhere was this more true than at The Golf Club, and Alice's total contribution to the game continues to be recognized. In February 1994, the Golf Course Builder's Association honored her with the Don A. Rossi Humanitarian Award.

When I began to sketch the ideas for The Golf Club, images of two golf courses built in the 1920s came to mind. Along with the Scottish courses and Pinehurst No. 2, the design features at Seminole and Camargo influenced many of the characteristics prevalent at The Golf Club.

Of all the great courses in our country, Camargo, built in 1921, is probably the most obscure. Respected golf instructor Jim Flick told me recently that like its sister course Shore Acres, which designer Seth Raynor also built, Camargo is the premier example of a "golf course that is meant to be played on the ground and not through the air."

While most articles written about me link my design ideas to Donald Ross, I have always been fascinated with Mr. Raynor, who was an engineering student from Princeton turned landscape architect. His relationship with Charles Blair Macdonald began when Mr. Macdonald asked him to survey the proposed acreage where he intended to build the National Golf Links of America. Raynor not only handled that assignment but went on to construct such wonderful courses as Piping Rock, Lido, Sleepy Hollow, and The Greenbrier for Mr. Macdonald.

At the age of forty-one, Seth Raynor, who possessed the artistic virtues of skill, imagination, and technology, began to design and build golf courses under his own name. Besides Camargo, he lists Fishers Island Golf Club, Fox Chapel Golf Club, and the Country Club of Charleston among his accomplishments. He often hooked up with Charles "Steam Shovel" Banks, known for his tendency to build large elevated greens and deep bunkers, and together with Macdonald, they are credited with designing many of the "Redan" type holes that can be found in the eastern half of the United States.

Since the membership at Camargo is exclusive, few people have seen the brilliance of Mr. Raynor's design. Set on more than three hundred acres, Charles Blair Macdonald's apprentice laid out eighteen holes that are each intricate parts of an intriguing puzzle. By taking great care to weave natural holes in, out, and around the property, Seth Raynor negotiated subtle as well as abrupt changes in elevation that leave the golfer every imaginable type of shot.

The fifteenth at Camargo, a Redan hole of 192 yards, symbolizes Mr. Raynor's belief in that type of design. *Redan* means fortress; such a hole normally requires the golfer to hit a long iron or wood shot to a green fortified by a strategically positioned deep bunker. That green is usually set at almost a 45-degree angle from the expected line of flight.

The key to this design is the slope of the green. The front portion is elevated and then a severe contour flows down and away. As a result, a good portion of the back of the green is blind or semi-blind from the tee.

The par-three fifteenth at North Berwick Golf Club in Scotland is probably the most famous Redan hole. Shinnecock, Piping Rock, the Chicago Golf Club, and Macdonald's The National Golf Links of America all feature these design characteristics, which challenge the golfer to hit just the right spot on the front of the green for the ball to roll down toward a back pin placement.

Since I am an admirer of this type of design, I have used the concept on several occasions. The design at the par-three thirteenth hole at Crooked Stick follows the Redan concept, as do the fourteenth at the Ocean Course at Kiawah and the seventh at the new Brickyard Crossing public course in Indianapolis.

I first appreciated Mr. Raynor's Camargo when I played it as a youth with my father. Many years later, I played it several times when the course was the site for USGA qualifying rounds.

In the mid-1960s, the membership at many of the older courses was interested in modifying the original designs. They thought their courses needed updating to bring them in line with the new ones that were being built. After I built The Golf Club, I was asked by the membership to consider revisions for the seventy-year-old Camargo.

I traveled down to Cincinnati and spent several hours walking around the course. Memories of my earlier days playing there waltzed through my mind, and I was once again fascinated with Mr. Raynor's ingenuity in carving out such a dynamic course.

I was finally escorted to Camargo's boardroom, where a group of distinguished business executives requested my views regarding what was wrong with their course. Sitting in my khakis among these elite gentlemen, I extolled the virtues of Seth Raynor's design, but the committee kept insisting I tell them what problems I saw. Finally, I bluntly told them that as far as I could tell, the only thing wrong with Camargo was its membership, and they would be wise to leave Mr. Raynor's course alone!

My early memories of playing at Seminole, which was built eight years after Camargo, are very rich and vivid. Ben Hogan told everyone that Seminole was his favorite course and probably put it best when he said, "If you can play well there, you can play well anywhere."

Most experts agree that Seminole, designed by Donald Ross, was the first great course in the South. Set along the sands bordering the Atlantic approximately twenty miles north of Palm Beach, the golfing experience begins with the drive up the tree-lined lane toward the clubhouse.

The ambience of Seminole gradually unfolds when the golfer enters the stately old clubhouse, signs the register, and climbs up the steps to the flagstone patio. Crossing to the locker room, one sees the Olympic-size pool and the bronze statue of the Seminole Indian.

A few steps then lead to the cathedral-ceilinged locker room. Oak walls dotted with plaques bearing the names of many of the greatest golfers ever to play the game hold heavy wooden lockers marked with discreetly carved identification numbers.

Outside the locker room, the American and Seminole flags extend fully in the wind. Standing close by, it is possible to see the first hole, the sand dunes of the third, the lake at the tenth, and the oceanside green of the eighteenth off to the right.

Even though the sound of the Atlantic Ocean crashing against the shoreline fills the air, it is the wind that makes Seminole so demanding. Some criticize the course as not difficult unless the wind blows, but I dismiss such charges, since the wind is a factor 95 percent of the time.

Seminole is laid out on a long ridge. Mr. Ross positioned more than 180 sand bunkers across the course, and the green of the lush fairways set against the sandy dunes provides a striking contrast.

Using multiple tees and alternate routes, Mr. Ross succeeds in presenting golfers of every skill level with a perfect balance of long tough holes, short risky ones, and intriguing par-threes where the direction of the wind may change the club selection three times in less than a minute.

The most impressive design characteristic at Seminole is Mr. Ross's use of alternating directional sequences. The famed architect confronts the golfer with a feeling that the drive should be played left to right followed by a right-to-left approach shot to a green where the main bunker is set to the right. The opposite will be true on the next hole, and this continues intermittently throughout the eighteen. While Donald Ross contributed many design innovations to the profession, this one took me a while to discover but then influenced me the most.

Number fifteen, a 495-yard par-five, is especially innovative, since it contains two distinct routings. The "AIA" route takes the player to the left of the water and the tall palms, and then around to the right to the slightly elevated green. Players with more courage who choose to try to hit the green in two may drive the ball over the large lake, providing risk/reward golf at its best.

My recollections of playing Seminole in my teens bring back wonderful memories, but some thirty years later I would have the experience of a lifetime. In the mid-1970s, I was asked to play the course with Ben Hogan, and I was more nervous than I have ever been before a round of golf.

I was sitting in Seminole's impressive locker room with my three guests when Jerry Pittman, the club professional, interrupted our discussion to ask me whether I'd like to play with Mr. Hogan. Very quickly I made arrangements for my guests to play with someone else!

The Ben Hogan Company had just come out with a new set of clubs that year, and I remember being afraid that Mr. Hogan might be offended when he saw I was playing with a set of Tommy Armours. Quickly, I ran to the pro shop and purchased a new set of Hogan Medallions. Then I thought Mr. Hogan might wonder why they had no marks on them, so I sneaked back behind the clubhouse and pounded the irons on a cement walk until they looked used!

All I can remember from that round is the purity of Mr. Hogan's swing, but years later we played again, this time with the fine amateur Billy Joe Patton. At the treacherous par-four dogleg-right sixteenth, I remember watching in awe as Hogan, whom I consider to be the finest ball-striker who ever played the game, hit one of those low, screaming two irons of his from the left side of the fairway into the teeth of the wind.

The magnificent shot from nearly 200 yards just cleared the front bunker and nestled less than three feet from the pin. Patton, one of golf's all-time great characters, ran out of the rough toward Hogan yelling, "Here's my phone number, Ben, so you can call me tonight and talk about that shot if Valerie [Hogan's wife] won't listen."

Contrary to what many might imagine, Mr. Hogan just laughed at Patton's antics. The Ben Hogan on the PGA Tour and in major championships might have seemed a bit dour, but playing with friends in private matches, Mr. Hogan is talkative and a great playing companion.

Fred Jones came from the same tough mold that produced Ben Hogan. An admirer of Mr. Hogan, he was a rigid, stern taskmaster who was meticulous in his preparation when it came time to select an architect for his dream course. Mr. Jones solicited advice from several people, including USGA Executive Director Joe Dey. Based on his recommendation, Mr. Jones called me, and I immediately flew to Columbus to look at his proposed site.

Fred Jones made it clear right away that he wanted his course to look as if it had been there for decades. He also told me unequivocally that I was in charge, that he wouldn't bother me, and that I would answer only to him.

Without hesitation, I can say Mr. Jones was true to his word. I knew what was expected and began to sketch out a series of routings indicative of the demanding course he envisioned.

I never doubted for a minute that Mr. Jones had the financing for The Golf Club, so when he was hospitalized and unable to function shortly after we broke ground, I took it upon myself to borrow $40,000 to continue construction.

When I visited him in the hospital, he seemed astounded I had borrowed the money. Mr. Jones asked what I would have done if he'd passed away, and I merely told him that I would have bought a lily and climbed in that pine box with him!

Other than the problems with the design of the first hole, my only mistake with Fred Jones was asking him where the housing sites would be. He had purchased nearly four hundred acres, and I knew I would use only a little more than half.

As soon as I asked the question, I knew it was a mistake. Mr. Jones took a minute to think, but then his stinging reply informed me in no uncertain terms that there would be no houses to interfere with the beauty of his golf course.

Besides his quest for privacy for The Golf Club, he demanded protocol whether it involved members, Tour professionals, or dignitaries who came to play.

Mr. Jones's dining room at The Golf Club enforced a dress code requiring a jacket. U.S. Senator Robert Taft learned firsthand about Fred Jones's wrath when he appeared in a sport shirt only to find himself scolded by Mr. Jones, who embarrassed the senator by asking him, "Where do you think you are, the Senate Dining Room?"

Fred Jones stories are legendary, since he never backed away from expressing an opinion. "He was a dictator, a lovable dictator," Alice is quoted as saying in The Golf Club's historical book. "But the best golf clubs in the world are run by dictators."

The proposed site for The Golf Club was a beautiful piece of land replete with huge oak trees, a winding creek, and rolling terrain.

Before the course had a name, we called it Blacklick Creek, after the meandering creek that snaked through the property. When I walked the acreage, I knew immediately that Mother Nature and Mr. Jones had provided a great setting for the golf course.

Based on Fred Jones's directives, the main objective at The Golf Club was to carve out a distinctive golf course that could be played by a golfers-of-all-skills membership in love with the game. Longtime member Pandal Savic recently complimented the course by saying The Golf Club is "cut into the terrain as well as any course in the country."

In the spring of 1965, I was making preparations to begin work at The Golf Club. Alice and I and the boys were living in Indianapolis, where we were still involved in the construction of Crooked Stick.

My course construction supervisor for The Golf Club was forty-year-old Cliff Compton, who had been farming the land where we built El Dorado. Cliff was the epitome of the midwestern Indiana farmer, complete with overalls, a red-checkered handkerchief, and great common sense.

Cliff Compton, who also assisted at Crooked Stick, was invaluable because he could adapt to any situation. He knew very little about golf or golf courses, but he was a man who could fix anything if he had enough baling wire.

Cliff brought his house trailer to New Albany, and he and his wife lived on the worksite. This sounded like a great idea to me, and so I brought Alice over to look at their spic-and-span trailer.

Believe me, nobody knows me as well as Alice, and she merely nodded her head and promised that we'd look into buying a trailer at first chance. Little did I know that she already had decided that she and the boys were not going to live in a trailer.

Early one Sunday morning after a lively evening of drinking

and dancing, Alice suggested we go trailer shopping. Ashamed to admit my dizzy, hung-over state, I agreed, and so we drove to a trailer sales lot on the west side of Indianapolis.

The temperature that morning was over 100 degrees. The thirty-two-footer we entered had not been aired out in months, and I almost blacked out the moment the salesman opened the door.

Sweat poured down my face as we began our tour. True to her plan, Alice made me see every nook and cranny of that trailer, including the small living area, pint-size kitchen, and a minuscule bathroom complete with a shower that only a skeleton could enjoy.

The trailer was on blocks and it rocked back and forth, increasing my nausea. I kept saying I'd seen enough, but Alice wanted to make sure I saw the boys' tiny bedroom and the cramped quarters that would be ours. She also asked the perspiring salesman every question imaginable.

When I finally left that stifling-hot cracker box Alice had made her point. I never, ever discussed trailer living again!

Alice and the boys stayed in Indianapolis and I went to Columbus alone. Several times I walked the four hundred acres Mr. Jones had chosen, attempting to find the best placements for the holes.

I first tried to find locations for what I call the natural holes, ones where there's a high point that overlooks a valley and then winds its way to a suitable level landing area. After I've routed those holes, I decide how many par-threes, fours, and fives I've discovered and how many I'll have to manufacture. The direction of these holes will be important, as well as length and topography, since I want to end up with four par-threes, ten par-fours, and four par-fives with as much variety as possible.

The amount of land I have dictates much of what I can do. At The Golf Club, it turned out that in addition to the four hundred acres Mr. Jones had purchased, I needed another forty-acre tract to lengthen a hole without disturbing the natural setting for the remaining holes.

My opportunity to fit the course to the land was the exception to the rule, for normally the acreage available is restricted. The luxury I had at The Golf Club was a throwback to the days of old, when the architect was permitted to choose suitable land before the purchase was made.

Locating those natural hole settings where there is high ground overlooking a valley area is critical, since I want the golfers who are hitting a long shot to the green to be higher than the green level so they can get an idea of the green location and the position of the hazards. If the approach shot is a short one, then the change in elevation is not as important, since the golfer has a better feel for the features of the green, the hazards, and the pin placement.

The site for The Golf Club contained flat wooded areas. I knew that if I brought in dirt and built up the green sites, they would look artificial, so I looked for natural positions for the greens where I could dig out in front of them. All but two or three of the greens at The Golf Club are ground level, and I get a big kick out of people who talk about how well Pete Dye is able to elevate his greens!

Once my green sites and the routing schemes are finalized, the real work to clear the land begins. Anything that might cause problems with shaping the fairways and roughs must be removed, and that includes all trees, stumps, branches, brush, and other big debris. When this area is cleared, we concentrate on grubbing and removing all the large roots, rocks, and other below-the-ground obstacles.

Blacklick Creek, which meandered through the property, was a mixed blessing. It provided a hazard for the players and supplied water for the lakes on the course, but it also overflowed with every central Ohio deluge. Cliff Compton and I and our construction crew spent many hours trying to extricate our heavy equipment from the mud and sludge.

I first used railroad ties on the short par-four thirteenth hole at The Golf Club, which former Tour professional Ed Sneed calls his favorite hole on the course.

My main reason for using railroad ties was to provide a bulkhead or transition zone between fairways and water hazards. In addition, the fairway became more defined and could be maintained easier, since severely sloped grassy banks were eliminated.

At the 185-yard par-three third hole, I had originally built four bunkers to surround the open green, but when Jack Nicklaus visited the course, he felt the hole was dull. Based on his critique, I went back and built a gigantic three-level bunker on the left-hand side and used more than 450 railroad ties for bulkheading.

I may have gone too far with that concept, since everybody and their brother copied that idea. I finally quit using the ties and have since discovered that chicken wire hidden with proper vegetation produces a similar steep slope on banks along water hazards.

It took us nearly two years to complete The Golf Club. Blacklick Creek came into play on four holes, and without a great deal of earth movement, I was able to undulate the fairways to give Fred Jones the natural look he wanted.

The Golf Club has incorrectly been labeled a "links" course; I call it "Old English." Like legendary high-fescue-grass courses such as Sunningdale and Wentworth outside London, I intended a rugged natural look for The Golf Club and used a combination of grass mixes to provide a contrast for the player.

While I was building The Golf Club, I often asked Jack Nicklaus, who was twenty-seven at the time, to come out and take a look at the course. Asking the opinion of someone so young was unusual, but Jack had already compiled a competitive record that most other golfers would never match in a lifetime.

Jack grew up in nearby Columbus and learned the game playing the Scioto Golf Club. By the time Jack provided input for The Golf Club, he had already won the United States Open *and* the Masters. I considered him to be not only a great player, but one whose sharp mind really understood the mechanics of golf course design.

When Jack and I walked The Golf Club, the course was in its early stages of development. Jack agreed with many of my design ideas but did not hesitate to express his dislikes as well.

While I can't match Jack's razor-sharp memory, which permits him to recall almost verbatim what he suggested to me on each and every single hole thirty years ago, I do remember very clearly our discussions regarding the potential for teaming up as designers. Obviously, such an arrangement would have been a bonanza for me, and I remember that Jack seemed quite interested in an association as well.

•　　•　　•

Fred Jones's fun-loving attitude at The Golf Club is evident at the treacherous par-three sixteenth. After failing several times to finish the hole, Mr. Jones installed a hangman's noose on the branch of the magnificent 270-year-old white oak that overhangs the green. A nickel-plated boxcar was used for a bridge at the par-three sixth, and someone with an unusual sense of humor placed the skull of a steer in the waste bunker at the second hole.

Mr. Jones always called Alice "Pot Walloper," either because she outdrove him or because he heard she banged around pots and pans in our kitchen. I knew he admired Alice a great deal, and when she attacked the first hole, Mr. Jones was as surprised as I was.

Of course, Alice chuckles when she remembers the startled look on his face when she blasted the opening hole as the "worst starting hole I've ever seen." Seventeen good ones out of eighteen isn't bad, but he was completely dumbfounded.

When I designed the opening hole, I intended players to drive off the elevated tee, over a huge sycamore tree, and then cut the dogleg if they chose to gamble. Unfortunately, several stately old beech trees hid two huge bunkers that guarded the right side of the fairway, and golfers had no idea they were there.

With overhanging trees, the hole was too severe for an opening one. Most players had to hit the ball way over to the left, where there wasn't much landing area, but while I thought it provided an exciting "wake-up" challenge, Alice believed it would prove too demanding for the first hole. To correct the problem, we enlarged the landing area by altering the Blacklick Creek bank and removing enough trees to make the bunkers visible.

When The Golf Club was completed, the goals that Mr. Jones had in mind were met.

The use of railroad ties, pot bunkers, sawed-off telephone poles, different grasses, long fescue grass around the bunkers, and the simulation of elevated greens were all novel ideas for the Midwest.

Three par-fours at The Golf Club have forced-carry shots to the green. Those who know of my current disdain for such things wonder why I ever created such holes.

I always design a golf course with all golfers in mind. At The Golf Club, I expected members to play, who were knowledgeable of the game and would be experienced enough to play the course from the proper tees.

In 1965 the idea of a forced-carry did not bother me. Augusta National had two such holes, the thirteenth and fifteenth, and no one seemed to throw a fit, so I deliberately allowed Blacklick Creek to run in front of the greens at the fifth and sixth. I also built a lake between the player and the green on the eighteenth hole.

I did not realize at this stage of my design career that such holes are overly difficult for most players. Many times they have to lay up, since they cannot carry to the green from where they lie.

I do not believe there is anything wrong with a forced-carry on a par-three. I know the exact distance from where the player is starting and can design the hole appropriately from the different tee positions.

The atmosphere surrounding The Golf Club provides the player with the same nostalgia reserved for courses built fifty years before.

Fred Jones asked me where the best clubhouse and locker room in the world was, and I told him Seminole. Fred then copied its cathedral-ceiling interior design for the clubhouse and built a locker room that is second to none.

The holes at The Golf Club are so far apart, golfers can actually lose themselves out on the course. Beautiful trees, a clear-running creek, and an abundance of wildlife welcome the player. I've played rounds by myself at dusk when I thought I was the only person on the face of the earth.

Since The Golf Club has hosted no national championships and received no national television exposure, the course remains a secret to those who haven't played it. Through the years, it has matured into an age-old beauty and its playing condition is as good as you will ever find.

I know many states lay claim to having the best golf courses in the country, but with The Golf Club, Muirfield, Inverness, Scioto, and Camargo, my home state of Ohio is difficult to beat.

Although I've had several memorable experiences in designing courses over the years, I doubt I've ever had more fun than during the time I worked with Fred Jones. He was a tough old bird, but he treated me with great respect and brought me honor by selecting me to design his dream course.

Mr. Jones's best asset was his ability to treat everyone alike. Jack Nicklaus found that out when he returned to play The Golf Club along with his son Jackie. Pandal Savic was in the foursome that day when Jack hit his tee shot on the long par-four twelfth into a pile of small stones along the right rough that served as a yardage marker.

Under the watchful eye of Fred Jones, Jack started to pick up his ball, only to hear Mr. Jones say, "Jack, what are you doing?" Pandal remembers Jack's startled look, and his firm response: "I'm taking relief."

"Not on my golf course, you're not," Mr. Jones explained, whereupon Jack proceeded to hit his second shot onto a cart path near the green. Despite Nicklaus's renewed protest, Fred Jones wouldn't allow him relief there either!

The Golf Club New Albany, Ohio Par 72		
Men		
Yardage:	7263, 6908, 6640	
Rating/ Slope:	75.3/140, 73.7/136, 72.5/130	

Harbour Town Golf Links

Success in this game depends less on strength of body than strength of mind and character.

Arnold Palmer

Bless Jim Colbert, wherever he may be!

Even though he shot a fourteen-over-par 85 in the second round of the inaugural 1969 $100,000 Heritage Classic at Harbour Town Golf Links and missed the cut, it was his first-round 69 that saved me and the golf course from extensive criticism.

Arnold Palmer later brought fame to Harbour Town by breaking a fourteen-month slump with his victory in that tournament, but signs of disgruntlement seeped to the surface early in the first round as many players stalked off the course shaking their heads. Tour professionals accustomed to lavish fairways and large greens found my narrow-appearing fairways and small greens difficult to play and many seemed displeased with the new course.

As sports reporters around the scorer's tent started scribbling down such words as "tricky" and "unfair" to describe the course, here came smiling Jim with a score of two under par and a mouthful of words extolling the course as the greatest since Pine Valley!

•   •   •

To understand the evolution of Harbour Town Golf Links, it is important to know the background of Sea Pines Plantation and its originator, Charles Fraser.

While golf may have had its origins in Scotland, the game in America is deeply rooted in the Carolinas. As early as 1786, the South Carolina Golf Club, the oldest club in our country, originated in Charleston.

Most of the settlers of that era emigrated from the British Isles and lived in stately manors beside huge oak trees hung with nets of Spanish moss. Many of these post Revolutionary War residents returned to visit Scotland and England and imported the game of golf to their new homeland.

In the late 1700s, the members of the South Carolina Golf Club competed at Harleston's Green, a local park that no longer exists. Use of the course by the general public led to the term *green fees,* because the golfer would compensate the city for the right to play. This procedure still exists at the Royal and Ancient Golf Club, where they pay the city of St. Andrews for use of the course.

Early photos of golf in this era show no tees, no greens, and no areas designated as roughs and fairways. In fact, no specified number of holes was required to be played, since most all of the competition was match play.

The player simply began a hole by teeing up within a club length or two from the preceding cup placement. Early greens were one club length long, then two, and so forth until the greens expanded to a more conventional size.

The term *forecaddie* originated in this era as well, although there are those who would argue that it had its beginnings in Scotland. Certainly, records in South Carolina indicate that in order to find a golfer's ball, another member of the foursome or a slave might speed ahead and locate the ball by driving a stake nearby.

Our present use of the golf term *fore* was evident in the late 1700s: the loud cry was heard on golf courses to warn those who might be horseback riding, playing cricket, or simply enjoying a lovely picnic with family members. Records indicate that strict rules did govern the game, such as playing the ball where it lies, but it is not clear what the penalty was for hitting an unsuspecting cricket player.

These notes of history were important to developer Charles Fraser, who personally researched the origins of the game in his native state. He was only nineteen when his father, lumber baron and Brigadier General Joseph Fraser, Sr., purchased controlling interest in eight thousand acres on Hilton Island in 1949. From the moment Charles graduated from Yale Law School, he dreamed of turning the land into a great real estate development complete with championship golf courses.

Bankers were dubious of Charles's ideas, but fortunately many of them finally financed his plans. In 1957 he incorporated the Sea Pines Plantation and began selling lots on the waterfront.

Charles Fraser had the most imagination of any developer I've ever known. He took a little desolate island that did not even have a bridge to it and convinced his skeptics that he could develop a multifaceted resort that would captivate the world.

Anticipating the boom in golf before it was apparent to most others, Charles Fraser began building his first golf course in 1959. Designed by George Cobb, the Ocean Course features the long par-three fifteenth, which provides a beautiful view of the Atlantic Ocean.

Mr. Cobb also designed Sea Marsh in 1967. Approximately 50,000 rounds are played on this course each year, where golfers face a heavily bunkered layout later modified in 1990 by architect Clyde Johnston.

With the second course completed, Charles Fraser focused on the four hundred acres of low land he considered a potential location for a true championship course. He had commissioned George Cobb to sketch out preliminary routings for the course as a part of his overall land plan, and I've always given Mr. Cobb credit for his innovative work.

From day one, Charles Fraser stated unequivocally that his goal was to develop a championship golf course that had an "old-fashioned look." Conscious of the need to connect the new course with an established name in golf, Mr. Fraser called Jack Nicklaus.

I first met Jack in 1957 when we tangled in a hard-fought match in the semifinals of the Trans-Mississippi, held at Prairie Dunes in Kansas. Alice had played there before, raved about the course, and encouraged me to enter the tournament.

I recall flying into Wichita, renting a car, and driving over toward Hutchinson, where Prairie Dunes Golf Club is located. Driving in the middle of nowhere with nothing but flat, barren wheat fields surrounding me, I thought Alice was crazy, but then I began to see enormous sand deposits just to the northwest of Hutchinson.

Former banker Perry Maxwell built Prairie Dunes. His incorporation of sand dunes into the course makes it similar to a Scottish links.

In the tournament, I began the semifinal match against the stocky, freckle-faced, sixteen-year-old Nicklaus. Midway through the front nine, my confidence waned when I found myself being *outdriven* thirty yards on every hole by this young kid half my age!

After he dusted me off 3 and 2, Jack went on to become the youngest champion in the history of the Trans-Mississippi. By the time he was twenty-five, he'd won two United States Amateurs, the North and South, the Western Amateur, and the NCAA while at Ohio State.

In 1965, when he first visited The Golf Club in New Albany, Ohio, Jack had what Bobby Jones called "the greatest performance in golf history" in the Masters when he conquered Augusta by shooting 67, 71, 64, 69 for a 271 total. That year he also won the first of his three British Open crowns at Muirfield, which gave its name to the great course he chose to design and build near his hometown of Columbus, Ohio.

When Jack came to visit The Golf Club in 1965, I believe he was already considering designing golf courses himself. While he did not form his own highly successful golf course architectural practice until 1974, Jack knew the profession was a natural for him, and he began to work with me and other designers in order to learn as much as possible regarding golf course architecture.

After Jack blessed The Golf Club as a great new course and said it was "his kind of design," we agreed to collaborate. To have this respected champion associate with me was an enormous boost to my confidence, and I will always be grateful for Jack's belief in me.

When the 1969 Heritage Classic was history and Arnold Palmer had been crowned champion, many reporters wrote articles featuring details of Palmer's win on the new *Jack Nicklaus* course. Jack did everything possible to include me in all the publicity.

While Charles Price termed Jack's contributions to be no more than "one percent," it was far more than that. In fact, I never would have been involved in Harbour Town if Jack hadn't introduced me to Charles Fraser and told him we were working together.

Charles Fraser knew the importance of having Jack Nicklaus's name associated with the course, but from our first meeting, it was clear that I would be the designer and Jack would be the consultant. Jack knew he was being asked to lend his famous name and ideas to a course for the first time, but I would have signed on even if we had been designated as codesigners.

Building Harbour Town Golf Links was quite an engineering challenge, far different from working in either the cornfield at Crooked Stick or the rolling hills in New Albany at The Golf Club. Those projects presented unique challenges of their own, but neither prepared me for building a course in the low country.

Since the site was soggy, our crew began by dredging out narrow canals to drain off the water. Eight separate lagoons were then built for a dual purpose: to handle the excess runoff and to create water hazards for beauty and challenge.

When the water was drained, the exposed property was unimpressive. The change in elevation between the highest and lowest points on the drained land was only four feet. Abrupt contouring and waste areas were used to emphasize elevation changes, but at Harbour Town I also experimented with using a variety of grasses for that purpose.

Throughout the years, I had learned that most northern courses featured bent or bluegrass in the fairways and fescue in the roughs. In the South, Bermuda was used for fairways, greens, and roughs, making the course the same color, lacking definition.

To distinguish Harbour Town and create the perception that the course had varying elevations, several varieties of grasses were used to highlight the contour of the land. Fairways and tees were sown in rich, green 419 Bermuda, while a duller-green Bermuda strain, Tift-Dwarf, was used for the greens.

The area in back of the greens was sodded with centipede, a thick-leaf, off-green grass that was once used on nearly every Florida course. To counterbalance that off-green color, I used bahia grass in the roughs, providing a multicolored border for the course.

I also intentionally spread sand and covered it with pine needles around many areas of the rough. Not only did this provide the course with the Pinehurst look, it decreased significantly the dollar amount required for maintenance.

In an ironic way, my design concepts at Harbour Town were influenced by the architecture of Robert Trent Jones, in that I took Mr. Jones's ideas and headed in the opposite direction.

The idea came to me as I drove by Mr. Jones's new course at Palmetto Dunes nearby on Hilton Head Island. As I watched the big machinery carve out long tees, huge bunkers, and large greens, I wondered how I could design something that would separate my identity from his. Somehow, the concept of designing small greens and a low-profile course seeped into my brain.

My decision to head in the opposite direction from Robert Trent Jones was intended to show no disrespect for him or his great collection of course designs. His contribution to golf course architecture is unequaled, but I simply wanted to establish my individual identity by building courses with design features unlike those seen on other modern American courses.

Instead of long tees, flowing fairways, and elevated large greens, I deliberately chose to design multiple-tee positions, small to medium-size "shot-making" greens, undulating fairways, long waste areas, and abrupt, steep pot bunkers.

At Harbour Town, several situations were deliberately created where it appears one type of shot is necessary when another may be required.

For example, on the par-five second hole, which measures 505 yards, there is a shallow bunker to the left side some 240 yards from the tee. The fairway appears open to the right, so the tendency is to hit the drive to that side to steer clear of the bunker.

While the normal width for a fairway is usually forty yards, the fairway on number two measures at least sixty yards. A false sense of security is created for players who decide to play to the open side, for any chance of hitting the green in two is virtually eliminated, since deep bunkers and overhanging trees block the entrance from that side.

The better play is to drive the ball down the left side, and even if it rolls into the bunker, the player will find that a shot out of the shallow, hard sand bunker is not difficult at all. The green is offset from the fairway, and birdies are plentiful for those who play the left side all the way to the green.

While the course became famous for its small greens, narrow-appearing fairways, and short length (6,600 yards), Harbour Town's bunkers may be its best asset. There are fewer than sixty on the course, but once again their strategic placement is the key.

I prefer sharp, crisp bunkers that give definition to the hole. A third of the bunkers at Harbour Town either assist in outlining the driving area or surround a green to frame the target.

Behind and to the left of the fourteenth green, I positioned what turned out to be a very controversial pot bunker. Former United States Open champion and CBS television commentator Ken Venturi once challenged me to get out of it, and I was smugly pleased to show him that I could handle the shot.

There was criticism of that bunker from the outset. Finally it was removed, and then I put it back a few years later. The second time we built the bunker I caught hell from a disgruntled Pete Dye fan who came along when I was working.

Spotting me in the bunker, this gentleman walked over and asked what I was doing. Believing I was softening it, the red-faced man proceeded to exclaim, "I'm traveling all over the country playing Pete Dye courses. You have no business messing with what Mr. Dye put there."

"I'm just following instructions," I told him, barely able to get a word in edgewise.

"Well, leave it alone!" he retorted as he made his way back to putt.

The term *waste bunker* originated at Harbour Town, but I'm not certain whether I or a member of the construction crew coined the phrase.

During construction, I was checking the course one day and spotted the local sewer patrol fighting a losing battle with a broken pipe near Harbour Town's border. With raw sewage about to pour over the area, I suggested the workers pump it into a long, narrow depression that was to be used for a bunker. As the waste water filled the bunker, somehow the term *waste bunker* was born, and it has been used to designate such areas ever since.

I tried stacking sod strips as bulkheads around bunkers as they do in Scotland, but with little success. Unfortunately, the sod in our climatic conditions won't sustain the banks like the fescue grass or the hard sand found in Scotland.

Maintenance crews on Scottish courses have to replace the sod only every six or seven years, which is cost feasible; replacement here is required every year. I therefore used weathered boards, telephone poles, and railroad ties to bulk up the various hazards.

This land had no streams, hills, or other natural elements necessary to guide the player. Bunkers and waste areas were positioned to steer golfers in, around, and through chutes to the greens.

When I design a golf course, it's really not just a Pete Dye golf course, since I draw on the expertise and advice of several people. The Harbour Town Golf Links is a great example: what I built there is a Pete Dye/Alice Dye/Jack Nicklaus/George Cobb/ Charles Price golf course.

Besides his fine articles lauding Harbour Town, respected writer Charles Price contributed to the design of the course through his candid observations. Charles also suggested submerging a lifeboat on the edge of the eighteenth green in Calibogue Sound.

As consultant, Jack Nicklaus was always quick to voice an opinion during the construction of the course. In spite of being known as a long hitter, Jack had a real sensitivity for what I wanted to do with the shorter yardage at Harbour Town.

Jack's input at the par-five fifteenth was especially helpful. We both recognized that the championship player would in all likelihood have hit in succession a short iron, a half-wedge, and a long iron as approach shots to the twelfth, thirteenth, and fourteenth holes. Sixteen, seventeen, and eighteen to follow would require another short iron, a medium iron, and then perhaps a long iron to the respective greens.

Based on that knowledge, Jack and I discussed what length would be appropriate for the fifteenth. To balance out the holes down the stretch, he suggested a par-five difficult to reach in two.

After some discussion, we decided that the third shot to the green should be no more than a nine iron. We then walked to the pint-size green site, where Jack surprised me by suggesting it be half the size I had in mind, since he felt there should be an extreme premium on the accuracy of the approach shot.

Based on Jack's input, the 562-yard par-five hole was designed. While a wide fairway driving area was provided, the golfer must play a controlled position shot to within 130 yards of the green and then place a short-iron shot onto the 2,500-square-foot putting surface. (This green was later enlarged.)

Jack could attempt to hit the green in two, since he could loft the ball high enough to scale the trees that protect the green. Other Tour players took a crack at hitting the green in two as well, and spectators at the Heritage Classic thoroughly enjoyed watching them blast away.

Over the years, those trees by the green have grown a great deal, but the powers that be have refused my repeated requests to cut the tops back. Unfortunately, the hole isn't as exciting as it once was because no one ever tries to go for the green in two.

The famed eighteenth with the trademark lighthouse in the background was more a product of nature than anything we did. George Cobb had originally intended the hole to parallel the tenth, and I was going to use the small amount of land where eighteen was built as the site for the par-three seventeenth.

When the construction company responsible for building the harbor dug out the bay, they had nowhere to take the sand. Someone decided the banks of the golf course would do, and soon truckloads of sand were being dumped all along the coastline that bordered the proposed seventeenth hole.

Dikes were built to keep the sand in place, but the construction company apparently underestimated the amount of sand it was depositing on the shore. The dikes kept breaking, the sand kept flowing outward into the sound, increasing the width. Pretty soon there was enough workable land to build not only the par-three seventeenth but also the par-four eighteenth.

• • •

Working with Jack Nicklaus at Harbour Town was a first-class experience. He has always been gracious enough to give me most of the credit, but the course would never have been so well accepted if it hadn't been for him.

We managed to associate on two other golf courses after Harbour Town, but Jack was interested in operating a large design company and I never considered anything but a small operation. Jack often jokes that we went our separate ways because he wanted to make money and I didn't.

In fact, I'm sure it *cost* Jack money to work with me, because the design fees in those days probably didn't match the cos of fuel for the trips Jack took in his Lear jet to the sites. I never once heard him complain about it, though, and Alice and I have had a lifelong friendship with Jack that we cherish to this day.

Unfortunately, I believe that over the years the media has presented an image contrary to the truth. For some reason, journalists wrote that Jack and I have been at odds over certain design concepts, and they have attempted to emphasize his criticism of my designs and even mine of his.

To be sure, we don't agree on every aspect of golf-course design. Mutual respect exists between us, and my opportunities to discuss the design profession with him are always a pleasure.

Jack has designed many great golf courses, but none better than Muirfield near Columbus, Ohio. I had suggested some initial routings for him, but Muirfield is all Jack Nicklaus. These days he's building golf courses all over the world, and I'm very proud to think that he first started in the profession with me at Harbour Town.

When asked who I would pick for the remaining three spots in my all-time greatest golf foursome, I choose Jack, Ben Hogan, and Alice Dye. The fact that Alice is my wife might enter into that decision just a bit, but I'd rather play with her than anyone.

Even though I could watch Alice's beautiful swing all day long, I'm fortunate that her playing prowess translates into an innate sense of what makes a great golf hole.

When golf experts invariably choose the best eighteen holes in the world, I'm always interested to see that the 358-yard par-four thirteenth hole at Harbour Town, the classic example of the short par-four, is included on many of those lists.

In 1969 the design of the thirteenth was unique, since very few new golf courses presented such a challenge. I wanted the player to back off the driver and hit a four wood or long iron to place the ball in position for the second shot, and then be required to hit a precision short iron in order to loft the ball onto a miniature-size green.

That thirteenth green, which has received so much publicity, was designed by Alice. I hadn't quite figured out how to top off the hole, and with the inaugural Heritage Tournament just a few months away, deadlines were staring me in the face.

I was on a tractor working on drainage problems at the fourteenth when Alice asked me about my plans for the green at thirteen. Since I had no clue, I asked her if she'd take a couple of the boys from the construction crew and a bulldozer operator named TeePee and see what she could do.

The next thing I knew, I looked over to see Alice directing traffic and signaling instructions. Before long, Alice had carved out a small heart-shaped green as well as a horseshoe sand bunker protecting the front.

Alice also came up with the idea to bulkhead the bunker with old gray cypress planks that present a dramatic feature.

Ironically, I was called upon to defend my wife's work in the early-morning hours of the first round of the inaugural Heritage tournament. My crew and I were still spreading sand in the bunker surrounding the thirteenth green when professional Steve Reid, first off the tee, came into view on the fairway.

The fact that we were still finishing up the hole as Steve was playing the very first competitive round in a PGA tournament on one of my courses wasn't surprising since the deadline to complete the course had been a tight one. The ten-man crew and I had risen before dawn to complete our work and we all climbed out of the bunker so Steve could have an unobstructed view of the green.

Dressed like one of the laborers, I stood at the back of the green and watched as two spectators discussed the hole. I heard one of them say, "Man, what a great hole Jack Nicklaus built!"

Unable to let that pass, I turned and said, "Jack Nicklaus had nothing to do with it. In fact, a very lovely lady designed and built this hole!"

Having said my piece, I sauntered away, but overheard one of the men exclaim, "Well, there's an early-morning drunk for you!"

As late as the first day of the practice rounds, I watched the players to see what possible alterations might improve the course.

Touring professional Jim Ferriell, a good friend and loyal supporter who became the head professional at Crooked Stick, says the first time he ever laid eyes on me, dressed in khaki shorts and work boots, he thought I was a maintenance worker. Jim spied me standing under a tree off to the side of the sixteenth hole watching intently as he and Davis Love and two other professionals played their practice rounds. Each drove down the fairway and bent their tee shots around a giant pine tree, which guided them away from the huge waste area.

According to Jim, when he came to the hole the next day that pine tree had magically disappeared, and without its presence to guide them, he and all of his playing partners pulled their drives in the crusty waste area. As Jim beat his driver into the ground, he said he saw me standing in the very same spot with a wry smile on my face.

Our attention to detail at Harbour Town paid off though, and most of the professionals were very complimentary about the course prior to the tournament. *Sports Illustrated*'s Dan Jenkins was labeling Harbour Town as "Pebble Beach East," and both Jack Nicklaus and I were very pleased with that comparison.

Even with the lavish praise, I still believe that if Jim Colbert hadn't shot that early first-round 69, momentum might have swung the opposite way. Anything new and different on a golf course always lends itself to criticism, and professional golfers are especially vocal.

Arnie's surge to the front quickly shifted the focus to him and away from the course. Despite recent cries of "The King is dead, long live the King," Arnold was returning to the throne to defy those who believed he was through winning.

After the opening-round 68, Arnold shot 71, 70, and then as

winds whipped off the Calibogue Sound, 74 to win the title and $20,000 by three strokes over Bert Yancey and Dick Crawford. Jack Nicklaus, who later won the Heritage in 1975, fired 71, 71, 71, and 75 to take home a paycheck of $3,250.00.

Palmer's post-tournament comments regarding Harbour Town were terrific. He pointed out that while the course was tight and the target areas small, a big hitter could adjust his game to play what he called "smart golf."

Palmer told reporters, "I guess I felt more anxiety today than I have in a long time . . . and I think I put more pressure on my-self than I really intended to. I wanted to win the tournament as much as if it were the United States Open or Masters."

Most observers were surprised that Palmer won on such a tight golf course. While there are those who recall Arnold as being long and wild off the tee, he was one of the straightest drivers I've ever seen when he was on his game.

After the tournament, officials noted that 80-plus rounds out-numbered subpar scores by two to one. The thirty-six-hole cutoff was the highest of the year, but Tom Weiskopf proved a player could score at Harbour Town when he shot 65 in the second round.

Despite the high scores, a great many of the touring profes-sionals were pleased with Harbour Town. Lee Trevino shot an eleven-over-par 295 yet called it "the greatest course I've ever played," and even the often-critical Art Wall paid the course slight praise by saying it was "very, very interesting."

When writer Dan Jenkins wrote a complimentary article after the tournament, entitled "What a Little Instant Character Will Do," people took note. That article was reprinted several times by the Hilton Head developers, prompting Dan to say recently that he's still waiting to receive his commission check for selling all those island homesites!

I believe the Heritage Classic at Harbour Town marked the first time that the architects of a golf course were featured along with the tournament and the course itself. Architects previously were unknown entities and the headlines were reserved for quotes about the course, its playability, and the tournament champion.

Jack Nicklaus's connection to Harbour Town changed all that, and because I was working with him, we both received a great deal of publicity. In recent years, architects' names have been displayed prominently with their courses, and today many architects are household names among the golfing public.

The list of champions at the Heritage since 1969 speaks well of the high caliber of golf it takes to win there. Besides Palmer, the select list includes Johnny Miller, Jack Nicklaus, Tom Watson, Nick Faldo, Greg Norman, and Hale Irwin, whose win in 1994, twenty-three years after his first one, is a tribute to his incredible shot-making ability.

Recently, Tour professional Craig Stadler remarked that Harbour Town "has character on every hole," while Chip Beck applauded the "unique strategy" required to play well there. Former Masters champion Larry Mize chided me by saying, "Harbour Town makes the player invent so many different shots you would think Pete Dye had stock in a third-wedge company."

Harbour Town Golf Links' successful debut in 1969 sparked a revolution on the island, and development took off like a rocket. A landowner near the seventeenth got mad as hell at me for muddying up the bay near his property and accepted $34,000 for his house, which brought $250,000 the next year.

While more flattering material has been written over the years about the Harbour Town Golf Links, perhaps it was writer Teague Jackson in *Dixie Golf* who wrote the most intriguing words about my work there. "Pete Dye," Mr. Jackson said, "is a mad doctor who created the monster and now loves his pet as only a Doctor Frankenstein can."

Despite Teague's devilish description of me, I choose to believe that Harbour Town made other designers and the golfing public aware that a golf course with short yardage could still be demanding. Small greens, pot bunkers, bulkheaded banks, and Arnold Palmer may have grabbed the headlines in that first year, but the Links proved that 7,000-yard-plus golf courses weren't required to challenge the top professionals.

	Men	Women
Harbour Town Golf Links **Hilton Head, South Carolina** **Par 71**		
Yardage:	6916, 6119	5019
Rating/ Slope:	74/136, 70/126	69/117

Teeth of the Dog

From the roaring oceans to the majestic lakes, the rushing streams and quiet ponds and burns, water adds a test to golf that entrances.

Robert Trent Jones
Golf's Magnificent Challenge
1988

As I made my way across the rocky terrain on the desolate southeastern coastline of the Dominican Republic in 1969, I was certain that my motor trip was just another wild goose chase. Attempting to find a suitable site for a golf course had proven difficult, and although I had traveled much of the Dominican, I had not yet found land that excited me.

Bumping along a narrow dirt road, I passed through the town of La Romana. Almost by accident, I saw before me the most beautiful seaside location for a golf course I had ever seen. Little did I realize that my wonderful discovery would be the start of a lifelong devotion to the Caribbean country and its warm, gracious people.

Teeth of the Dog, or "Cajuiles #1" as it was first called, opened eighteen months later. My Dominican friends and I would not only succeed in building a world-class golf course but also improve the economic conditions of the area.

With its temperate climate and vast amount of coastline, the Dominican was ready-made for tourist trade. Despite the potential, there was little progress until the late 1960s, when a Cuban named Alvaro Carta came to the island.

Having fled Cuba in 1960 in a daring escape to the United States in Fidel Castro's brother-in-law's stolen plane, Mr. Carta first lived in Miami and then came to the Dominican to run the financially troubled South Puerto Rico Sugar company. With the financial backing of the huge Gulf and Western empire, headed by Charles Bludhorn, Mr. Carta formed a new division known as Gulf and Western Americas.

Soon 330,000 tons of raw sugar a year were being produced by the sugar mill in La Romana. This production made the mill the largest single producer of sugar in the world, and Mr. Carta began to consider investment options for the millions of dollars flowing into the company each year.

Mr. Carta's interest in alternative revenue for his new country evolved from his firsthand experience in Cuba, where the government had unsuccessfully put all its economic eggs in the sugar-export basket. In addition, Mr. Carta believed that it was important to take money earned through sugar sales and put it back into the country to bring new industry to impoverished areas, improving the economic conditions for the people.

Armed with this vision, Alvaro Carta focused on the potential for establishing a tourist trade and set out to locate land where a lavish resort with a golf course could be built.

Mr. Carta's first site was six hundred acres of land near the Santo Domingo airport, and I first walked that property with him in 1968. Plans were drawn up, but I was not enthused because the site lacked an adequate source of water.

After discussing the proposed course for over a year, I asked Mr. Carta about alternative sites. He told me of a location near the sugar mill where 400,000 acres were available that was too dry for growing sugarcane and too sparsely vegetated to graze cattle.

An industrial free zone to attract foreign business ventures had been proposed for the oceanfront acreage, and since construction had already begun, Mr. Carta was reluctant to abandon those plans for a golf course. In addition, the site was nearly sixty kilometers from the Santo Domingo airport, and the road was unpaved. The nearby city of La Romana had no tourist facilities.

I actually persuaded Mr. Carta to let me get started by promising him a nine-hole "executive course" that could be played by the employees of the sugar mill. Scouting treks along the coral cliffs further convinced me that something extraordinary was possible, and after some persuasion Mr. Carta agreed that a championship course could be built.

How many dollars could be allocated for the course was the question, though, and for a time I wondered whether there would be sufficient funds to build the course I had in mind. Determined to confront the issue, I decided to talk to Mr. Carta because I'd caught wind of a rumor that only $50,000 had been allocated for the entire course!

At our meeting, I told Mr. Carta that $50,000 wouldn't be enough for one hole, let alone an entire golf course. When I came back from the meeting, my sister and her husband, Tom Doss, remembered, I had a big smile on my face. When Tom asked about it, I said, "Tom, Mr. Carta told me that the $50,000 I'd heard about wasn't for one hole or the entire course, but an allocation made for *each day* of construction!"

The course known as Teeth of the Dog could not have been built without an energetic man named Bruce Mashburn, or Señor Bruce, as he became known to the admiring Dominicans.

I first met Bruce when we were building a course for TRW in northern Ohio. I didn't know much about him when he was signed on as a laborer, but it soon was apparent that Bruce had experience in golf course construction and design. He'd encountered some personal problems in past years, but I soon realized I had found not only a talented sidekick but a great friend.

A native of Pine Bluff, North Carolina, Bruce worked first with Donald Ross and then George Cobb after Mr. Ross's death. Not only had Bruce been a good player in his early days, but working with Mr. Ross had provided him with a perspective on golf course design very similar to mine.

Bruce always dressed in a starched white shirt, khaki pants, and cordovan shoes. At age sixty-two with frosted hair and a ruddy complexion, he had the look of a prosperous Philadelphia banker.

I truly believe Bruce was the only man alive who could have

built the golf course in the Dominican the way I wanted it. He read my thoughts, and his ability to work with the laborers was miraculous.

Bruce had built golf courses atop high mountains and in deep swampland. He'd even been to Kenya, where he was shot at by tribesmen who didn't share his vision for the construction of a golf course.

Bruce's ability to lead the willing but inexperienced Dominican workers was the key to our success. They took to him right away, and he gained the respect of all those who worked for him.

Over the next year, more than three hundred Dominicans molded the course. We emphasized manpower instead of horsepower. Because the cost to import special machinery was prohibitive, we had to rely entirely upon the machinery used at the sugar mill.

I penciled out potential course routings for Teeth of the Dog on scratch paper, and Bruce Mashburn and I continued to improvise by drawing diagrams in the dirt.

Bruce did his sketching with a knotty, hardwood "crooked stick" he always carried with him. It became his trademark, and when Bruce passed away in September 1971, only months before the course was completed, hundreds of Dominicans claimed to have the original stick.

The land Bruce and I encountered was covered with thick underbrush, stubby tropical trees, and cactus. Gulf and Western provided me with a helicopter, but I never got a sense for the jungle-like density of the site from up there.

I borrowed a small metal boat with an old Johnson outboard motor and puttered along the coastline. From there I tried to envision how we could fit as many holes as possible along the top of the rocky bluff.

Once I had a ballpark idea where the holes could go, Bruce and I made our way through the underbrush. Using machetes to clear the way, we measured foot by foot the centerlines where I anticipated routing three of the back-nine holes.

Encouraged by the prospect of three one-of-a-kind oceanside holes, I laid out the remaining five for the back nine. I knew the eighteenth would need to take the golfer from my last ocean hole up to the clubhouse, and the first five would be inland leading the seaside.

Moving farther along the coastline, I found enough land to position four additional seaside holes on the front side. Unlike the three on the back, which were for the most part naturally in coves set along the coast, these ran in a straight line.

Having selected the locations for the seaside holes, Bruce and I picked three hundred laborers, who gripped their machetes and cleared the remaining underbrush. Bruce directed the Dominicans like a proven squad leader, and soon they cleared most of the land, giving me a better idea of how to route the remaining six holes of the front nine.

The opportunity to carve out Teeth of the Dog was a once-in-a-lifetime experience. The land was scintillatingly beautiful, but most of it was bare coral rock and limestone. Even though the guinea grass and other native flora grew right through the coral, such conditions would not be conducive to growing fairway grass.

Without the proper heavy machinery to crack the coral, the tireless Dominican crew used sledgehammers, pickaxes, and chisels. We also tied a large steel bar behind one of the small bulldozers so the Dominicans could slam the bar into the coral, breaking off larger points to smooth the surface.

There was very little good soil available near the coastline, so the crew had to dig by hand some that was discovered a mile from the site. It was put into sugarcane carts pulled by oxen and transported to the course site.

As incredible as it may seem, those oxen-drawn carts brought the soil one square yard at a time. I can still see the long line of cane carts strewn across the countryside as load after load was transported down by the tireless animals.

After much research, we came up with the idea of using cachaza, a by-product of sugarcane, as the chief ingredient of our topsoil. An organic material much like peat moss, cachaza was used for a similar purpose in the cane fields, and we decided we would mix sand and red dirt with the cachaza to formulate the needed topsoil.

Bruce and I knew this mixture would be a success since Bruce pounded green wood survey stakes into the ground and ten days later they sprouted! Despite that success, we still had soil samples analyzed in the United States to make certain our formula was correct.

Patience can be a great virtue, and I learned firsthand that land responds more positively to the raw-boned hands of the laborer than to the steel-faced jolt of heavy machinery. Whatever delicate features Teeth of the Dog possesses are a direct result of the hard work of those Dominicans who took such pride in their work.

Besides the problems with the coral and the lack of topsoil, there were also hundreds of large boulders lying in the proposed fairways. One by one, the Dominicans loaded the boulders onto sugarcane carts and then pulled the carts to the borders of the course, where they built four-foot-high stone walls.

Creative builders, the workers demonstrated an instinctive ability to take the smaller pieces of rock and pile them alongside the largest of the boulders. The Dominicans approached this arduous task with a great sense of pride; as the walls became taller, they could point to something tangible they'd built that would be not only part of the new course but an artistic legacy for generations. When done, the wall would extend nearly two miles and contain more than twenty thousand tons of rock.

Alvaro Carta's name for the course was Cajuiles, which refers to the beautiful cashew trees that grow in the mountains. I suggested changing the name when I heard the natives refer to the sharp coral rock as "diente del perro" (teeth of the dog, in Spanish), after the canine-teeth appearance of the sharp rock edges.

Water was critical to our operation. The crew built open aqueducts for water to flow from the Romana River across the course and into the irrigation pond. However, these eventually fed too much fertilizer into the pond and the water had to be piped underground.

Sand for bunkers and the coconut palms were brought in from El Maceo, a fishing village eighty-five kilometers away on the north coast.

In early August 1971, we planted the fairways with 419 Bermuda, the roughs with Bahia grass and guinea grass, and the tees and greens with Tift-Dwarf, providing the contrast of green colors I'd experimented with at Harbour Town. On many holes the fairways were painstakingly planted sprig by sprig, blade by blade, by workers using a little pointed stick.

With 400,000 acres available for me to build a 200-acre golf course, one would think I could have kept Teeth of the Dog on Mr. Carta's property. However, Rudolpho Escabar, a vice president of the sugarcane company, informed me one day that the construction had wandered too far east, and that I was actually violating Dominican law by digging on someone else's land. Mr. Escabar was quite excited, and his extreme nervousness caused him to stutter. He said, "Señor D-D-Dye . . . we own f-four h-hundred th-th-thousand acres a-a-and you're n-n-not even on our p-p-p-p-pro-property!"

Mr. Carta purchased those additional acres the next day. When Mr. Escabar approached me with the good news, he was quite relieved and his stutter was gone.

In the late fall of 1971, the course, which featured seven holes on the sea, was ready for play. The front nine holes were more gentle in their "links" way of sloping off onto the rocky beaches, while the back nine appeared to have been molded out of solid coral rock.

The first four inland holes lead down to the sea, while the fifth, sixth, seventh, and eighth play along the sea and the ninth heads back up toward the clubhouse. The eighth was a long-term project, as it initially would have played in a straight line along the water.

I wanted the back tee to be at least thirty feet out in the Caribbean so the drive would carry over water. When I continued to pile rocks out there, the natives thought I was building a causeway to Puerto Rico, but the promontory tee made a magnificent hole.

Plans to build three holes along the sea on the back side worked out even better than expected.

The fifteenth is a medium-length par-four dogleg right around the cliffs of the sea. The sixteenth became a treacherous, long par-three across the sea to a kidney-shaped green, and the seventeenth a long par-four that winds left to right along the coastline to a small green perched along the rocky cliffs.

Each of these holes, which television commentator Jack

Whitaker called the "soul of the course," has a spectacular view, and oftentimes golfers must drive with salty sea spray pelting their faces.

From day one, Teeth of the Dog was a hit with golf enthusiasts. Its beauty caused amateurs and professionals to compare it favorably with another great seaside course, Pebble Beach.

Even as spectacular as it may be, Pebble Beach doesn't have as many seaside holes as Teeth of the Dog. In fact, one observer remarked that "Pebble Beach may have several holes along the sea, but only Teeth of the Dog has seven holes *in* the sea."

In 1973, Alvaro Carta decided to add to the beauty of the inland holes in preparation for the 1974 World Amateur Team Championship. Hundreds of African tulip trees, hibiscus, sandbox trees, gumbo limbo trees, quick stick trees, and bougainvillea were planted, dressing the course in tropical finery.

Just prior to that tournament, I decided to move the eighth green down flush with the sea. I rounded up my loyal Dominican crew and we began to construct a new green protected by a wide sand bunker across the front.

With the tournament date so close, Mr. Carta violently disagreed with my endeavors, and with no warning I looked up the fairway to see him coming at me with a two-by-four. While fending off his attack, I promised that the green would indeed be playable by the first day of the tournament!

A severe grass bunker was built behind the green, making recovery extremely difficult. Many of the competitors hated it, but Keith Mackenzie, secretary of the Royal and Ancient Golf Association, labeled it "a lovely, grassy hollow."

In 1974, Teeth of the Dog hosted the World Amateur Team Championship. The United States was represented by future Tour players George Burns, Curtis Strange, Gary Koch, and Jerry Pate, who took lessons from Alice when his driver wouldn't behave. Only three of the 590 rounds produced subpar scores, and the windy, intimidating seaside finishing holes easily won their battle with the top amateurs, earning them the nickname "Reload Alley."

Gary Koch experienced the difficulty of the two finishing holes by turning an even-par round into 76. He pushed his tee shot on the seventeenth into the Caribbean and his second shot into the pond on the final hole. "This course will come out of nowhere," Gary told reporters, "and it will throw you down and stomp on your head."

Teeth of the Dog has received its share of plaudits throughout the years, including exposure on ABC's "Shell's Wonderful World of Golf" in the spring of 1994. The eighteen-hole competition pitted Fred Couples against his Ryder Cup teammate Raymond Floyd, but that day Raymond was no match for Fred, who recorded two eagle threes on the way to a 68.

Despite his loss, Raymond told ABC commentators Dave Marr and Jack Whitaker, "Teeth of the Dog ranks with the great courses in the world."

When I told Dave Marr that the holes along the Caribbean were built mainly by the Man upstairs, he kidded me by saying that fortunately I didn't "mess up what the Old Skipper had done."

Based on the success of Casa de Campo's first course, Mr. Carta gave the go-ahead to design a second course on adjacent land. Also set on coral rock, the Links would be an eighteen-month project where a brilliant protégé of mine, Lee Schmidt, was in charge.

The Links was intended to be an entirely different type of challenge from Teeth of the Dog. Seven natural seaside holes built mostly by the Lord are difficult competition, and Keith Mackenzie told me, "Pete, you better make the Links damn notable, or nobody will ever play it."

Lee Schmidt was partly responsible for the routing scheme on the Links. I say partly because he had staked out the course in 1975 and cleared out the corridors through the thick guinea grass. He then flew to Miami en route to his scheduled wedding date in Indiana with a lovely lady named Jean Fruth and left me in charge.

Ten days later Lee and his bride met me at the Miami airport on the way to their honeymoon in the Dominican. He asked me how things were going at the Links and my answer drained every bit of color from his face.

"I only changed one thing, just one," Lee remembers me telling him. "I kind of reversed everything. Where you had the greens, I put the tees and vice versa." With that, I ambled away to my plane, leaving poor, bewildered Lee to begin his honeymoon.

Though not a true "links" course, since the land was never covered by water, the Links has that flavor. Wide swinging fairways and beautifully contoured greens distinguish the Links, which is enclosed by yard-high guinea grass.

Hopefully we succeeded in building "a damn notable" course. The Links contrasts greatly with Teeth of the Dog and with La Romana Country Club, the third Dominican course, built in 1990.

By this time, Alfy Fanjul, a spirited Florida businessman who loves the game of golf, had purchased Casa de Campo. A low-handicapper who once partnered with Jay Haas to win the Bing Crosby Pro-Am, Mr. Fanjul wanted a private membership club that could stand alongside its two Dominican partners.

Although water confronts the golfers on only two holes at La Romana Country Club, the players can admire spectacular views of the Caribbean Sea. Hundreds of citrus trees frame the splendor of the course, built under the direction of a dedicated prospective architect, Mike O'Conner.

While La Romana Country Club and the Links are outstanding courses, Teeth of the Dog still continues to overshadow both. I've tinkered with the course many times over the years, but for the most part it remains the handcrafted beauty that the Dominican people built in 1971.

Over the years, stories surrounding play at Teeth of the Dog have been legendary. Fashion designer Oscar de la Renta built a home on the bluffs just behind the fifteenth tee, and play is often held up as golfers pause to watch Oscar's voluptuous models sunbathing by his pool.

Guests also rave about the dedication of the Dominican caddies, even though they have been known to follow instructions to extreme. One youngster was told to report to the first tee and accompany the first gentleman who hit from the blue markers.

Somehow the order of the foursomes got switched, and after

two groups preceded his, the caddie's assigned golfer could not locate his caddie or his clubs. The golf professional, caddiemaster, and all the staff frantically looked everywhere for the clubs, but they were nowhere to be found.

Finally the unhappy gentleman was loaned a set of clubs and he went out to play. Some four and a half hours later, the young caddie was spotted carrying the missing clubs as he approached the eighteenth green. True to his orders, he had simply followed the first man who teed off from the blue markers!

Certain visitors to Teeth of the Dog also have become legendary. One balding, seasoned New Yorker, originally scheduled to play Teeth of the Dog for three days, stayed a fourth and then a fifth. When asked by golf director Gilles Gagnon how long he might be around, he said, "I'm not going to leave this !@#%&° course until I hit one of those !@#%&° damn par-threes with my first shot."

By the time the determined gentleman had played thirty-six holes a day for six more days, his sunburned face was blistered and bloody. Finally, this golf-crazed New Yorker reached the tee at the thirteenth, a 141-yard hole aptly named "Donut" since it is surrounded by a sand bunker.

After applying more suntan lotion to his painful forehead, the never-say-die player bladed a six-iron shot onto the green inches inside the back apron. Too weary to celebrate, he headed straight for the hotel without even bothering to retrieve his golf ball!

Teeth of the Dog La Romana, Dominican Republic Par 72		
	Men	Women
Yardage:	6888, 6057, 5571	5571, 5041
Rating/ Slope:	74.5/144, 73.2/137, 69.8/126	75.6/141, 69.3/122

Oak Tree

I suggest that the construction of bunkers on various courses
should have an individuality entirely of their own which arouse
the love or hatred of intelligent golfers.

Charles Blair Macdonald
Scotland's Gift—Golf
1928

"If you want to play well on a Pete Dye creation, aim for the
bunkers!"

That was former touring professional Ernie Vossler's response
to a question about what strategy to use on my golf courses.
Nowhere is this more true than at Oak Tree, a hard-as-they-come
test built outside Edmond, Oklahoma.

When Ernie Vossler and Joe Walser, Jr., contacted me in 1975
to design the golf course for them in Edmond, their instructions
were very straightforward. "Build us a championship golf
course," Joe told me. "One with no compromise."

Going first class was the only way Ernie and Joe knew how to
do things. Though they were both talented golfers, their ultimate
contribution to the game would come through the development
of some of our nation's finest golf courses.

I first met Joe Walser when he competed in the 1961
PGA Tour's 500 Festival Open in Indianapolis. Good play
through the first three rounds placed him in the final threesome
with Dave Marr and Gene Littler, and although he didn't win, a

respectable paycheck was most welcome for the young professional.

Joe Walser is Oklahoma born and raised and his dad started him in golf at an early age. An Oklahoma State Amateur Championship landed him a spot on the Oklahoma State golf team, and after a successful college career he turned professional in 1954.

Joe competed on the professional Tour with some limited success for the next eight years. While crossing the country from tournament to tournament, he became close friends with Ernie Vossler, another touring professional.

Ernie Vossler and I first met at a United States Amateur Championship in the mid-1950s and again later when he competed in the PGA Tour's 500 Festival Open in Indianapolis. Actor James Garner was the grand marshal for the race that year, and he and Ernie and I spent some time together.

Originally from Fort Worth, Ernie, a fine shot-maker and a great scrambler, won the Texas State Amateur title and then turned professional in 1954 at age twenty-six. Ernie competed on the Tour for seven full years, winning five events, including the Carling Open.

Ernie vowed to his wife, Mary, that he would leave the Tour when their daughter Judy reached twelve. He intended to keep that promise, and while playing in his third Masters, Ernie learned from amateur Charlie Coe that a new golf course development in Oklahoma City called Quail Creek was looking for a head professional.

In the fall of 1961, Ernie accepted the position at Quail Creek. Joe joined him as an assistant and not only worked in the golf shop but helped the construction crew in building the course.

Both men were interested in the real estate portion of the Quail Creek development, and they monitored its progress closely. In 1968 Joe then moved on to become the head professional at the Oklahoma City Golf and Country Club, designed by A. W. Tillinghast.

Ernie and Joe believed that while the Oklahoma City area had some excellent courses, there was not one to compete with the legendary Southern Hills layout in Tulsa. Whenever it came time for a major championship to be staged in the state, Southern Hills won out.

Intent on building a golf course that could compete with Southern Hills, the two men scouted several pieces of land. While they were looking, their interest in a local golf course turned in another direction. An attorney from New York named John Russell asked them to join him in building a course in Greensboro, North Carolina.

While Russell handled the financing for the course—to be known as The Cardinal, Joe and Ernie searched for a golf course architect.

When Ernie first contacted me, he asked if I could suggest someone to accompany them on a tour of my courses. David Pfaff, one of my assistants, took them to Crooked Stick, The Golf Club, and Harbour Town.

"I was impressed with the fact that every hole Pete Dye designed was different from another," Ernie told reporters in 1986. "There was never any confusion about his holes. They were exciting and caused a golfer to have mental replay of exactly what the hole looked like."

After visiting my courses, the two men showed up on our doorstep in Delray Beach with a roll of maps. I had just completed Harbour Town and was working on Teeth of the Dog, but I listened earnestly to the two aspiring golf course developers.

Without much fanfare, Ernie, Joe, and I came to a handshake agreement, and the Greensboro course was started in 1973. Little did I realize that my working relationship with these two men at The Cardinal would blossom into a long-term association.

Ernie also discovered firsthand at The Cardinal the loyalty of the young men who worked for me. A devoted crew member named John Gray was the project manager, and one particular Thursday Ernie asked John when he expected me to fly in to visit the course.

"Mr. Dye told me to pick him up at the airport," John told Ernie. When Thursday, Friday, Saturday, and Sunday went by and I had not shown up, Ernie wondered what had happened to me. When John and I finally arrived at the course on Monday, Ernie asked John where we had been. John told him he had met every flight from my home city for five straight days, figuring I'd show up sooner or later!

While The Cardinal was under construction, Ernie and Joe

turned their attention back to Oklahoma and merged their company, Unique Golf, with Landmark Land Company.

Ernie and Joe knew I wasn't too excited the first time they showed me the Oklahoma site they had chosen for their dream course. Looking back, I don't believe it had as much to do with the characteristics of the property as the fact that the course would be way out in the middle of nowhere where I was sure nobody would ever find it.

Ernie and Joe convinced me otherwise with their commitment to building a first-rate course that could receive national recognition. While we were walking the property one day, Joe tentatively asked me if I really could build a championship course there. I told him I could already envision at least fourteen of the eighteen holes just lying there ready to be molded into a great layout.

When I make preliminary plans to design a golf course, I call upon every reference I can, whether it be from textbooks, photos, the influence of other architects, or my own playing experience.

After Alice and I played the courses of Scotland, we scoured the bookstores in London searching for old books about golf course architecture. We bought every publication we could find, including *The Links,* by Robert Hunter, *Golf Architecture in America: Its Strategy and Construction,* by George Thomas Jr., and *The Architectural Side of Golf,* by H. N. Wethered and T. Simpson.

My bible on the subject has been a four-by-seven, faded-green 135-page handbook entitled *Golf Architecture,* written by Dr. Alister Mackenzie in 1920. My copy is tattered and scarred with pencil lines that mark Mackenzie's most pertinent words. I treasured the book so much that I scribbled "$500 reward if returned" on the inside cover along with my name and address.

I certainly haven't followed every bit of advice that Dr. Mackenzie sets forth in the book, but his common-sense approach to the game captivated me from the first reading. The English doctor may have had his education in medicine, natural science, and chemistry, but his transformation into a golf-course architect has had a lasting and profound effect on the profession.

Golf Architecture is a compilation of several lectures given by Dr. Mackenzie prior to 1920. Published in London and featuring an introduction by the eminent designer H. S. Colt, the book captured for posterity Dr. Mackenzie's fabled thirteen "essential features of an ideal golf course," which are as apropos today as they were then.

While these principles set out Dr. Mackenzie's basic views, the pages that followed embellished the object of his directives. On page thirty-eight of the text, Dr. Mackenzie wrote thirty-nine eloquent words that have become the creed by which I have built each and every one of my golf courses: "In discussing the need for simplicity of design, the chief object of every golf course architect or greenskeeper worth his salt is to imitate the beauties of nature so closely as to make his work indistinguishable from nature itself."

In accordance with these principles, my goal at Oak Tree was to create a demanding course, one that did not disturb the beauty of the land.

I rarely use a set of grading plans for construction, relying instead on my gut feeling as to what works and what doesn't as I go along. At Oak Tree, Ernie and Joe told me the bank demanded a set of plans, so they hired an engineering firm to prepare them.

Ernie says he learned an expensive lesson, since the cost to prepare those plans was $25,000. He swears I never referred to them, and he's right!

On the day we were to break ground, a well-intentioned young fellow from the contractor's office drove up in a utility truck. Carrying rolls of plans under his arm, he announced to Joe and me that he would be the construction superintendent.

Joe says that I chuckled to myself, took the plans from the startled gentleman, threw them into the bed of his truck, and said that we wouldn't be needing them. Joe also recalls saying to himself, "Oh my God, what have I gotten myself into?" apparently fearful that I was going to strike off in some direction that would end up in gigantic cost overruns.

Joe used to call Alice at home and say, "Hey, I'm just a driving range pro, and the only thing I ever worried about was how many balls to put in a bucket. Now I have Pete out here and I can't quite tell what he's up to. Listen, Alice, does Pete really know what he's doing?"

Mutual respect between owner and designer is critical to the success of a golf course, and regardless of Joe's doubts, he, Ernie, and I shared the same vision. Although they spent a great deal of time at the course, they trusted me to make critical decisions and heeded my advice when it came to important design features.

Since Ernie and Joe were both former Tour players, I knew they would recognize playability and still permit me some latitude with innovative ideas, but I will admit that Joe was more tolerant in many aspects than his partner.

Ernie says he learned not to question my judgment again after an episode at the third hole. Touring professional Johnny Pott was visiting the course during its construction and apparently suggested to Ernie that the green on this 590-yard into-the-wind par-five was way too small.

Ernie called me over and we discussed whether the meager 3,600-square-foot green was appropriate. He wanted it to be larger, so I acquiesced; a day later I had moved all kinds of earth to the green site and built a green three times as big, which satisfied Ernie.

"I returned ten days later," Ernie remembers, "and I'll be damned if that tiny green hadn't reappeared. I asked Pete why he'd changed it back, and he mumbled something about 'you were wrong' and went on shoveling dirt. That was the last time I ever questioned Pete's work, and of course when Oak Tree opened, the small green at the third was a favorite of everyone."

I decided par would be 71 since I just couldn't fit in the usual four par-fives without manufacturing artificial holes. With just three par-fives and four par-threes, the eleven par-fours would mold the character of the course.

The prevailing wind at Oak Tree came out of the south-southwest, and that was a big consideration when I designed the par-fours. Since they served as the backbone of the course, I wanted to make certain most of them played either into the wind or across it.

I deliberately toughened the first four holes to demand accurate play from the beginning. Most of the competitors in the 1988 PGA said the secret to playing Oak Tree was to get off to a good start and not find themselves three or four over par after the difficult opening holes.

Veteran touring professional Doug Tewell called the 441-yard par-four first hole (the Oaks) the "toughest starting hole of any we play." Length is not what makes it difficult, since the hole plays downhill, but the second shot to the three-tiered, hillside green requires precision. Holes two (Dubsdread), three (Coe's Corner—named after former National Amateur Champion Charlie Coe), and four (Waterloo) are all demanding holes that rise up to confront the golfer.

Ernie Vossler's earlier comments about bunkers is appropriate at Oak Tree, since an essential design feature is the positioning of bunkers in strategic locations.

In Scotland, bunkers were natural scars on the links that were a result of animals sheltering themselves in the sandy hillsides. Golfers played in and around the indentations, and as time progressed, they became a design feature of every course.

When I consider the use of bunkers, I have three basic questions to answer: What purpose do I want the bunker to serve? What type of bunker is needed? What will be the best strategic position?

When deciding the purpose I want a bunker to serve, I take into consideration the overall severity of the hole, whether water comes into play, the desired angle for the shot, and how best to challenge the aggressive player.

Many times a bunker is used to guide the golfer on the intended route to the green. The severity of that bunker depends on the concept for the hole; the degree of difficulty is based on the exact purpose the bunker serves.

Alister Mackenzie compares placement of bunkers on golf courses to the positioning of fielders in cricket to combat opposition opportunities to score unmolested. Nowhere is this placement factor more evident than in the British Isles. All the great courses there place a premium on dodging the bunkers, and unlike in the United States, often the player has to consider a sideways or backward shot to escape the severe banks of the bunker.

In Scotland, you rarely see bunkers on both sides of the green, since that provides a guide for the player through the chute. That pattern is followed on my courses, and very seldom are opposing bunkers placed anywhere.

I also try to alternate the placement of the bunkers between the left and right sides of fairways and greens so that the player's perspective changes with each hole. Strategic placement subconsciously forces the golfer to head away from the bunkers when the better route may be to hug them.

Except on par-threes, I very rarely position bunkers directly in front of the green requiring a forced carry. Professionals and low-handicap golfers usually hit the ball pin high or beyond, so lateral and rear bunkers are built with their shots in mind.

My overall philosophy is to make the hole appear more difficult than it really is, and great care is used in selecting the type of bunkers. Variety is the key, since I want to inspire golfers to surpass their own talent. Often a good recovery shot will lift the competitors' spirits and help them play better.

In my arsenal are several types of bunkers that may be used as guardians of the course: shallow, grassy-banked bunkers, waste bunkers, steep-walled bunkers, and the infamous pot bunker.

All except the pot bunker are familiar to American golfers. Pot bunkers, which resemble a small kettle or pot, have never been accepted in this country. In contrast to players from the British Isles, who are weaned on courses peppered with straight-banked pot bunkers, most American golfers are not accustomed to them. Foreign players adjust mentally to the exciting challenge presented by these severe bunkers, but in our country they are perceived as gimmick golf and too punishing.

Pot bunkers are used on my courses to intimidate the professional or low-handicap golfer more than the medium- to high-handicap player.

Great players have little trouble recovering from a regular sand bunker, while the higher-handicap player will be unsuccessful more times than not. By strategically positioning deep pot bunkers where they can lure the best players, I provide a hazard that challenges both their physical and mental skill.

Higher-handicap golfers have trouble with all kinds of bunkers, so they do not get too upset if they fail to recover from the pot bunker. If they do hit a good shot, they are ecstatic. If they hit a poor one, it becomes a "war story" to tell their golf friends.

On the other hand, skillful players who fail to recover from a pot bunker are very upset when they do not meet the challenge.

They rave about how terrible Pete Dye is for throwing such an unfair obstacle at them!

At the par-five third hole at Oak Tree, with water bordering the left side, I carved a tiny pot bunker into the left front of the elevated green. It's normally a three-shot hole, and that bunker protects the small green from those who don't position their second shot to the right side of the fairway.

The pot bunker to the left of and behind the fourteenth green at Harbour Town is a small target to hit, but many of the professionals roll into it during the Heritage Classic. They struggled with that tiny bunker in 1981, and Bill Roger's ability to save bogey there was critical to his ultimate victory.

Recently I've included three pot bunkers at the short par-four fourteenth hole at the Brickyard Crossing course in Indianapolis. Owner Tony George is a real golf traditionalist, and he believes that the public golfers who play his course will enjoy the challenge presented by those unique bunkers.

Just prior to completing the bunkers at Oak Tree, Alice decided we should take a trip to South Africa to look at golf courses in that country.

We had a wonderful time there as guests of Gary Player, who would return to the United States that spring to win the Masters. We visited Gary's ranch and played many notable courses, including Royal Johannesburg, Royal Durban, Houghton Golf Club, and the East London Golf Club.

While we were on our journey, David Postlethwait sculpted the Oak Tree bunkers as instructed, but when I returned, I told David to rebuild them in line with the subtle design I had seen on our trip.

Joe Walser took one look at the bunkers and told me he was not pleased with the bland style. He labeled them "Pete's South African bunkers"—not a term of endearment.

I finally admitted he was right and reshaped them so that the slopes were much more severe. When we made the changes, two interesting developments occurred that improved not only the look of the course but how it could be maintained.

Once the abrupt slopes of the bunkers were sodded, we watched the growth patterns of the Bermuda grass. Quite to our surprise, we discovered that the grass grew much slower on the steeper banks and, as a result, required less maintenance. In addition to cutting maintenance costs, the sheer slope of the bunkers at Oak Tree made the course look much more dramatic.

While I had free reign to design the holes at Oak Tree, Ernie and Joe were insistent that the clubhouse be positioned on top of a sizable hill. They couldn't be convinced otherwise, so I had to be innovative with the design concepts for both the ninth and eighteenth holes.

I don't like to build uphill golf holes, and so a scheme was devised to present an optical illusion that would actually make the golfers believe that they were level with the green when they hit the approach shot. By slightly elevating the tees, a big valley between the tee and the landing area was created so that the landing area appeared level. Another valley area in front of the green was dug, so the area of the approach shot appears just level or even a little above the green.

Since Oak Tree is located near Oklahoma City and Oklahoma State University, which has proven to be a training ground for many future PGA professionals, the course was under close scrutiny from the moment I started construction. When such fine players as Bob Tway, Gil Morgan, David Edwards, Mark Hayes, Doug Tewell, Willie Wood, and Andrew McGee are watching the progress, the end product had better be spectacular.

Initial reaction from these players and the membership was very positive when the course opened on May 1, 1976. Just eight years later, the course was the site for the 1984 United States Amateur, won by Oklahoma native Scott Verplank.

Shortly after that tournament was over, I recall strolling down the par-five sixteenth hole, which plays 479 yards from the back tees. Scott was playing with some friends, and he told me he thought fifteen was a *great* par-five.

I pressed him to tell me why. Instead of mentioning the winding stream, the severe bunker to the left side of the green, or the plateaued putting surface, all Scott could talk about was the fact that if he positioned his drive, he could then use a five iron to reach the green in two.

Scott's observation hit me dead center, for it was emblematic of the mind-set of the good player in the modern era. With the advancement of golf-equipment technology, the current professionals and low-handicap amateurs believe that a great par-five is one they can reach with a medium iron.

What a difference that is from the days when Ben Hogan used to discuss the *great* par-five tenth hole at Pinehurst No. 2 by pointing out that if he positioned a big drive and then "striped" a fairway wood, he could then hit a short iron to the green. I guess the term *great* depends on your viewpoint.

The exposure gained through hosting the 1984 United States Amateur propelled Oak Tree to prominence and increased its chances for being selected to host a major tournament. When it was announced that the course would be the site for the 1988 PGA, I was extremely pleased for Ernie and Joe, since they had fulfilled their dream of bringing a major championship to Oak Tree.

Most of the pre-tournament talk in 1988 was about Oak Tree being such a monstrous test. "Oak Tree is regarded as a most difficult course, even by those who have played the Stadium Course at PGA West," spouted David Eger, who was the PGA Tour's tournament director. "It has a bit of everything . . . sand, water, railroad ties, and undulating greens. It's not meant to be a Winged Foot or an Inverness . . . it's a modern course with all the hazards and obstacles," he added.

Scott Verplank described the course as "intimidating . . . when I first played it, I really didn't like it too much . . . so hard . . . so different from anything I'd ever seen, but now I feel it's one of Pete Dye's greatest courses."

Doug Tewell summed up the feelings of many of the players prior to the first round. He told of seeing Tom Watson, Craig Stadler, and Tom Purtzer after a round at Oak Tree and watching them as they "rolled their eyes" in amazement at how difficult the course played.

Despite these comments, expectations that Oak Tree would bury the finest professional golfers in the world never materialized because Mother Nature decided to reverse the weather conditions that normally consume August. Instead of dry conditions with lashing southwest winds, the course was besieged with alternate days of heavy thunderstorms and windless conditions during the four days of the championship.

I remember a conversation I had one time about wind with my friend Jack Leer, the force behind Wolf Run Golf Club in Indianapolis. Jack pointed out that in his opinion Seminole wasn't nearly as great a golf course on the days when the wind didn't blow.

I responded by telling Jack that since the wind blows 95 percent of the time at Seminole, the course is demanding almost every day. In Oklahoma, the wind normally blows 99 percent of the time, so I built a course where wind is a definite factor, only to have that 1 percent catch the course on the days when the PGA was being played.

The 1988 PGA champion was a long-shot: thirty-one-year-old Jeff Sluman, whose twelve-under-par total of 272 beat Paul Azinger by three shots. Jeff started the final round three behind Azinger but zapped the breezeless Oak Tree for a six-under-par 65 that included a holed-out 115-yard wedge-shot eagle two.

Since the wind was not a factor, the professionals could not play Oak Tree as it was intended. Its extraordinarily difficult nature never surfaced, and the local members were disappointed that the competitors weren't required to battle the course the way they usually play it when those gusty Oklahoma winds roar through the prairie.

Despite the lenient conditions that week, *Golf Digest* architectural editor Ron Whitten summed up Oak Tree when he said the course is "unlike most championship ones in that there is not as much room for error. Pinpoint accuracy is the call of the day," Ron adds, "and a great example of target golf at its best."

The ability to be accurate off the tee paid dividends for Jeff Sluman, who recalled recently that he "drove the ball so well during the PGA that it was impossible to play poorly." Jeff also pointed to his ability to get up and down out of the bunkers as a key to victory, echoing Ernie Vossler's profound comments.

Oak Tree is fairly wide open on the front nine, but beginning with the second shot on number twelve, the holes are bordered with dense woods filled with giant oak trees.

Based on that observation, Ernie and Joe told me they had

decided to call the course Oak Tree. I really laughed at the suggestion and told them that the name was a silly one that would never catch on. They certainly proved me wrong: the Oak Tree name and its accompanying emblem have become one of the most recognized trademarks in golf.

Besides the enjoyment I had working with Ernie and Joe, one of my fondest memories at Oak Tree is staying at the "Martin House," an old farmhouse located between the fifth and sixth holes. During the summer, Alice and I set up temporary living quarters there and all the crew members called it their second home.

Alice attempted to dry our laundry on a makeshift clothesline only to discover that the blustery Oklahoma winds spread our family underwear across the plains. When a husky bulldozer operator retrieved a pair of Alice's panties one evening, she decided we had better dry things inside.

Building Oak Tree was a very positive experience for me. Ernie Vossler and Joe Walser's commitment to excellence resulted in the first of a long line of great golf courses that they would develop in our country. Oak Tree stands as a tribute to them, and Alice and I were elated that the two former golf professionals realized their dream of establishing a championship golf course in their home state of Oklahoma.

Oak Tree Edmond, Oklahoma Par 71	
	Men
Yardage:	7015, 6475, 5986
Rating/ Slope:	96.9/148, 73.2/138

The Stadium Course at TPC

A good golf course is like good music or good anything else.
It is not necessarily a course which appeals the first time
one plays it, but one which grows on the player the more
frequently they visit it.

Dr. Alister Mackenzie
Golf Architecture
1920

When 1984 Masters champion Ben Crenshaw first played the
new Stadium Course at the Tournament Players Club in 1982, he
couldn't believe his eyes or his 80-plus score. "This is Star Wars
golf," he bellowed. "The place was designed by Darth Vader!"

Gentle Ben was obviously talking about me, but I have to
share the credit for the controversial design of TPC with Alice
and former PGA commissioner Deane Beman.

Deane has been a winner all his life. Besides being a highly
successful insurance executive whose early golf career produced
two United States Amateur Championships, Deane won four official PGA Tour events after turning professional in 1967.

Deane also won the British Amateur Championship in 1959,
and I watched as he and the rest of the United States Walker
Cup team beat back the British at Turnberry in 1963. Deane
played the courses in the British Isles well, and his appreciation
of our design at Harbour Town apparently reminded him of
those Scottish courses where he was so successful.

When Deane first considered architects for the Tournament

Players course, he thought a great deal about me because he was familiar with the work I did at Harbour Town. He liked the fact that it was a strategic golf course, had small greens, and was a throwback to the older style of golf courses.

Deane's main goal was to build a home course for the Tour professionals. He also wanted to establish the Tournament Players Championship as the fifth major tournament alongside the British Open, Masters, United States Open, and the PGA Championship.

Deane decided that the way to build this championship course and make it significant in the eyes of the professionals and the press wasn't to compete with the other majors but to create a separate identity. In his opinion, that is just exactly what the concept of stadium golf could accomplish.

Deane has admitted over the years that he "wanted to build another Harbour Town," due to the similarity of the terrain. I understood his intention and realized that if the greatest players in the world were going to play at TPC, I would need to create a course that would be every bit as unique as Deane's idea for stadium golf.

Interestingly enough, Deane really felt that while he was certain I could build a great golf course, it would be the reception the professionals and fans had to "stadium golf" that would make or break the facility. He had first discussed the concept in the early 1960s with then-Commissioner Joe Dey, and over the years the idea for a course where the fans could see every shot close-up never left his mind.

Deane Beman's stadium-golf principle was not a new one, but no one had ever taken the innovation as far as Deane envisioned. In effect, he wanted to create several hubs of activity where spectators could watch the competitors on as many holes as possible.

In Scotland, many of the natural sand-dunes make wonderful spectator areas. Turnberry, with its seaside elevations, is probably the best of the lot, and I've often wondered whether the stadium idea was imprinted in Deane's mind when he played there in 1963.

To learn more about the concept, Alice and I traveled to the Glen Abbey Golf Club in Ontario, Canada, which was designed by Jack Nicklaus in 1976. Although Jack's Muirfield course was a natural amphitheater layout, Glen Abbey was the first to have constructed spectator mounds.

Jack explains his design this way: "The theory of Glen Abbey was that a spectator could stand in the central core and see the greater part of play on fifteen of the eighteen holes. I then designed a mid-core where the golf fan could come closer to the competitors and really feel like they were part of the action."

After viewing Jack's work, and with Deane's thoughts in mind, I sketched the routings for the course on the back of a place mat. My intention was to build a combination club, resort, and public course where business executives, vacationers, and the public links golfers could enjoy a course the Tour professionals play in a major championship.

I had to submit a complete set of plans for the Stadium Course. I suppose Deane's bankers must have been afraid I'd kick off midway through the job and they would be left with half a golf course!

Prior to 1970, the number of fine championship courses that the ardent nonmember golfer could play was severely limited. Since all of the major championships were normally played on private clubs such as Oakmont, Merion, Olympic Club, and Augusta National, ardent golfers could only dream of playing the prestigious courses they'd seen on television.

Beginning with Harbour Town, and including the Tournament Players Course, Teeth of the Dog, the Stadium and Mountain courses at PGA West, Blackwolf Run, the Ocean Course at Kiawah, and Brickyard Crossing, I have been able to design courses where championship tournaments are also held. Coupled with Deane Beman's innovative TPC stadium-golf-course development, and the work of other designers who have built demanding courses open to the public, there exists a great number of courses where the public golfer can compete on the same holes the Tour professionals play.

When I first inspected the proposed site for TPC, my only compatriots in the impenetrable jungle were deer, alligators, wild boar, and deadly snakes. In order to cut a path, I followed the deer tracks, and they led me to areas in the swamps where I nearly drowned in the depths of the marshland.

At TPC we must have killed sixty or seventy rattlesnakes, all of them five or six inches around. Since rattlesnakes live in pairs, our crew had to watch out for momma when we killed her mate.

While I had a pretty fair idea of what Deane Beman intended at TPC, writer Peter Dobereiner summed up in a *Golf Digest* article the mission he felt Deane had in mind for me when I began construction of the course. "Deane Beman sent for Pete Dye and said: 'Behold this tract of jungle swamp. Pray turn it into the world's first golf stadium.' Dye glanced over the uncompromising acres of marsh and impenetrable scrub. 'Certainly,' Dye said. 'Bring me a bulldozer and two quarts of Mountain Lion's Sweat.'"

Based on the current environmental rules, it would be impossible to build the Stadium Course at TPC today. Reclaiming usable land from swamps and marshes by draining the water into lagoons was allowable then but would not be permitted today.

The easiest way to build a golf course on flat land is to dig a big hole for a lake and then use the dirt to elevate certain areas of the course. Continuing the pattern begun at Harbour Town, the fairways were actually lowered, leaving the roughs unchanged so the fairway would flow up to the adjacent rough area.

At TPC we wanted a sandy-soil base to grow the Bermuda grass. We therefore dug out all of the muck that was on top, removed the sand below it, and then flip-flopped the two.

When we emptied out space for a lake or pond, the resulting muck was piled up in the areas along the fairways and roughs and alongside the greens. Using this excess muck, we began to build the large spectator mounds that would provide perfect viewing areas for the golf fans.

The spectator mounds that have become so famous at TPC were never envisioned to be anywhere near the height they rose to be. If I had told Deane Beman that he would have mounds as high as three-story buildings beside his low-profile greens, he would have fired me right then.

During the months of constructing the course, the huge mounds simply evolved. The more muck I dug up, the higher the mounds became, but to our pleasant surprise they looked great.

We planned on ten- to twelve-foot-high mounds, but soon they approached thirty to forty feet and provided an amphitheater effect that really embellished the course.

Even the hundred-year-old Cabbage Palm trees, which stood forty to fifty feet high, still appeared stately when almost buried by towering mounds that cut their height to less than twenty feet.

These spectator mounds were positioned on the right side of the hole so the gallery would be looking into the golfers' faces, and they were built on the northwest side to block out the prevailing wind. This also permitted the walking gallery plenty of room to move about the course.

In order to clear out the vegetation that bordered the fairways, my construction superintendent, David Postlethwait, imported a small herd of goats. Prickly palmetto plants could have been hand-cleared, but goats are great because they will eat all that undergrowth without damaging any of the short fairway grass.

This experiment, which had been successful on many of the courses in the British Isles, worked for a time. Unfortunately, the goat population grew to almost fifty; Deane Beman said he'd seen enough and the steely-eyed critters were sent away.

I thought the goats added atmosphere to the surroundings, but I think Deane grew weary of hearing that "Old Prunes," the largest of the lot, was climbing the struts to the top of the clubhouse roof. In addition, Prunes and his mates apparently nudged a few too many golfers as they teed up the ball!

Both Alice and I had great respect for Deane Beman and the PGA Tour. We dedicated ourselves to building the very best golf course we could, and in order to make certain that we were overseeing the project on a daily basis, we moved into a motel very near the constuction site.

While building TPC, our crew frequently worked well into the night using lights to guide us. Many times we altered the paper plans as we went along.

Just as the incredible height of the spectacular mounds at TPC had not been in the original drawings, neither had the island green at the seventeenth hole. If we hadn't been on the scene to supervise construction, there would never have been such a green at the Stadium Course.

In 1946, Alice and I had played architect Herbert Strong's Ponte Vedra Club, located just minutes from the TPC course, which featured a massive green set out in the water. Surrounding the green were large sand bunkers and lots of grass berm, providing multiple bail-out positions for players.

Such a hole was the furthest thing from my mind when we set the green site marker some 150 yards from the tee for the seventeenth hole. The area around the green site contained the best sand for the course, and the more we dug it out to use on the fairways, the deeper and wider the cavity became.

Soon I was amazed to see that nearly three-quarters of the land around the green site was gone. The idea for an island green flashed in my mind, and I called Alice over to discuss it with her.

Perhaps it was the memory of Strong's island green, but I knew we had happened onto something special. Alice's enthusiasm matched mine—and Deane Beman's when we told him.

The plan had been to have only a small lake to the side of the seventeenth green. But since the green was going to be surrounded by water, we were now confronted with how large it should be. I had planned to build all small- to medium-size greens for the course, but now I needed to decide whether the seventeenth could match the others.

When we finished the hole, the apple-shaped green was twenty-six paces long and thirty paces wide. On the bottom of the apple was a single pot bunker with the narrow stem leading to land. Otherwise it was green or water from the tee.

At the time I didn't really think the seventeenth would be all that difficult, so I sloped the back portion of the green toward the water. Alice told me that if I left the green that way, she could envision the television announcers notifying the viewing audience that play in the championship was being held up because twenty-five foursomes were still waiting on the seventeenth tee for the lead player to keep his ball on the green!

After some thought, I was convinced Alice was right, so that portion of the green was raised. The hole is played with a short iron, and if it wasn't for the water lurking on all sides, the seventeenth would be quite easy.

Golfers who have played the seventeenth say it's a once-in-a-lifetime experience. Words fail to describe the dry-mouth sensation that grips the player seconds before the short iron leaves the safety of the setup position and heads into the take-away.

In the split second while the club descends toward the ball, golfers realize that the slightest deviation will cause its flight to miss the green and disappear in the water.

The island green at the seventeenth made me realize that I had created a hole that was planted in the player's mind from the very first tee. Knowing they ultimately have to confront the do-or-die seventeenth, competitors subconsciously realize that no lead is secure until their ball is safely on that green.

Even though the hole plays from a fixed distance, the varying wind conditions at seventeen add another element to the difficulty. If the water near the green is smooth, the prevailing wind is against the golfers, but if the water is choppy, they have the wind at their back.

When the course was completed, I told a reporter that while someone probably would shoot 64 at TPC, another player might shoot 104. "Everything here," I told a reporter the week before the tournament, "is the dead opposite of Augusta. . . . That course is pretty pretty; TPC is mean pretty."

During the practice rounds, there were as many compliments as complaints while the Tour players tried to make up their minds as to how they felt about their new course. Based on their comments, and those of the amateurs who played the course, I felt I'd succeeded in establishing the multiple-use type of demanding layout we'd envisioned from the outset.

Jack Nicklaus's pre-tournament comments were interesting, especially when compared to the critical comments he made after missing the cut. "Golf is not a fair game and was never meant to be," he told reporters. "By and large this course is finished, and a British weekend player would enjoy it because he's used to hitting shots while standing on his head."

Craig Stadler, whose outrageous antics at seventeen in the tournament would cause the gallery to roar in laughter, lamented, "There's just too much luck involved out there." And Jerry Pate, after hitting four golf balls into the water during a windless practice round, told the press, "If the wind blows, they may have to call off the tournament because the seventeenth will be unplayable."

When I played with Raymond Floyd, whose competitive desire reminds me of Ben Hogan, in the pro-am and provided suggestions to him as to where to hit the ball, he was eight under for seventeen holes. Somehow we got separated on the eighteenth, and without my advice he hit the ball on a flat area of the green and it bounded way over. Even with a double-bogey on the eighteenth, Ray shot 66.

Based on Floyd's round and my belief that we had built a well-designed championship course, I felt the professionals would fall in love with TPC. Unfortunately, when the first round was over, criticism was the call of the day, and the verbal assault against our new creation hit like a stake in my heart.

I felt bad for Deane Beman. He was the lifeblood of the course, and now he had a full-fledged revolt on this hands.

Tom Watson, who eventually finished sixth, led the parade of those disenchanted with my creation. "It's a joke, a real joke," he roared. "This course needs some major changes before it can even be called fair." Jack Nicklaus added, "This course plays all around my game and never touches it. I've never been very good at stopping a five iron on the hood of a car."

Tour jokester Fuzzy Zoeller, who missed the cut, chirped in with, "Where are the windmills and animals?" and John Mahaffey told reporters, "There's no mystery here. All you have to do is to hit a perfect drive, a perfect second shot, and a perfect putt. What I'm trying to figure out is whether you win a free game if you make a putt on the last hole."

With Watson the main spokesman for the rebel golfers, the protesters expressed complete displeasure with the course. The greens were too small and severe, the fairways too narrow, the mounds artificial and out of place and, to top it off, my prized seventeenth was a "ridiculous piece of s--- reminiscent of some putt-putt carnival course," according to one unidentified professional.

Watson also took Stadler's words about luck one step further when he complained that there was nothing "but sheer, unadulterated luck involved in hitting fifteen of the eighteen greens" and then added, "Is it against the rules to carry a bulldozer in your bag?" J. C. Snead, never one to hide his opinion, echoed Watson's comments, saying, "This course is ninety percent horse manure and ten percent luck."

Even the merry Mexican Lee Trevino bashed the course after he shot the first 82 of his Tour career in the first round and "X" in the second. Veteran professional Dave Eichelberger added, "I was out-mounded." In all, nine players withdrew, there were twenty-five rounds in the 80s, and veteran PGA scorekeeper Dom Mirandi told a reporter, "I've never put up so many 8s in my life."

Prior to the tournament, Deane had given the professionals the choice of whether to play the original TPC course at Sawgrass or the Stadium Course, which was still in rough form. The Tour regulars voted to play the Stadium Course, and now they were blasting away at the very conditions that Deane had warned them about.

While potshots were taken at almost every aspect of the design, most of the criticism was leveled at the greens and their severe contours. Tom Watson summed up the players' feelings: "The greens are too unfair now . . . too many slope away or slope sideways . . . you can't get the ball close to the hole." Miller Barber added, "Nice course you got here . . . when are you gonna put in the greens?"

At TPC, all eighteen greens were a medium-size 6,000 square feet or less. Deane Beman wanted to have four separate flat spots for permanent pin placements for each day of the tournament.

During construction, I would build a green and Deane would look it over and make suggestions. I took these seriously and tried to incorporate his ideas.

Judging the severity of greens during construction is very difficult since the dirt surface looks softer, gentler, and more receptive than when it is covered with grass. At many of my other early courses, I was often fooled, but over the years I have learned that valuable lesson.

When Deane and his associates Bob Dickson and Clyde Mangrum observed my progress, they judged the severity of the greens in relation to those of other great courses. In the end, the greens they approved had very severe contours, but not in comparison to such great courses as Pine Valley and Oakland Hills.

While putts with no break might seem preferable, the professionals hate them. They want to gauge the anticipated movement of the ball. The flat pin placements left them with dead-straight putts that could and did fall either way.

While I felt that the first-day pin placements were extremely difficult, and that the professionals would calm down after their initial outburst, I was ready and willing to give in where warranted. After all, this was to be their home course, and I wanted them to love it.

To appease the protesters, Deane assembled Tom Watson, Jack Nicklaus, and some of the other interested golf professionals and Tour officials. Alice and I joined them to inspect the course, and the group offered constructive ideas, which led to later modifications of the course.

Looking back, I realize that the radical design of the Stadium Course wasn't something the Tour professionals were ready for. They had never seen anything like it, and they were displeased when a wayward bounce or unexpected roll off a green ruined what they felt was a perfectly hit shot.

But while the professionals rebelled, the fans loved the course. The spectator mounds were packed all day long, especially at seventeen and eighteen, as the fans cheered the successful shots and groaned with those players who found the water.

Though the seventeenth was an immediate success with the fans and the media, many of the professionals hated the hole because there was no bail-out area. But the audience—at the course and watching television at home—loved seeing their favorite players struggle to hit the green.

Tour professional Victor Regalado made back-to-back sevens on the seventeenth, and Seve Ballesteros splashed one in the final round after he had pulled into contention. Even when the players were successful, their animated sighs of relief brought huge roars from the fans.

Despite his pre-tournament criticism of the seventeenth, Jerry Pate, winner of the United States Open in 1977, won the inaugural tournament by shooting 70, 73, 70, 67, 280 to win by two strokes over runners-up Scott Simpson and Brad Bryant. Jerry played flawlessly, and ironically a fifteen-foot birdie on the controversial seventeenth provided the key to victory.

Just as Arnold Palmer's incredible win at Harbour Town and John Daly's miracle victory at Crooked Stick were significant moments for our courses, Jerry Pate's decision to push Deane Beman and me in the alligator-filled lake and then dive in himself made headlines around the world. Jerry was a great champion, and my happiness for him was well worth the soaking.

Jerry had warned me that he would throw me into the lake at eighteen if he won, but I really didn't take him seriously. Once he had the nerve to throw Commissioner Beman into the murky waters right in front of millions of television viewers, I knew I was next. True to his word he pitched me in the pond right alongside Deane.

When asked if he got the $90,000 check wet during his brief swim, Jerry told the press, "No . . . I wanted to keep it dry so I can give it to Pete to help pay for re-doing some of the greens!" Commenting on Jerry's dip in the lake, writer Dan Jenkins wrote, "If Pete Dye is the Leonardo of golf course architects, then Jerry Pate is surely the Esther Williams of touring professionals."

In recent years, Hal Sutton, Fred Couples, Calvin Peete, John Mahaffey, Mark McCumber, Tom Kite, Jodie Mudd, Steve Elkington, Davis Love III, Nick Price, and Greg Norman have followed Jerry Pate into the winner's circle as the Tournament Players Champion. Respect for the TPC from the Tour professionals has increased over the years. During practice rounds it has become a ritual for the professionals to allow their caddies a chance to hit the famed seventeenth green, much to the delight of the gallery.

Amateurs from across the country, low- and high-handicap players, enjoy this public course as well. Along with players' consultant Jerry Pate and architect Bobby Weed, I built a second eighteen at TPC called the Valley Course, which has hosted a Senior Tour Event, but when amateurs come to TPC, their first priority is to play the Stadium Course.

In spite of the horror stories that have beset the touring professionals over the years, the Stadium Course, which hosted the 1994 United States Amateur, has become a challenging test for those amateur players who are courageous enough. Four separate tees make it playable for everyone, and the public golfer gets to test the same course the professionals play in a major championship.

While the seventeenth is enjoyed by the amateurs, the excitement really builds when spectators gather to watch the professionals in the Tournament Players Championship try their skill at hitting that evasive island green. Those great players could take a hundred balls down there in practice and hit every one on the putting surface, but when the flag goes up, they get the same knobby-knee feeling as the rank amateur.

Over the years, the Tournament Players Championship has risen in stature. Deane Beman's vision of stadium golf has become more popular, and the seventeenth now rivals the sixteenth at Cypress Point as perhaps the most famous par-three in the world.

In the last ten years, many changes have been made to the Stadium Course. Bobby Weed, who first modified the course with me in 1983, says he was the only course superintendent to have the cost of a dump truck, a bulldozer, and a track-hoe built into his maintenance budget!

Bobby and current course superintendent Fred Klauk have implemented the Tour players' directives. Greens have been stripped and rebuilt, slopes altered, waste areas cleared of grass, holes lengthened, fairways narrowed or widened, and recently some waste bunkers have been converted into sand bunkers.

On the greens, Bermuda grass was replaced by bent, then Bermuda was brought back again. As Ben Crenshaw said recently, "The course has evolved into what it is today . . . it was a radical beast in the early days, but through evolution it has become very playable."

Ben's words to the contrary, the Stadium Course came under assault before, during, and after the Tournament Players Championship in 1994. Unlike twelve years earlier, when the professionals ripped it for being unfair and too difficult, this time the criticism centered on the course being too soft and easy for play in a tournament that is being billed as a fifth major.

The leader of the opposition to the setup and maintenance of the Stadium Course was normally mild-mannered Tom Kite, who blasted Tour officials for permitting the difficulty of the course to "deteriorate." Tom told reporters that tournament officials were "in love with the color green," and the soft fairways and greens took the demanding nature from a course he felt "used to be worthy of hosting a major championship."

Greg Norman's opening-round nine-under-par 63 did nothing to lessen Kite's conviction, prompting him to inquire of reporters: "Is it going to take subpar to make the cut in the Players Championship? Is that right?" Kite, who shot 65 himself, was answered by Fuzzy Zoeller, who chastised him by saying, "Tom Kite has a short memory. He's forgotten how big and tough this course can be. He caught it when it was a pussycat this morning. Put him out there with a thirty- to forty-mile-an-hour wind and see what he says."

Controversy continued for the remainder of the tournament, which became a two-man battle between Norman and Zoeller. Tom Kite eventually finished tied for ninth at nine under par, eleven shots behind Fuzzy, and fifteen behind Greg, who blew the prestigious field away with an incredible twenty-four under par total.

Ironically, Greg came close to predicting his fate when he told me the Monday before the tournament that he was going to "shoot twenty-two under" on my course. We both laughed at the time, but Greg's incredible play may be one of the great tournament performances in the history of golf.

The fact that the Stadium Course was being labeled "easy" and "soft" brought a chuckle to me, since in twelve years the comments had come full circle.

While I don't have anything to say about the highly manicured condition of the golf course these days, I do believe the rustic nature of the Stadium Course has been lost over the years. That has lessened its demanding design features, but no wind and soft greens have probably contributed more to the low scores, since the course was originally designed to play firm.

Even more than Greg Norman's birdie barrage, I was interested in his post-tournament comments regarding the pressure he felt on the incoming holes in the last round.

Even though he had a five-shot lead over Fuzzy Zoeller heading into sixteen, Greg admitted that he hit a lay-up shot to that par-five to steer clear of the water on the right side. He also told reporters that the tension began to build as he tried to block out the image of having to hit his tee shot on seventeen to the island green.

"I have to admit seventeen flashed in my mind at the fifteenth hole, since I knew it would be the shot of the tournament," Greg told reporters, "but I immediately blocked it out of mind." Later he would call the seventeenth "under pressure, the hardest 142-yard par-three in the world."

NBC's Johnny Miller also discussed the "strategy" of playing the finishing holes at the Stadium Course. Regardless of the low scores, his analysis of the drama that begins to build at the sixteenth was right in line with the intent of my design.

In spite of the accusations that the Stadium Course played soft in 1994, I still believe it is a formidable foe for Tour professionals and amateurs alike. Nick Price recently said that golfers need their "A" game there and that he attempts to play "conservatively aggressively," since there are locations on the course that "severely penalize the player."

John Daly echoed those thoughts when he said a championship course like TPC demands "extreme patience to play," and Chip Beck said that "TPC causes the player to hit exacting shots from unusual locations not seen on other championship courses." Ryder Cup player Ian Woosnam told reporters the course can force the golfer to play "negative golf" by worrying about where not to hit the ball. Fellow British professional Colin Montgomery agreed, suggesting to reporters that his ninth-place finish in the 1994 TPC was due to making good "percentage-shot decisions."

More than anything else, the 1994 Players Championship proved that the Stadium Course at TPC continues to be controversial. Many journalists have tried to describe the type of person who would design it, but I believe Peter Dobereiner may have outdone them all in that September 1981 article for *Golf Digest*. Having just failed to post a score at the Stadium Course, Peter wrote: "While I have never met Pete Dye, I know him well. He is 500 years old and has absorbed the wisdom of the ages. He wears a pointed hat and a flowing robe embroidered with occult symbols. When he speaks, he becomes extremely animated, and gesticulates a lot, with flashes of blue static crackling from his long fingernails."

Thank you, Peter. I must have done my job well.

The Stadium Course at TPC Sawgrass, Ponte Vedra, Florida Par 72		
	Men	Women
Yardage:	6857, 6394, 5761	5034
Slope/ Rating:	74.0/135, 71.9/130, 68.7/126	64.7/123

Long Cove

Putting greens are to golf courses what faces are to portraits.

Charles Blair Macdonald
Scotland's Gift—Golf
1928

While most journalists wrote favorable articles regarding the Stadium Course at TPC, noted writer and historian Charles Price hated it. I think he believed island greens belonged somewhere in the middle of the South Pacific and that the stadium concept was best left for watching Michael Jordan's jump shots.

In 1982, when it came time for Charles to evaluate Long Cove on Hilton Head Island, he chose to compare it with TPC. In an article published shortly after Long Cove opened, Charles found a way to poke fun at TPC while praising the new course: "To compare Long Cove to the TPC Course is to compare the Last Judgment to a cartoon . . . [This time] Pete Dye left himself out of the design, giving the course a timeless transparency as though it had been designed by no one in particular."

On the whole, I have always felt my courses have received a fair shake from journalists. Regardless of their personal views, most of the time they have presented an objective picture and even surprised me with their commendations.

When we were building Harbour Town Golf Links, Charles

Price not only supported what we were doing but even made suggestions as we went along. More than anyone else, he popularized Hilton Head Island, and neither Harbour Town nor Long Cove would be as nationally recognized if it were not for his effort.

Shortly after the first PGA Heritage Classic at Harbour Town, Dan Jenkins wrote his wonderful article in *Sports Illustrated,* "What a Little Instant Character Can Do." In just seven prosaic paragraphs, Dan elevated the course into the ranks of the elite when he wrote that "Harbour Town is a sort of Pine Valley in a swamp, a St. Andrews with Spanish Moss, and a Pebble Beach with chitlins."

In addition to Charles Price and Dan Jenkins, Herbert Warren Wind also wrote an informative two-part article entitled "Pete Dye: Improving On Mother Nature" for *Golf Digest.* His question-and-answer format allowed me to speak out about my design concepts at Crooked Stick, The Golf Club, Harbour Town, Teeth of the Dog, and Oak Tree.

Dick Taylor, George Peper, Jerry Tarde, Tim Rosaforte, Peter Dobereiner, Brad Klien, and *Golf Digest* architectural editor Ron Whitten, among many others, have also been supportive of my golf courses over the years.

My relationship with Long Cove began when Joe Webster, project director at the Sea Pines Plantation Company, oversaw the construction of my course at Amelia Island. When Sea Pines ran into financial difficulties, Joe ventured out on his own and obtained an option on 675 acres three miles from Harbour Town.

Joe and his partners David Ames and Wes Wilhelm made it clear to me that they needed a championship golf course that would make an immediate impact. By this time, Harbour Town's success was evident, and Joe believed another course that attracted national attention could take advantage of the coming real estate boom he foresaw for Hilton Head Island.

At Long Cove I was pleased that my younger son, P.B., joined us and made the experience, like Crooked Stick, a family affair.

Over the years, I have collaborated with my sons Perry and P.B., and my brother Andy, who passed away in April 1994 after a courageous battle with cancer.

Three years younger than I and a Yale graduate with a degree in chemical engineering, Andy started to work with me in 1969. He assisted Lee Schmidt and me at Wabeek in Michigan and then supervised the construction of Little Turtle Club in Columbus, Ohio, in 1971 and Fowler's Mill Golf Club (formerly TRW Country Club) outside Chesterland, Ohio, in 1972.

Andy also designed the majority of Waterwood National in Huntsville, Texas. His work at La Mantarraya Golf Club in Las Hadas, Mexico, where actress Bo Derek displayed her wares in the motion picture *10*, is indicative of my brother's flair in design.

At Las Hadas, which is located between Acapulco and Puerto Vallarta, he surpassed himself. Working for Antenor Pitino, a Bolivian tin-mine millionaire, Andy carved out a lavish golf course, which features a spectacular eighteenth hole bordering the ocean.

Indicative of Andy's initiative was his determination to secure a few acres of land adjacent to that owned by Mr. Pitino. Mexican Ejido Indians owned the property, which included a small one-room school.

No one had been able to obtain that land until Andy came up with a novel idea. Recognizing that the Indians needed paint to refurbish the school, he forged a deal whereby he agreed to paint the structure in exchange for their permission to extend his golf course onto their land.

Besides my work with Andy, and in the tradition of other great father-son design teams of the past such as Old Tom and young Tom Morris; Trent, Bobby, and Rees Jones; and Ellis and Dan Maples, I have been fortunate to work with my sons Perry and P.B.

Perry first began working with me when he was only twelve, hauling water, pounding stakes, raking sand in the bunkers, and driving small equipment at Crooked Stick. By the time he was seventeen years old, Perry staked out the routing for the John's Island Course, and at nineteen he supervised the construction of the Harbor Tree Course north of Indianapolis.

After a successful stint in real estate, Perry founded Dye Designs, Inc., in Denver, and has built memorable courses in the western part of the United States. In the mid-1980s, Perry began to research the golf industry in Japan, and beginning with the Mariya Country Club in 1987, he has built outstanding courses there. His style more than anyone else's has greatly influenced architecture in Japan.

Extending his talent eastward, Perry now has courses in Korea, Taiwan, Thailand, and Australia.

When my younger son P.B. was in his early twenties, he was just a step away from being good enough to compete on the professional golf tour. P.B. was swinging a club when he was five, outdriving me by the time he was fifteen.

P.B. was for all practical purposes born on a bulldozer, and he might be the most innovative operator of a small dozer I've ever seen. His ability to sculpt three-dimensional shapes is exceptional, and his work at Long Cove produced some of the finest mounding ever created.

Being a good player and having visited Scotland and played in the British Amateur gave P.B. many visual ideas. Shot values are crucial to him, and my second-born is a hands-on designer whose favorite pastime is sitting square on a bulldozer and moving earth.

P.B. has done some fine work on his own since he formed his own company, P.B. Dye, Inc., in the mid-1980s. His designs at Loblolly Pines, Palm Beach Polo Club, Harbour Ridge, and the exquisite nine holes on Fisher's Island where they played the Merrill Lynch Senior Shoot-out in 1993, are very innovative Florida courses. Debordieu, Prestwick, and The Legends are as good as anything that can be found in South Carolina, and P.B.'s new series of Gauntlet public courses along the Eastern Seaboard are first rate.

In 1993 P.B. added nine holes to my dad's initial nine at the Urbana Country Club. When that nine matures, it is going to blend perfectly with my father's work seventy years ago.

We never dreamed our sons would become golf course architects, even though they had been exposed to construction from their youth. When both showed interest, we divided the country: P.B. could design courses east of the Mississippi and Perry took the western half.

Being Pete and Alice Dye's sons has not been easy for the two boys. While we have attempted to assist them in their aspiring careers wherever possible, they have had to fight some tough battles.

Perry and P.B. often confront situations where the developer or financier wants Pete Dye and not his son as the designer. Even though I know that either one of them can build as good a golf course as I can, the recognition my name brings to a course and the accompanying sale of real estate has sometimes kept developers from hiring them.

Based on Perry's work in Japan and the western part of the country and P.B.'s in the eastern half and France, I have no doubt that both will continue to establish their own prominence apart from mine.

Twenty-five-year-old native South Carolinian Bobby Weed, now the chief architect for the PGA Tour, was the construction superintendent at Long Cove.

Bobby Weed was working in St. Augustine, Florida, when I was first introduced to him. I told Joe Webster that I had this hotshot coming to ramrod our crew, and Joe immediately put Bobby on the payroll and forked over the expense money to move him to Hilton Head.

For the first two weeks he was on the island, Bobby never saw the property at Long Cove. I had him remodeling some bunkers over at Harbour Town, and he remembers that I and a tall, scowling gentleman approached him over there one day.

"Bobby," I said, "this is Joe Webster, the owner of Long Cove." The two men started to shake hands when Joe looked at his ghost employee and said bluntly, "So this is the man I've never seen who is on my payroll."

Bobby's local knowledge at Long Cove was very useful, but his hiring of a construction company that normally built roads caused some confusion. At hole number ten, we decided to excavate a three-foot-deep waste bunker all the way down the left side of the hole, and Bobby and I called over the bulldozer operator to give him instructions.

The gangly bespectacled man chewing a huge wad of tobacco listened intently. He smiled and nodded in all the right places, and Bobby and I left believing the area would be dug out when we returned.

Two hours later we walked over to the tenth hole, but the dozer operator hadn't moved. I asked him what the problem was and he just hitched up his pants and rubbed his hand slowly across his forehead before saying, "Look here, sir . . . is there a two-lane or four-lane highway going through here?"

P.B. says Long Cove was built by "people who love golf," and he's right. Of the nine or ten construction men who worked there with us, seven of them could break eighty and all dearly loved building golf courses. In fact the nucleus of the crew were all turf-school graduates who wanted to stay in the golf business either as superintendents or architects.

P.B. also believes that we can teach a kid who has no experience, but loves golf, to run a bulldozer in a day while it might take thirty years to teach an experienced operator who has no feeling for the game to sculpt mounds. He says that the greatest courses in the world were designed by people who really love the game and its great tradition.

This love for the game created a camaraderie at Long Cove, and those young men on the crew were inseparable. Legend has it that they drove golf balls off a pad near Spanky's Pub across the Savannah River. I understand the balls ricocheted off a Russian freighter, but thank goodness I wasn't there to see it happen.

I also never competed in their after-midnight "Hilton Head Open," an event played across the highway from Long Cove over to Shipyard Plantation using flashlights to guide the way!

During construction of Long Cove, Bobby Weed, P.B., and I began at daybreak, but Alice would wait until late afternoon to check our progress each day.

Bobby is right when he says that we held our collective breath in anticipation of Alice's thumbs-up or -down reaction. Sometimes she liked what we had done and sometimes not.

One day, after a stifling-hot day's work on the fifteenth green, I proudly showed Alice my masterpiece. Without hesitation, she jolted me with, "I think the inside shapes on that green make it look like a toilet bowl!" Bruised egos aside, she was right, and I went back and fixed the damned thing.

There would be comparisons of Long Cove with Harbour Town, and so it was important to provide it with a distinct personality of its own.

The course was to be played mainly by the homeowners, so we purposely concentrated on opening the landing area and locating the difficulty near the greens. Even though it appears narrow from the tees, there is ample room to land the ball on safe ground before the demanding approach shot to the green.

Since it is difficult for a strong person to imagine the shot facing a frail player, Alice used to lecture Perry and P.B. and me about making certain there was access to roll the ball to the green as if we were playing the course left-handed with a putter.

At the beginning of construction, our delightful seventy-year-old friend LaJunta Stowall began building a home just off the seventeenth green. Every time Alice saw us constructing a hazard fronting a green, she would mention LaJunta and the need for her to be able to play the course.

Bobby Weed recalls that whenever we began a design concept, we'd ask ourselves, "How can LaJunta play this hole?" Keeping that dear lady in mind helped us stay on track with a membership-type course, and she deserves equal billing for the end result at Long Cove.

To give the course a hole like no other on Hilton Head Island, we built the unusually short (317-yard) par-four fifth hole. Water protects the left side from the tee to the green, and there are pine woods to the right. Once players have safely found the fairway, they face the anxiety of hitting their second over a fifteen-foot-high mound that completely blocks any glimpse of the green.

We patterned this hole after similar ones in Scotland, and three-time Indiana State Amateur Champion Kent Frandsen says its unique feature brings the element of fear into play, since once the ball is lofted in the air, there is "no certain knowledge of its fate." Even though the approach shot is a short one, Kent, who competed in the 1991 United States Mid-Amateur at Long Cove, believes the "golfer's mind plays tricks on him since the unknown forces him to rush the swing in anticipation of learning the outcome of the shot."

While the fifth presents an American oddity for the players, Bobby Weed says the success of Long Cove is due to the variety of holes. All are blended into the terrain, but Bobby believes that by designing holes that meander through the oaks, the pine upland areas, and the manmade lagoons, golfers experience playing three golf courses in one.

If I'm known for one thing when I leave this earth, I hope people will say that Pete Dye knew how to build a set of first-class greens.

Unlike the Stadium Course at TPC, where I built putting surfaces for the touring professionals, I knew Long Cove would be played mainly by its residential members and their guests.

The first consideration in designing greens is what type of golfers are going to play the course (resort, private, men only, mixed membership, Tour players, etc.), the number of golf rounds expected per year, and the climate where the greens will be built. Knowledge of these factors allows me to scope out a preliminary plan for the green, although it may change several times during construction.

The second consideration is to fit the size and shape to the intended site. Greens can be pint size, giant size, or somewhere in between. Configurations include greens that are perfectly round, oblong, heart-shaped, or kidney-shaped, but mine must always have depth.

My third consideration is to decide on the potential elevation of the greens. They can be ground level, elevated, or appear to be elevated; terraced; mounded; concave; or they can slope toward or away from the golfer.

If I had ever imagined that Harbour Town would become as popular as it did and host more than forty thousand rounds per year, I would never have built such small greens. Problems with the condition of those greens will persist, for there is nowhere for alternate pin placements to divert foot traffic and allow a portion of the green to recover.

Joe Webster envisioned the potential for no more than thirty thousand rounds a year at Long Cove. With this in mind, I designed medium-size greens in a variety of shapes for the course.

Since Long Cove was to be a membership course first and foremost, I built low-profile greens that were receptive to diverse shots. The first thirty feet of the greens and the areas in front slanted inward. Mounds were employed on either side of the approach to kick errant shots back toward the green. This feature assisted most players, who often hit short, bouncing shots, but did not help expert players, who normally carry the ball all the way to the putting surface.

By the time I designed Long Cove, I was much more conscious of the increased speed of greens.

This factor was not a consideration in the Hogan/Nelson era, since mowers could not cut the greens shorter than one-quarter of an inch. At that height, the grass would lay over, creating what is called grain. The direction the grass would lay over depended on the prevailing wind and the slope of the green. To increase speed, greens were rolled, causing the grass to lay over even more. Rolling makes reading the line of a putt and judging the speed more difficult.

Designers of the legendary courses built in the early part of the twentieth century never imagined that the grass would ever be trimmed to lengths shorter than a quarter inch. Putters like my father's wood-shaft Silver Scot Tommy Armour were all lofted to help skip the ball over the shaggy grass to the cup, especially when the putt was against the grain.

Ancient courses such as Pinehurst No. 2, Seminole, Pine Valley, Merion, Oakmont, and Augusta National never considered cutting their greens to threadbare length, since their many contours were designed to be putted at speeds of their day. The grain factor on those courses also affected the player's attempt to chip the ball, since a shot could include surfaces on which the ball moved with the grain, against it, and across.

In the early 1980s, a new word, *stimpmeter,* entered golf's vocabulary and the game has never been the same. Invented by John Stimpson, the stimpmeter measures the speed of the greens. A golf ball is placed at one end of a three-and-one-half-foot narrow aluminum trough. The end with the ball on it is raised until the ball rolls down onto the green. The distance the ball rolls is measured. Then the procedure is repeated in the opposite direction and that distance is measured. The two distances are then averaged, providing the stimpmeter reading.

If the ball rolls ten feet in one direction and eight back the other, the stimpmeter reading is nine. The larger the number, the faster the speed of the green, and if a certain speed is desired, the greens are then cut to heights that will produce that number.

If a stimpmeter had been used in 1953 when Ben Hogan won the Masters at Augusta and the United States Open at Oakmont, the reading would never have been more than six or seven. This means the downhill reading might have been ten, and the uphill reading, against the grain, maybe four.

In the 1960s and 1970s, the speeds increased to eight or nine, but in the early 1980s, decisions were made to increase the stimpmeter readings for PGA Tour events to eleven or twelve.

In my opinion, the decision to increase green speeds has definitely hurt the game of golf. This development has not only caused many of the greens on the great old courses to be nearly unplayable, but greatly hampered the ability of member players to negotiate the new speed levels.

In effect, emphasis on putting surfaces as smooth as glass has shifted the skill-level balance in favor of the modern-day touring professional. Before green speeds were increased, the art of putting depended more on stroke, and golfers like Bobby Locke, the greatest putter I ever saw, kind of hooked the ball around the green and corralled it into the hole.

Cutting greens today to an eighth of an inch causes the grass to stand straight up, virtually eliminating the grain factor, and putting has become more of a test of nerves instead of skill. In addition, the necessity of constantly watering the closely mowed greens on the PGA Tour has made them more receptive to spin shots than the old firm greens.

All this talk about green speed on the Tour has in turn convinced golf clubs and even municipal courses to speed up their putting surfaces as well.

In a day and age when course superintendents are attempting to find ways to cut back maintenance costs, increased green speeds are adding to them. The need to cut the greens short in order to make them lightning fast requires more course maintenance, since the surface must be mowed and watered so often.

In addition, the grass is under constant stress, making it susceptible to disease and requiring more chemical-spray treatments. Footprints and spike marks are more evident, and the frequent mowing increases the mower wear marks.

To understand the idiocy of all this, Jack Nicklaus told me that at his Memorial Tournament at Muirfield Village, greens got up to a *sixteen* reading, which means the professionals were putting on ice-fast surfaces. Imagine playing the severely contoured greens of Pine Valley, Merion, or Oakland Hills with that reading.

At Long Cove, I purposely contoured the greens with more gentle slopes to accommodate increased green speeds.

In an effort to reduce maintenance for Long Cove, I began to experiment with growing grasses that didn't require much attention. Since my mounds and bunkers may have steep slopes, I needed to find slower-growing grasses so that mowing costs would not be prohibitive.

My experiments at the Stadium Course at TPC never got off the ground because Deane Beman needed to get the course up and going for the Tournament Players Championship. At Long Cove, however, I found that a blend of centipede grass was perfect for the steep inclines.

That grass grew very slowly and needed to be cut only three or four times each summer. In addition, the combination of centipede, carpet grass, love grass, and the blends of Bermuda provided Long Cove with great color contrasts.

Waste bunkers, which need no water or mowing, slow-growing grasses, many unirrigated rough areas, and moderate green speeds also kept the maintenance costs reasonable.

When the course was completed, our "designated player," LaJunta Stowall, could enjoy every hole. Touring professional Davis Love III recently said that he wants to design golf courses his mother could play, and that type of playability is the key to Long Cove's success.

Just as Joe Webster had desired, Long Cove gained instant national attention. In 1991, the 11th annual United States Mid-Amateur was played there. One hundred fifty-six of the finest twenty-five-year-old and older golfers in the country gathered to compete for the championship, which was won by Jim Stuart of Macon, Georgia.

Over the years, the course has matured and become a favorite with members and guests. Joe Webster was pleased with the course, but I believe he was even more impressed with Alice.

When asked what would happen if I passed to the hereafter in the middle of building his golf course, Joe promptly replied, "Alice would just finish it—cheaper, better, and faster!"

Long Cove Hilton Head, South Carolina Par 71		
	Men	Women
Yardage:	6900, 6420, 5873	5873, 5002
Rating/ Slope:	74.1/140, 71.1/130, 69.2/120	74.6/138, 69.5/121

The Honors

Amateurism, after all, must be the backbone of all sport—
golf or otherwise.

Richard S. Tufts
The Amateur's Creed

No one in the world believes more in the spirit of the amateur golfer than Jack Lupton, the founder of The Honors course, near Chattanooga, Tennessee. Since the first golf courses appeared in our country, The Honors is the only course built specifically for and in "honor of" the amateur golfer.

In spite of the possible temptation to do so eventually, it's doubtful that Jack will ever agree to host a professional event. His dedication to amateur golf brings to memory how the game was first brought to the United States in the late 1800s.

While the first three- and six-hole courses were actually built in and around Yonkers, New York, the very first eighteen-hole golf course was built by Charles Blair Macdonald in Belmont, Illinois, in 1893. A native of Chicago, Macdonald first learned about the game when he attended St. Andrews University in the mid-1870s.

Soon after his arrival in Scotland, Macdonald's grandfather took him to the golf shop owned by Old Tom Morris. Besides introducing the young university student to its famous proprietor, grandfather Macdonald bought Charles his first set of clubs.

Charles Blair Macdonald's fascination with the game was instantaneous. Before long he was playing with the likes of Old Tom, Young Tom, and Davy Strath, a fine player for whom the intimidating bunker at the eleventh green on the Old Course is named.

By the time Macdonald returned home to Chicago in 1875, he had golf boiling in his blood. St. Andrews and the other great links courses in Scotland were still fresh in his mind, but he had no eighteen-hole course upon which to continue his passion for the sport.

Seventeen years would pass before Macdonald got his chance to use what he had learned in Scotland. Chicago was the site for the World's Fair, and to prove themselves hospitable to their English visitors, several Illinois businessmen decided to build a golf course. They contacted Macdonald about designing it. Within weeks he had built seven holes on the estate of U.S. Senator John Chatfield.

Shortly thereafter, some thirty members of the Chicago Club invested ten dollars each and Macdonald built a separate nine holes in Belmont, Illinois. In the spring months of 1893, he completed another nine holes, providing the United States with its first eighteen-hole layout.

Charles Blair Macdonald was also a great golfer as evidenced by his United States Amateur title in 1896. His playing prowess and love for the Scottish courses propelled him to choose golf course architecture as a profession.

Over the next decade, Charles Blair Macdonald returned to the British Isles several times to prepare for his future design work. Reminiscent of my trip to Scotland with Alice in 1963, Macdonald studied the ancient courses carefully and returned with surveyor's maps and sketches for many of his most famous holes.

Macdonald's finest creation is the National Golf Links of America. He incorporated the design concepts from the holes at St. Andrews, North Berwick, Prestwick, and other famous Scottish courses into the layout, and the result was incredibly imaginative.

Charles Blair Macdonald was definitely a hands-on designer, and he worked on the National Golf Links until the day he died.

He was quite passionate about his design there, as evidenced by a run-in with a relative.

Apparently a nephew of Macdonald's wasn't all that impressed with the par-four first hole and bragged to his uncle that he could drive the green. Macdonald told him that was impossible, but the nephew continued to boast.

Soon the two men ascended the first tee, whereupon the nephew hit a perfect tee shot that cleared all the bunkers at the seam of the dogleg, bounced on the fairway, and then leaped up and on the green. The nephew stood by proudly, awaiting his laudations, only to have Macdonald stomp from the tee into his house, where legend has it he promptly struck the name of that nephew from his will!

In the true spirit of men like Macdonald, Jack Lupton and several of his friends purchased a 460-acre tract of land in the rural Tennessee village of Ooltewah, a Cherokee word meaning "resting place." History books indicate that the Spanish explorer Hernando de Soto led an expedition through Ooltewah Gap as early as 1540, making camp on the western side of White Oak Mountain where the course now stands.

Jack first approached me about his proposed course as Alice and I were standing on the tenth tee at Seminole. He rather commanded me to build a golf course for him that would honor the amateur player.

When owners like Jack Lupton hire Alice and me, they don't attach themselves to some sort of corporate conglomerate. A phone call to our number in Delray Beach, Florida, either brings one of us to the phone or reaches that fancy answering machine Alice bought. Up until 1992, when we were away we call-forwarded our phone to my mother's house, and anyone who called had the pleasure of speaking with her.

My mother was a delight, and she handled the phone duties right up until she died at the age of ninety-four. She would even take her portable phone to the bathroom with her, and oftentimes wondered what callers would have thought if they'd known they were talking to a ninety-four-year-old woman standing naked just out of the shower!

Alice and I have nothing against large-scale design operations, but we've enjoyed keeping the business simple. A loyal, competent secretary named Diane Darsch efficiently manages our home office.

We very rarely work on more than one or two courses at a time. Our home is scattered with routing plans, and there's not a room that isn't full of golf course literature, maps, correspondence, photos, or memorabilia.

We do not own a car; renting works out fine for us. The rental-car folks and I have a longstanding relationship, even though I have been pretty rough on their cars.

One time they called, telling me that they had located my car outside a motel. They were certain someone had trashed the car by throwing shovels, sandbags, dirt, and wooden stakes inside. The dispatcher went on to say that the outside was covered with mud, and that the oil pan seemed to be dragging from underneath the automobile. I professed innocence, but had to confess I was the culprit when I realized I needed the shovel!

I'm also a friend of the airlines, since I buy so many one-way tickets, but some of my trips have caused problems.

During the work at The Golf Club, I found a baby raccoon and decided I would take it back to Indianapolis for P.B. I hid it in my heavy jacket, and none of the flight attendants noticed the cute little critter.

When I dozed off, the raccoon eased himself out of my jacket, crawled along the seats, and somehow ended up in the bouffant hairdo of the woman sitting behind me. Recently the captain of that flight introduced himself to me in Kansas City and explained that if it wasn't for his sense of humor I'd be taking the train these days!

My tendency to pack my own lunch for airplane flights got me in trouble when I flew the Concorde to Paris. French developers asked me to take a look at a potential site, and when they offered a ticket on the Concorde, I accepted.

I sat beside a rather stuffy English gentleman dressed impeccably in an expensive English-cut tweed jacket replete with cravat and a diamond stickpin. He took one look at my khakis, faded golf shirt, and work boots and immediately dove into the *London Times*.

I was engrossed in a paperback mystery, but I noticed that the man kept waving his hand across the front of his face in an attempt to swat away what appeared to be gnats. Since he had ignored me, I hated to bother him, but I finally asked what seemed to be the problem.

Extending the index finger of his left hand, he pointed directly at my duffel bag and brusquely said to me, "My good man, there seem to be bugs flying out of your case."

He was right. Passengers were swatting gnats until we got to Paris, all because I had forgotten about a black, three-week-old banana in the duffel bag!

As we made our way toward the site, Jack Lupton told me, "Frankly I am sick and tired of professionalism and its commercialism. I want a course dedicated solely to the amateur, but molded in the tradition of Charles Blair Macdonald, Donald Ross, and Alister Mackenzie."

Jack Lupton's link with Mackenzie came through his membership at Augusta National. He also was a lifelong friend of Bobby Jones, and told me of Jones's fond wish that an amateur would win the Masters.

"Amateur golf is the last bastion of sport," Jack extolled. "It is a gentleman's game and is played by strict rules that are enforced by the United States Golf Association."

If Jack Lupton used the word *straightforward* once during our construction of The Honors, he used it a hundred times. He was insistent on carving out a formidable golf course, but one that held the line when it came to trickery.

Jack escorted me to the course site and expected to walk the property with me. Jack recalls, "I was ready to plow through the underbrush with Pete, but he told me to head downtown and come back in five or six hours. I did so, and when I returned Pete told me I had a wonderful piece of property for my course."

During my visit to the site, I could easily visualize the potential routings and even the placement of many of the greens. I usually walk a piece of property many times before I can visualize holes, but at Ooltewah the routing was easy.

"Pete Dye has the capacity to walk raw land and see a vision of the finished course," Jack told reporters shortly after the course opened. "I couldn't see a damn thing but somehow Pete could look ahead and visualize golfers attempting a downhill five-footer on a severely contoured green that didn't exist at the time."

Many times the scenic beauty of a piece of property can actually be a problem if the owners have fallen in love with their site. If the owner isn't prepared to see massive changes in the landscape after bulldozers sweep through, it can be very disturbing. Many times I've almost been fired a few days into the job, and I'm sure Jack Lupton considered it several times.

While we try to save all the trees possible, the proposed fairway areas must be cleared. This creates a problem, as we must find a way to dispose of the timber.

Many owners don't realize that while a standing tree takes up very little ground space, its massive branches spread out everywhere when it's downed. Chainsaws are required to section it, and then the sections have to be burned, buried, or hauled away.

If possible, I like to bury the trees, but at The Honors we decided to burn them. Unfortunately, our first blazing fire triggered an allergic reaction in a neighbor woman, and our burning permit was revoked.

Hauling those downed trees to a location near holes seven and eight and burying them there was costly and time-consuming. While understanding the neighbor woman's problem, Alice commented that it would have been cheaper to send her to Palm Springs!

Our son P.B. was the project manager at The Honors, and he provided valuable input regarding construction of the course.

Big bulldozers relocated hundreds of tons of dirt, and we used a bushelful of dynamite to remove stumps and crack the tough White Mountain stone. During the building of The Honors it rained so much we considered drawing plans for an ark. We also faced the challenge of dealing with Tennessee red chert, a glue-like substance that still makes me shudder when I think about it.

P.B. says chert is lousy soil, since there's no nutritional value to it. It doesn't percolate and the only way to deal with it is to spread sand over the top and hope.

Alice was instrumental in the design of the tenth hole, but it cost Jack Lupton a bundle. At a point when construction was nearly complete, my tell-it-like-it-is wife joined Jack and me for an inspection of the layout.

As we stood on the tenth tee, Alice blurted, "This fairway won't do at all. It needs to be lowered at least ten feet." Jack and I looked at each other with rolling eyes, but as usual Alice was right.

When the construction crew dug down two feet, they reached a bedrock of limestone. Three hundred thousand dollars later, Jack jokingly told Alice to leave the premises and never come back!

Besides this little cost overrun, Jack Lupton's checkbook was pried open on several other occasions. I normally can provide owners with an estimated dollar figure to build their course, but the unexpected has to be expected when you're dealing with Mother Nature.

Building golf courses is not for the financially timid. I built Heather Hills for $80,000 and Crooked Stick for $500,000, but today's costs can escalate to as high as six or seven million dollars, or even more. If a bank or other financial institution is doing the financing, a full budget must be prepared.

My developer friend Joe Walser once said, "Pete Dye is the only golf course designer who was ever given an unlimited budget, and then exceeded it." Joe's observation may be true, but most times any escalation in cost is beyond my control.

Cost overruns most often occur when weather delays construction or destroys work already completed, the land provides surprises that escalate construction cost, or the owners decide that they want to modify the design of the course.

At The Honors, that Tennessee chert proved more formidable than I expected, and with the steady rainfall, more man-hours of work were expended than we had in our budget. Jack adjusted a few holes as we went along, always to the improvement of the course.

Costs increased when the amount of local sand needed to build the USGA greens proved insufficient. Truckloads had to be hauled in from fifty miles away to supplement and to provide sand for the approaches to the greens when the chert would not mold.

When the water supply proved inadequate, Jack Lupton's costs increased again. Additional property needed to be purchased across the road from the course to build a new lake.

While it was expensive to dig up that limestone from the tenth fairway, P.B. put it to use bulkheading the lake in front of the ninth green. Jack liked the look so much he ordered all the lakes framed with rock, which made for another cost increase.

When it was time to choose the grass mix for The Honors, I was drawn back to my initial fascination with turf in the 1950s. Experts agree that in that decade and the one following it, most courses in the United States began to have very poor turf quality, which was a mystery to everyone.

In the 1950s the USGA studied the problem very carefully, and I closely followed their research. Several theories emerged, but it was only when they began to explore the use of arsenic in the soil that progress was made. Officials discovered that in the period beginning in the early 1900s and up until World War II, most golf courses used a fertilizer called Milorganite, which contained a small percentage of arsenic.

Milorganite was very popular because worm and bug counts were virtually eliminated. Every superintendent was pleased with the results, and for years Milorganite dominated the market.

Further research indicated that during World War II, the lead used to make arsenic was needed by the government for the manufacture of bullets. By order of the military, arsenic was removed from the Milorganite mix. When the war was over, arsenic was not remixed into the Milorganite, and so none of the turf on golf courses had that ingredient. In the early postwar years, *Poa annua* began to infiltrate the greens, and then left bare patches when summer heat caused it to die.

The USGA Greens Committee and other experts did their best to find out why this occurred. They devised a plan to provide better percolation, creating more drainage for the greens, but that didn't eliminate the *Poa annua.*

Finally, researchers discovered a direct correlation between the absence of arsenic and the growth of *Poa annua.* Soon it became obvious that the arsenic, acting as a preemergent, kept the undesirable annual grass down and let the good grass grow through.

After that revelation, fertilizer companies introduced three different variations of a new mix that contained varied amounts of arsenic: Mil-Arsenate, Lead-Arsenate, and Cal-Arsenate, which had the greatest amount of arsenic.

When I learned of these new fertilizers back in the mid-1950s, I ordered them for the Country Club of Indianapolis. Using this miracle cure, I was certain I would become a hero to the members by restoring lush grass to their pockmarked course.

Never being one to go halfway, I chose the hot Cal-Arsenate. We bought bags and bags of the chemical, and I began my assault against the demons of the fairways.

The unfortunate result of my well-intentioned efforts was to burn off sections of the fairways, sterilize them, and leave them bare! Pete Dye had struck again, and it was a lengthy time before anything at all would grow there. For a long time, I refused to answer the door at our home for fear of a lynching party!

Actually none of the organites worked because no one could administer the correct dose in gradual applications as had been done during the years prior to World War II.

Another reason there was not as much of a problem with turf in the early 1920s and 1930s was because fairways were not watered. *Poa annua* will not grow without sufficient water, so it became a problem only when artificial irrigation was introduced.

The texture of the soil and the type of grass that can be grown in different parts of the country have a tremendous influence on the design of a golf course. I would love to introduce more bump-and-run shots, but the soil must be sandy and firm. Spill a little water on the sand in the British Isles, where the weather is cool and windy, and you can drive a car up and down the hard surface. Put some water on the sand in the United States and most times you will sink to your heels.

Only in certain locales such as Long Island, northern Michigan, and Maine can turf be grown that will allow bump-and-run shots.

At The Honors, we had clay soil and hot, humid summers, so we used a variety of grasses: bent, fescue, Bermuda, and bluegrass, known collectively as "The Honors Mix."

On the fairways, Jack Lupton wanted us to use a hybrid Bermuda that is rather uniform. I felt zoysia might be more appropriate, but Jack was the boss.

Zoysia was my preference because it permits the ball to sit up better for the golfer. Professionals are able to spin the ball, but a high-handicapper can still hit a three wood off the fairway.

After a few heated discussions, we planted the Bermuda. But without my knowledge, my resolute son planted a patch of zoysia on an approach area in front of the sixth green. Jack was upset when he learned of this bit of trickery, but I assured him we'd replace it.

Winter kill took its toll on the Bermuda, but the zoysia just kept on growing. Even I was somewhat amazed, and P.B. was trying not to gloat.

Shortly thereafter, I received a phone call from Jack. "I love the zoysia, and I want it on the rest of my golf course," he told me. I assured him that I could do it and have the fairways playable in less than two years.

"Pete," he retorted, "I'm afraid you're not listening to me . . . I said I want zoysia on my golf course."

He had to say that three or four times, each more loudly than before, for me to finally get it through my thick head what he meant. He wanted zoysia and he wanted it immediately!

The owners of every nursery between Cincinnati and Tulsa must have thought they'd died and gone to heaven when we called and bought every single yard of zoysia they had. Trucks were blazing the interstates toward Chattanooga, and within a week Jack had his fairways sodded with zoysia.

P.B.'s hunch had paid off and we learned a great deal about zoysia grass. There's a "crabgrass belt" that runs through the central United States where zoysia can be grown, and if you grow it long, cut it back, and then leave it alone, it will flourish.

The window of time to plant grass at a course like The Honors is a short one. The golf course superintendent chosen must work with the designer to never miss a beat in getting the land in shape so that the grass will grow and the course can be playable the next season.

To nurture The Honors along, we wanted to hire the finest golf course superintendent we could find. When P.B. played a

Donald Ross course named Holsten Hills in Knoxville, Tennessee, he met an impressive young man named David Stone.

David is probably the best thing that ever happened to The Honors. He not only succeeded in growing lush grass on the fairways and greens but also was able to grow field grasses that gave cover for the mixture of wildlife that would inhabit the course.

David traveled the countryside around Chattanooga to see what grasses were natural to the area. He found tall fescue that blooms green and turns a straw color, and native broomsedge, a stiff-stemmed plant whose tall stems produce a yellow blossom.

Cedar, pine trees, blackberry, and honeysuckle bushes were also planted, giving a variety of colors. Robins, meadowlarks, quail, and woodpeckers were drawn to The Honors, and David even struck up a lasting relationship with a bluebird named Bubba who ate mealworms from his hand.

The New York Audubon Society took note of David's work. In 1991 The Honors was chosen as the first golf course to receive an award for wildlife habitat preservation.

David continues to experiment with grasses at The Honors. With Jack Lupton's support, he now has more than twenty-seven varieties of bent grass and five of zoysia under study on four acres set aside for his research.

Jack Lupton's input at The Honors was evident at the eighth hole, where I told him I was very frustrated with not being able to provide any depth perception to the green from the tee.

A solid eight-handicapper, Jack took a quick look down the fairway and then toward an elevated location less than thirty feet from us. "Look, dumb ass," he said while pointing out the obvious. "What about putting the tee up on that hill?"

One glance told me Jack was right. I just nodded and wandered away, realizing he was probably saying to himself, "And this guy is a big-time golf course architect!"

Prior to hosting the 1991 United States Amateur Championship, The Honors, true to Jack Lupton's word, had already established itself as a mecca for amateur golf. The 80th Southern Amateur Championship was the first major event played there. It was followed by the 50th anniversary of the Tennessee Women's Amateur and the 75th anniversary of the Tennessee Men's Championship.

In his pretournament assessment of The Honors for the USGA Amateur Championship, journalist Sam Woolwine wrote:

> Pete Dye's creation is tough, but fair. Keep the ball in play and the competitor is rewarded. Out of the fairway and the love grass is hardly as lovely as its name. The Honors is a startling contrast between the immaculately groomed fairways and the wild that is the rough, between the ecstasy of a good shot and the pity of a poor one.

The "wild" Mr. Woolwine refers to is kept that way so the indigenous wildlife on the course can coexist with the golfer. During the tournament, competitors could spy swallows, bluebirds, killdeer, bluejays, and midnight-black grackles who traverse the course in wonderment of the tiny white spherical objects that invade their jet stream.

The Honors, and especially its tough finishing holes, is perfect for match play. Multiple risk/reward opportunities exist for gamblers who find themselves anxious to hit that one shot that either takes charge of a match or permits them to catch up when they're behind.

The 91st United States Amateur Championship was a success from start to finish. Headlining the field was Phil Mickelson, the new superstar on the amateur circuit, who had not only won the 1990 Amateur and NCAA, but captured a professional Tour championship at Tucson. Only Jack Nicklaus had ever won the Amateur and the NCAA in one year, and even he had never won a professional Tour event as an amateur.

Mickelson faced a strong field, including Alan Doyle, John Harris, Jay Sigel, and the eventual victor, Mitch Voges, who beat Manny Zerman in the final. Mickelson played well but lost in the third round.

"I couldn't have been more proud than to have hosted the United States Amateur," Jack Lupton told reporters. "Mitch

Voges is a great champion, and it's the ultimate compliment for the USGA to have selected The Honors."

Shortly after the Amateur, The Honors hosted its first international event, the Devonshire Cup matches between Great Britain, Canada, and the United States. The year 1994 brought to Chattanooga the prestigious Curtis Cup, a competition between the women of Great Britain, Scotland, Ireland, and the United States.

While The Honors and its "straightforward" design have received praise since the day the course opened, this tribute to amateur golf is best summed up, as it should be, by its founder, Jack Lupton. When asked just prior to the 1991 United States Amateur Championship about his expectations for the course, Jack replied, "There should be an ambience about playing The Honors. The golfer should feel the serenity, the quietness of the place, the feel that regardless of how you're playing, it simply is an honor to be there."

The Honors Chattanooga, Tennessee Par 72		
	Men	Women
Yardage:	7064, 6606, 6372	5651, 4902
Rating/ Slope:	75.4/151, 73.1/143, 72.3/139	73.7/126, 69.7/117

The Stadium Course at PGA West

The Mountain Course at La Quinta

An ideal golf expert must not only have a knowledge of botany, geology, and particularly agricultural chemistry, but should also have what might be termed an artistic imagination.

Dr. Alister Mackenzie
Golf Architecture
1920

"Spiteful. Hateful," cried Raymond Floyd. "Awful. Artificial," bellowed Tom Watson. "Silly," added Bernhard Langer.

In spite of my high hopes, these quarrelsome outbursts greeted me after the first round of the 1987 Bob Hope Desert Classic played on our new Stadium Course at PGA West in La Quinta, California. Criticism from the touring professionals is something I've learned to live with over the years, but their bombastic comments really hurt this time.

My relationship with the Tour professionals in the desert actually began on a positive note when I built the Mountain Course at La Quinta in 1981. My colleague Lee Schmidt was right when he said it was a pleasure to build a course in the mountains, since even if the layout wasn't perfect, the majestic scenery would cover any mistakes.

The opportunity to design La Quinta and PGA West's Stadium Course was a direct offshoot of my continued relationship with Ernie Vossler and Joe Walser. Oak Tree was a successful venture

165

for them, and the two club professionals decided they were going to continue to develop championship golf courses.

Both men had scouted prospective properties along the California coast. Besides Carmel Valley up on the Monterey Peninsula, where I would build a course in 1980, Ernie and Joe focused on the Palm Springs area for future development.

To their amazement, they found that there were many fine resort courses such as Bermuda Dunes, Indian Wells, and Thunderbird in and around Palm Springs, but nothing that compared with a course like Oak Tree. They scoured the Palm Springs area for potential development sites and finally focused on the 1,200 acres adjacent to the old La Quinta Hotel.

The city of La Quinta was formerly part of Lake Cahuilla, which covered most of the Coachella Valley. The ancient desert Cahuilla Indians who inhabited the valley felt the cove was hallowed ground and called it "Land of the Eternal Sun."

The La Quinta Hotel and Resort was founded in 1926 by Walter Morgan, the youngest son of a wealthy San Francisco businessman. He styled a charming country hotel surrounded by secluded cottages.

La Quinta's private atmosphere appealed to Hollywood's "Golden Era" film community. Famous luminaries such as movie director Frank Capra and film stars Errol Flynn, Clark Gable, Bette Davis, and Greta Garbo stayed there.

Through a friend, Ellsworth Vines, the only athlete to win both a Wimbledon title and a PGA Tour event, Ernie Vossler and Joe Walser were introduced to the owner of the hotel, Leonard Eddleson. A Chicago banker, Leonard had built the La Quinta Country Club next to the hotel, but the equity members disliked guests crowding their course.

While Eddleson professed interest in permitting a golf course/ real estate development to be built on his adjacent property, he told Ernie and Joe that cost estimates were prohibitive, since the land was located in the middle of a floodplain. Undeterred, the two prospective developers persuaded Eddleson to retain them as consultants to research different means of solving the problem.

Soon after they were hired by Eddleson, Ernie moved to La Quinta and attempted to find a cost-effective way to deal with the floodplain restrictions. Although it rained rarely in Palm Springs, an occasional downpour deluged the area, causing water to cascade down the Santa Rosa Mountains, flooding the hotel and the city.

Months went by until Ernie convinced the local authorities that he could build the entire golf course as a flood retention area. A channel was created at the base of the mountains directing the flood waters to the golf course area, thus protecting the hotel and the city of La Quinta.

Building the Mountain Course at La Quinta was a back-breaking experience, since the course snaked in and around the rocky terrain.

On the 208-yard par-three sixteenth hole, the proposed tee was set back on a plateau. I kept eyeing an alternate site way up the side of the mountain, and tried to figure out how to build a tee up there.

All at once, here came Ernie flashing through the dust in a golf cart. "I understand you want to put a tee way up there," he said.

"You'll have a hole that everyone will talk about," I countered. "Magazine covers will love it!"

Ernie took another look up the mountain. "What about the cost?"

"You'll never know it," I offered. "Maybe twenty-five thousand dollars, tops!"

Ernie looked away at the desert and smiled. "It'll cost at least a hundred and fifty," Ernie sighed, "maybe more."

Later, Ernie reluctantly gave in and we built the tee. It did end up on the covers of various golf magazines, and according to Ernie, the cost was just a little more than a hundred thousand!

Working in one-hundred-degree-plus heat left me drained at the end of the day and prompted a return to the hotel to relax in the Jacuzzi.

Quite to my surprise, Judy Vossler, Ernie's lovely daughter, told me there would be a brand new set of clothes (white golf shirt, underwear, black socks, khaki shorts) waiting for me beside the Jacuzzi every evening. I thanked her warmly, not quite sure why she was going to all that trouble.

I later learned that Judy was concerned because of my habit of jumping in the Jacuzzi still wearing my dusty work clothes. Not only did the warm water relax me, but I could wash my clothes at the same time—and then wear them the next day.

When Judy told her father that Pete Dye was ruining the Jacuzzi by clogging up the drain with sand and dust, Ernie just laughed and suggested giving me a new set of clothes every day!

The Mountain Course was warmly received when it opened for play in 1982. It was quickly included on everyone's top one hundred list and has played host to the PGA Club Professional Championship, the World Cup, and the Senior Skins Game.

I'm pleased that the course opened to the public in the summer of 1994 so that amateurs from all over the world can enjoy it. Because the lower holes are in the floodplain, Lee Schmidt calls it "the golf course built in a bathtub," but the Mountain Course's majestic rocky sideshow makes for great desert golf.

Four years after the Mountain Course was completed, Ernie and Joe's orders were to build "the hardest damn golf course in the world" to bring recognition to their next real estate development in the desert.

Alice and I have built golf courses in cornfields, grazing meadows, swamps, and coal country, but the worst piece of land we ever started with was the featureless, barren acreage that became the Stadium Course at PGA West.

In order to build the tough golf course Ernie and Joe desired, I went back to the drawing board and called upon every design feature I'd ever seen or heard about. Together with Lee Schmidt, Ernie, Joe, and Commissioner Deane Beman, whose PGA Tour would play an active role in promotion of the course, I searched everywhere in an attempt to offer the Tour a showcase for their talent and amateurs an opportunity to emulate great shots seen on television.

Length alone would not be the ultimate test for the new course, but I believed strategic hazards, deep bunkers, difficult angles across fairways, slightly offset greens, parallel lakes, and desert plants when combined with cross-current winds could provide the type of course Joe and Ernie expected. Because of the intended difficulty, extra care was taken to make the course manageable for every caliber of player, man or woman.

•   •   •

Forward tees for women had been instituted in 1964 at Crooked Stick and built on all Dye courses since then. History will show that Alice was a true pioneer in designing tees for women, seniors, and juniors. More than anyone before her, she has improved conditions for women on courses all over the world, and her contribution to that element of the game is unparalleled.

Alice believes that many things have occurred to make golf more difficult for women. The fast, firm fairways have been watered into lush, spongy strips, greatly diminishing any roll. Mowers now cut fairways very short, making for tight lies. Sparse old fescue roughs are now irrigated into dense thickets. Approaches to the greens have been closed in with rough grass.

Architects and greens chairmen have elongated old bunkers to wrap around the front of greens. Bunkers have been deepened, so more strength is needed for the recovery shot. Increased green speeds have made putting and chipping more difficult for women. Contrary to common belief, this is the weakest part of their game.

Alice also points out that when the great architects of old designed their courses, length was calculated with a long roll expected. Today's lush fairways have added so much more playing yardage that neither men nor women golfers can reach many greens in regulation.

To restore the architect's intent, Alice proposed that tees for women be moved forward. How far depends on the length of the hole and finding a suitable location to provide a playable angle.

On dogleg holes, Alice suggests that the forward tee should be placed on the side that diminishes the dogleg so that a long hitter does not drive through the fairway. Since women have an even greater spread of strength than men, they need two tees.

Based on Alice's research, the "back" tee for women should measure from 5,400 to 5,900 yards and the forward one 4,600 to 5,200 yards, depending on conditions. Separate back tees do not need to be constructed, since this set can be positioned by using additional markers on a combination of the forward tees and the men's member tees.

Any tournament may be played from different tees. The golfer using the higher-rated tee receives extra strokes. For example, if player A uses the tees rated 68 and player B uses the tees rated 72, four additional handicap strokes would be given to player B.

Playing a shorter, more manageable course will not make the golfer's handicap index go down, as it will be computed from a lower rating and slope.

Based on Alice's input, I've built forward tees at Harbour Town, Teeth of the Dog, La Quinta, Long Cove, and The Honors, among others. Nowhere were we more careful with our placement of women's tees than in the design of the Stadium Course at PGA West.

Since we knew the course would play extremely difficult, we strategically positioned the women's tees so that the tee shot would be hit from favorable angles. Using the same philosophy we employ with the men's member tees, we believed it was critical that the women be able to hit the tee shot to a good position for their next shot. At the Stadium Course, there are two sets of women's tees, the gold at 5,675 yards and the red at 5,087. Women still face the same demanding challenge the men do, but they do so on a manageable golf course.

Besides different tees and hole angles for the women golfers, Alice and I provided three sets of tees for the men, permitting PGA West to play anywhere from 6,200 yards up to almost 7,300 yards for the professionals. Overall yardage lengths are always deceiving, however, for the length of individual holes is what really matters.

At PGA West, male golfers may play the par-five sixteenth, named San Andreas Fault, from the white tee at 479, the blue at 521, or the black at 571 yards. Whichever tee is chosen, each player will find that I have calculated the distances in view of my perception of where their drive will be, what range of second shot will follow, and from what point I believe the player will attempt the critical third shot.

The par-fours are set up the same way, so that if the men don't want to play the par-four "Turning Home" fifteenth hole from the 470-yard black tee or even the 439-yard blue tee, they can compete with par from just over 400 yards. If they hit a good tee shot from the appropriate tee, they will then be in the same fairway position as the touring professional and can experience the rigors of that hole just as the professionals do.

While length is not the main problem with either the par-fours or par-fives at PGA West, it added difficulty on the par-threes. "Alcatraz," the shortest par-three, measures only 166 from the back, but two of the par-threes stretch out to more than 220 yards. Those par-threes, however, are just as challenging from the blue and white tees, and may in fact be better holes from there.

Coming down the stretch at any golf course should always be a challenge, and at PGA West I intended something very provocative. Sixteen, seventeen, and eighteen may be the most difficult finishing holes I've ever built, and it's hang-on-to-your-hat time when you turn back toward the clubhouse.

At the par-five sixteenth, I may have created the deepest greenside bunker this side of Mars. Like many of my controversial design features, this one evolved somewhat by accident.

My purpose was to create a bunker shot that no one would forget. I intended that the player be required to attempt an almost impossible shot with the potential for a once-in-a-lifetime thrill if they could pull it off.

When I decided to position the bunker to the left front of the sixteenth green, I told the bulldozer operator to scrape out a medium-size bunker.

When he asked me one day how deep the bunker was to be, I told him to keep digging until he hit water. I don't know if he thought I was kidding or not, but his bulldozer finally found water at twenty-two feet, and we leveled off the depth at twenty!

At first Ernie Vossler was dubious of the bunker at sixteen. No sand had been put in, so Ernie took a bucket of sand or so and scattered it at the deepest part. From his pocket he produced a shiny new golf ball and placed it on the sand. Tossing me a sand wedge, Ernie then challenged me: "If you can get it on the green from there, then the damn bunker's all right with me."

Without apprehension, I used my flip-wrist sand wedge swing and safely elevated the ball up to the green site. While the Tour professionals don't believe that bunker is a laughing matter, just think of all the fun that golfers would have missed if I'd left the ball in the sand.

No one can describe the jubilation of hitting a shot over the twenty-foot steep bank of that deep sand bunker. Television audiences around the world did experience the trials and tribulations of former Speaker of the House of Representatives Thomas "Tip" O'Neill, whose ball came to rest there. Tip became an instant folk hero that day when, after flailing away several times, he finally threw the ball out.

After the Stadium Course opened, there were those who thought the depth of the bunker was ridiculous and unfair. Ron Whitten and other writers of note believed I had gone off the deep end, and were highly critical of the design. They believed that 99 percent of golfers had no chance of escaping the depths.

Like Seth Raynor's twenty-foot-deep bunker built at Fisher's Island, New York, in 1917, the crater at sixteen has caused much controversy. It's truly a love-it-or-hate-it design feature, but players who have peered up from the bottom of that sand pit never forget the moment of anticipation just before they try to clear the steep slope of the bunker.

The seventeenth hole on my golf courses has always been special to me. Even though eighteen is the finishing hole, I have focused more on the seventeenth, because I always feel that it sets up the closing drama for eighteen.

Obviously, I wasn't the first to believe in the principle. Many of the great holes in the world appear at seventeen. Three come to mind immediately: the 224-yard par-three at Merion, where Ben Hogan made two in the playoff in the 1950 United States Open title; the rigorous par-four Road hole at the Old Course at St. Andrews; and the illustrious par-three seventeenth at Pebble Beach, where Tom Watson's chip-in in the 1982 United States Open will live for posterity.

Most all of the courses I've built have a treacherous seventeenth hole, and the par-threes at the Stadium Course at TPC and the Ocean Course at Kiawah exemplify my attempt to challenge the player toward the end of a round. Although I often say there's been nothing new in golf since Queen Anne, I never like to attempt to duplicate a design I've already built. Due to the incredible popularity of the seventeenth island green hole at the Stadium Course at TPC, however, Ernie Vossler, Joe Walser, and Deane Beman asked me to build a similar hole for PGA West.

I was not crazy about the idea, since I felt that TPC's seven-

teenth should retain its precedent and be the only one in existence. Of course, other architects have copied the concept, but I
was afraid that if I built another island green, both holes would
end up losing their uniqueness.

My colleagues believed that a second such hole should be built
on the West Coast, and that if I was going to build the "hardest
golf course in the world," it had to have an island green. With
some trepidation, I agreed to do so, and we carved out a lake
surrounding the green site.

To provide contrast with the hole at TPC, rock was used instead of railroad ties to bulkhead the green. In order to match
the color with the mountains, the rocks were sprayed with an
oxidizing material that gave them a pinkish tint.

I also lengthened the distance for the hole, dubbed "Alcatraz,"
and increased the green size by a half. Like its partner, though,
the seventeenth in the West matches the seventeenth in the East
when it comes to pure unadulterated excitement.

Designing a finishing hole at PGA West to follow San Andreas
Fault and Alcatraz wasn't easy. Utilizing the lake I'd built along the
tenth hole, I designed a rugged 440-yard par-four, named "Coli-
seum." It requires the player to drive the ball over the right side of
the lake and then hit a long iron back to the left toward a heavily
bunkered green that is nestled kiss-close to that same lake.

In order to compete with the lush, green Palm Springs-area
courses that had palm trees, flowers, fountains, and waterfalls, we
wanted to go in the opposite direction and plant only desert
bushes and trees.

The Sunrise Company developing the house lots around the
course was very skeptical that winter visitors would accept the
native look, but after much persuasion they finally agreed.

We planted nearly 20,000 desert trees at the Stadium Course.
Those, combined with fairways bordered with gorse-like bushes,
produced a Scottish look that was a whole new concept for the
Palm Springs area.

Doing this was very risky, but the course was so distinctive,
home sales soared.

•   •   •

With its confrontational design, angled water hazards, monster bunkers, and desert aura, I felt I had created not only the hardest golf course in the world but also a showcase for the talent of the PGA Tour. I couldn't wait for the professionals to show their stuff against PGA West in the first round of the Bob Hope Chrysler Classic, and I anticipated very positive comments.

To my utter amazement and undeniable disappointment, I couldn't have been more wrong. Instead of glowing reports for the course, I was lambasted with personal, cutting remarks to the effect that I had lost my mule-headed mind.

While the use of words like *spiteful, hateful, awful,* and *silly* certainly bothered me, comments that I had built an artificial course featuring gimmicks and foolish trickery were really upsetting. I also knew that Ernie Vossler, Joe Walser, Lee Schmidt, and Deane Beman were quite disappointed at the reaction as well. Together we'd put our hearts and souls into the Stadium Course, and each one of us felt we'd been attacked unfairly.

Amazingly enough, the professionals even drew up a petition, which they presented to Commissioner Beman, requesting that the Stadium Course be banned forever from the Bob Hope Tournament or any other PGA Tour event.

Alice wasn't with me when the mutiny occurred, but she helped me try to understand the reasons behind the professionals' violent reaction. Over the telephone, she carefully asked me what had taken place, and together we began to try to understand what had thrown the professionals into such a frenzy.

To begin with, Tour professionals support themselves and their families solely on the paycheck they earn from each tournament. Unless they make the cut, there is no paycheck, and they need a good finish to cover caddie, travel, and other expenses.

Touring professionals make their living shooting low scores and cannot afford risky shots ardent golfers love to try. Low numbers mean cash and high ones mean potential loss of that lifeline Tour card, so most touring professionals love to play straightforward golf courses where low scores are relatively predictable. Bogeys and double-bogeys are death threats to the touring professional, and they don't want to compete on golf courses where they can't scrape it around on a bad day and still shoot a decent score.

With that mind-set, the touring professionals come to Palm

Springs every year to assault the Bob Hope courses. Unfortunately, they fall in love with the less-demanding ones played over the five days of the tournament, and when they encountered a much stiffer challenge, like the Stadium Course, they rebelled.

The professionals forget that the whole idea of a Pete Dye golf course is to require good players to hit a wide variety of shots. Touring professionals have a much better overall game than they think they do, and I know they can handle this challenge.

Shots that Hogan hit fifty years ago weren't any more demanding than those faced today, but unfortunately changes in maintenance standards and technological advances in golf balls and clubs give the professional too much control over a course. The Stadium Course was built to offset that advantage and permit those professionals to perform their skills at the highest levels.

Although most of the professionals hadn't seen much of the Stadium Course, they knew that it wasn't like the courses they were used to in the desert. Resentful of its being included at all, they approached the first round at PGA West with a spiteful attitude that worsened as their initial rounds continued.

Mother Nature decided to compound the problem on opening day by providing cold temperatures that one could expect in North Dakota but not Palm Springs. Donning bulky cold-weather gear, the professionals then proceeded to play a five-and-a-half-hour round with amateur partners bent on hitting every shot and counting every stroke.

Looking back, I should have expected such a reaction, especially since the weather was so awful. The petition to ban the course was absurd, but the Stadium Course was so different from anything the professionals had played.

I've always felt that a good player who's playing well wants to play a difficult golf course because he knows the winner won't be someone who can just out-putt him.

In the modern era, Hale Irwin, Lanny Wadkins, Raymond Floyd, Tom Kite, Greg Norman, Fred Couples, Jack Nicklaus and Lee Trevino, all boosters of my courses over the years, thrive on tough courses because they're exceptional shot-makers.

Perhaps Chi Chi Rodriguez put it best when he told Shawn Glick, a reporter for the *Los Angeles Times,* "Most of the courses today, the guys shoot twenty under par and think they've accomplished something. They can't do it at PGA West because you can't hit it crooked and score.

"Golf was meant to be a game of skill, not just strength. To get around here, you have to have the skills," Chi Chi added.

When news of the PGA Tour players' refusal to play the course hit the media, the zealous golfers of the world came to play. They wanted to see what they could do on a course the professionals found too difficult.

From their well-positioned tees and shorter yardages, women found that they could score even better than on their own home courses. In fact, so many women joined PGA West and played it so well that they were pushing the men players.

Complaints came to Ernie, who came to me and asked that I do something about these tees that made the course so manageable and enjoyable for women. I balked and told him, "I will do anything for you except take out Alice's tees."

Fortunately, the seething commentaries regarding the Stadium Course dimmed, and PGA West became the most popular home for NBC-TV's Skins Game in the ten-year history of the competition. The PGA Club Professionals also return year after year to hold their national tournament, and the Stadium Course has become a "must-play" for golfers all over the world.

Golfers stand in line at PGA West just as they do every morning at St. Andrews, just hoping there is a cancellation so they can play. Many of them can't post a score, let alone ever think of shooting par, but the potential to hit that one great shot just like the professionals do is what keeps them coming back.

Ernie Vossler and Joe Walser's legacy in the 1980s may never be duplicated. I know of no developers in the world who can match their success for building as many superior golf courses as they have, and I have never worked with finer gentlemen than Joe and Ernie.

Oak Tree, La Quinta, the Stadium Course at PGA West, and the Ocean Course at Kiawah Island are just some of their achievements, and history will record the enormous contribution they have made to golf.

Despite our varied lifestyles, Ernie, Joe, and I formed a friendship that lasts to this day. I know sometimes they both must have thought I was a bit crazy, as evidenced by the time I took the impeccably dressed Ernie to a discount department store.

I ran in and purchased a nifty royal-blue suitcase sale-priced at $19.95 and one of those red marking pens. Back at the car, I scribbled all over the outside of my new suitcase.

Fascinated by now, Ernie asked me what I was doing. "Ernie," I told him, "I travel a great deal and sometimes I don't get to pick up the luggage right away. People steal bags all the time, but they'll never take one that looks like this!"

Ernie just shook his head and started the car.

The Stadium Course at PGA West
La Quinta, California
Par 72

	Men	Women
Yardage:	7261, 6753, 6164	5675, 5087
Rating/ Slope:	77.3/151, 74.4/139, 71.2/130	72.3/126, 69.0/119

The Mountain Course at La Quinta
La Quinta, California
Par 72

	Men	Women
Yardage:	6803, 6307, 5775	5775, 5005
Rating/ Slope:	74.3/146, 71.4/136, 66.7/117	77.3/137, 68.4/120

Old Marsh

The greedy golfer will go too near and be sucked into his own destruction.

John Low
Concerning Golf
1902

While there are critics who believe my courses are too difficult, the ardent golfer would play Mt. Everest if somebody put a flagstick on top.

A significant part of the enjoyment of the game, however, comes from the player's awareness of the beauty of the golf course and the abundant wildlife that wanders freely there. My opportunity to build not only a demanding course but one that would be quite aesthetic came in 1986 when I was hired to design Old Marsh.

The proposed site for the course was a 440-acre sliver of property enclosed in 40,000 acres owned by the MacArthur Foundation. First glance at the proposed site made me wonder whether a roaring lion might appear from deep in the high grass, since the marshland's rich vegetation and abundant species of wildlife reminded me of Africa.

If it hadn't been for an old dirt road a rancher had constructed, walking the property would have been impossible.

Closer inspection of the land was critical, even though a murky muck stuck to my faded khakis for months.

Despite the isolation and anticipated construction problems, developer Bob Whitley knew he had discovered something very special. Fitting eighteen holes into this environmentally protected area would be a real challenge, but the result could be a spectacular golf course set in the middle of a wildlife sanctuary.

When the go-ahead was given, I began the two-year process required to obtain the city, county, state, and federal permits necessary for work on the course. Unfortunately, these days it takes more time to secure *permission* to build a golf course than it does to actually build it.

While I'm a firm believer in protecting the environment, the incredible bureaucracy that has festered within local, state, and national agencies severely penalizes even the well-intentioned, experienced designer. Severe limitations hamper our efforts, and it has reached the point where the cost expended by developers and other financiers on attorneys and engineering firms may easily be as much as 25 percent of the total cost to build the entire golf course.

One of the problems these days is that nobody knows whether a piece of ground will be a protected "wetland" until someone requests permission to use the specified areas. To add to the problem, every state has different criteria and regulations defining wetlands.

Even though abundant acreage may appear available, golf course architects are interested in "usable land." The proposed acreage may total 350 when plans are first made to build a course, but the loss of property designated as wetlands may take a large portion of that land.

Defining *wetlands* is difficult, but the term generally includes marshes, swamps, or other areas that are either used to assist with flood control and irrigation or are natural feeding grounds for certain species of wildlife. Florida claims to have lost at least twelve million acres of wetlands in the past twenty-five years, and so authorities are very touchy when they hear the "w" word.

Aerial photos taken of a proposed property delineate the marshes' location, and everything is put on computer. A spreadsheet is then produced, which indicates the amount of protected wetlands as well as dry areas that are included within the acreage.

Under the regulators' "mitigation rules," if one acre of marsh-land is to be utilized, the developer must create three to replace it. At Old Marsh, approximately ten acres of wetlands would be converted, so we had to come up with nearly thirty acres of manmade marshes within the boundaries of the property.

In addition, the new marshlands must be contoured in terms of depth so that the same species of wildlife that inhabited the old will inhabit the new. Deep, medium, and shallow shelves must be constructed to produce a variety of aquatic grasses.

Many agencies have several hundred employees working for them. The bureaucratic process is frustrating because each department has its own agenda, and no one seems to have the big picture in mind.

While all of the various aspects of keeping a course environmentally sound are important, I believe recycling is the least publicized. At Old Marsh, we were never required to meet any type of standard, but we went beyond the call of duty by inventing a new type of recycling system.

Although I take full credit for the system whenever possible, it actually came about somewhat by accident. Not wanting golfers traipsing out into the marsh trampling the grasses looking for their golf balls, I designed a six-foot-wide moat at the edge of the border of the marsh. To keep golf balls from disappearing into the moat, the near edge was raised and sloped back into the fairway so a ball would have to roll uphill to drop into the water.

Having the borders of the hole tilting toward the middle of the fairway produced a bathtub effect: all the water from rain and the sprinkler system drained toward catch basins buried in the middle of the fairways. These basins connected to a ten-by-ten cement-enclosed "basement," which housed a sump pump. When the water level triggered the float, it pumped the excess water through a six-inch line to an irrigation lake.

That water is used to irrigate the course, and the cycle keeps repeating itself. Chemicals used to treat the fairways and roughs never enter the natural marshes because all their runoff falls into these drains that lead back to the irrigation lake.

Many times an architect can actually improve the condition of land when it is modified to build a golf course. Nowhere is this more true than with the comparison between the old marshes that were drained and the new ones we created to replace them at Old Marsh.

The main objective should be to improve the aesthetics of the course by establishing vibrant, attractive marshes that enhance the beauty of the land. With a little care, the architect can not only produce clean, clear marshes, but actually attract new species of wildlife that never existed in the area before. At Old Marsh, the wildlife actually preferred the new marshes to the old ones.

The three-foot-high, stately sandhill crane is most predominant there. Ibis, egrets, blue herons, great white herons, endangered wood storks, Florida deer, and even American bald eagles also inhabit the course.

The sight of the sandhill crane leaves golfers entranced. The birds' ramrod-straight elegance and unusual pattern of high-stepping across the fairways is quite compelling, and the fearless cranes come so close that players can reach out and touch them.

Two of the more curious sandhill cranes actually became quite friendly with club professional Buddy Antonpoulous and his staff at the pro shop. Dubbed "Pete" and "Alice" by Buddy's kids, the two demanded attention by constantly pecking away at the pro shop door. When Pete and Alice decided to bear a "cranelet," it was named P.B. after our younger son.

In the initial stages of construction, I sometimes sit for hours on a certain fairway and just gaze up and down a particular hole.

What I'm doing is visualizing every potential shot a golfer may hit. I take into account potential wind conditions, varying yardages, the angle of the shot, the obstacles to be overcome, and the intended route I foresee to the green.

Since I am only five foot eight, I make certain that a golfer my height can see greenside bunkers and portions of the green from various locations in the fairway and rough. Lee Schmidt, who is nearly six inches taller than I am, used to tell me that everything was visible from a certain point, but I always check it out myself because even half a foot can make a great deal of difference.

Many times I've changed the setup for a hole after either Alice or I discover that there is a design flaw that makes the hole unfair. Demanding is one thing, but prohibiting the golfer from having a fair chance is quite another.

The specific approach taken to build a golf course varies each time, but there is a general procedure we normally follow. Once the routings were approved and the proper permits issued, we embarked on a twelve-month construction process that ended in 1987 when Old Marsh opened for play.

The positions of the usable marshes and the locations of homesites dictated where I could position the holes.

Prior to breaking ground, I assembled my team of workers. Scott Poole was my construction superintendent, and he and I rounded up a crew of several aspiring Lake Central Community College graduates who wanted to learn more about building golf courses.

Since I don't have an in-house construction company, I rely on the expertise of local contractors for the specific jobs required. My construction crew and these workers are all placed on the payroll of the developer.

The first thing we do is to stake the holes and clear an eighty-foot-wide corridor down the middle of each proposed hole. We don't start from hole number one but first clear the holes nearest the construction trailer and move outward.

At Old Marsh, we then dug out the oblong eight-acre lake that separates holes nine and eighteen. Another lake was created behind the eleventh green, and the dirt from these craters was spread around on different holes that needed to be elevated.

To handle the grading, my construction superintendent rented scrapers, wide-tracks, and D-5, D-6, and D-7 bulldozers. Even if a young man has virtually no experience, I'll let him take a crack at contouring the fairways.

At Old Marsh, we had several men shaping the fairways; they were instructed to contour them very gently. I envisioned a low-mounds-and-greens look for Old Marsh that would enhance the elevation of the marsh grass.

In tandem with this procedure, our crew began to carve out the tees. Most are elevated only one to two feet, and we built three sets of tees for the men and two for the women.

Fairway bunkers are also roughed in at this time. Greenside ones are shaped when the greens are built.

Building greens is a process that involves constant modification. I may have a rough idea of what I expect to achieve, but many times I climb on a tractor and wheel around trying to find the right shape or contour.

My intention is to provide a putting surface with a half-inch fall every ten feet or so. The human eye can detect only a two-and-one-half-inch fall every ten feet, so I attempt to make a putt appear straight when it actually has some curvature.

We design the green size to be eighteen inches larger than its final form. Since collars will be added, I leave room for their placement after the green size is finalized.

Since the course at Old Marsh was so low profile and the greens a little more than two feet above the water table, we followed USGA green specifications precisely to provide proper drainage. A handy-dandy Smithco with a small blade like the ones used in sand bunkers is ridden around to provide the final contour. These surfaces are then watered for two to three days to watch for puddles.

Old Marsh is a bit more subtle and the putting surfaces are natural extensions of the fairways, much like the great courses of Scotland.

The approaches to the greens roll in and onto the putting surfaces, but the greens are relatively flat, with the mounds abutting. One contour on the green is counteracted by another to prevent the ball from exploding by the hole.

Once all of the contours were balanced out, we proceeded to plant the greens with Bermuda stolens. Fairways and roughs were also planted at this time, with special care taken not to allow different grasses to blow or wash together.

Buddy Antonpoulous was present throughout construction at Old Marsh, and he likes to say that he was influential in convincing me to move the championship tee on the fourth hole forward. Believing the carry over the marsh to be too long, Buddy and his assistant pros, all former Tour professionals, took bags of balls to the tee. They tried repeatedly to carry the water but 99 percent of their attempts splashed.

Bob Whitley called me with this news, suggesting that if three ex-Tour players couldn't find dry land, maybe the carry was too long. I told Bob that he now knew why they were all *ex*-Tour players!

Buddy did get back at me once the course opened. I had hit all but one of my supply of balls into the marshes by the fourteenth hole, and when I got to the next tee, Buddy says I told him, "One more lost ball and I'm in your pocket, pro." Unfortunately I hit a snap hook into the marsh and turned to Buddy for help.

"Oh, no, not this time, Pete!" he announced loudly as he made his way toward a portable phone. Unable to play, I just stood there without a ball and watched as he called the clubhouse and had his assistant pro announce over the loudspeaker, "Your attention please, Pete Dye has just run out of golf balls on the fifteenth tee!"

Similar to the fifth hole at Long Cove, I built a love/hate hole with a short approach shot to a green hidden behind a huge two-story mound. Most golfers who have traveled to Prestwick in Scotland find the design reminiscent of the 391-yard par-four "Alps" hole there. While I don't pretend to have re-created the exact atmosphere of that great hole, the fifth offers a similar mental challenge.

Before I believed in the design of "blind" holes, I mentioned my dislike for them to Tommy Armour. The silver-haired Scotsman bluntly told me I knew nothing about golf, adding, "Laddie, a blind hole is blind only once to a man with a memory."

Tommy Armour believed blind shots were effective since they created anxiety in the golfers by delaying their knowing the result of their shots. I know Ben Hogan hated them, but I think they can play an important part in the mix of holes on a particular course.

What a blind hole like the fifth does is break up the flow of the golf course. An entirely different shot is required, and anticipation of the unknown makes the shot harder than it really is.

Golfers of all levels love to walk up and look around the mound, check the placement of the pin, and then try to imagine the line-of-flight to the green. The whole experience is topped off when they finally hit the shot and then race to the side of the fairway to see where the ball is.

Blind Man's Bluff at Old Marsh measures only 320 yards from the back tee, but there is water to the right that borders the entire hole. If the tee shot is properly positioned, a small obelisk rock sitting on top of the mound signals the line to the green.

Learning how to play the hole is the key, since the approach shot is more feel than anything. Effective calculation of distance and then complete trust in the golf swing will bring the best result for a player. Allowing a blind shot or another optical illusion to intimidate the golfer is sometimes my intention, but clever players can keep their composure and take advantage of birdie opportunities on this type of hole.

Mental preparation for the game is vitally important. Players who are intimidated by knowing they will be playing a trouble-laden Pete Dye course never have a chance at success and are beaten before they start.

While I'm extremely proud of the manner in which the golf course blends in with the natural environment at Old Marsh, I believe there's a real tempo about the course that tests and measures the players much in the same way they are tested on the old Scottish courses.

Since the native yellow colored grasses grow fairly tall in the marshes, and the elevation level of the land is low, Old Marsh has a look even the ancient courses could envy.

A connection to those great courses exists through an important display of history that is located in the clubhouse. Bob Whitley forged a friendship with Laurie Auchterlonie, the transplanted St. Andrews club maker who served for twenty-five years as the honorary professional of the Royal and Ancient Golf Club of St. Andrews. The presence of Auchterlonie's family collection of golf clubs in a glass-enclosed case at Old Marsh, many of which date back to the 1700's, serves as a reminder of the great traditions of the game.

Just after Old Marsh opened, Greg Norman, one of the greatest players in the history of the game, became a member. His presence at the club led to our striking up a friendship that resulted in a designer collaboration for the Medalist Club course in Hobe Sound, Florida.

Greg has designed several golf courses in Australia, Asia, and in the United States, including the Experience at Koéle, Hawaii, and Royal Melbourne outside Chicago. He knows exactly what type of championship course he wants us to build.

At the Medalist Club, which will host the Shark Shootout in 1995, we have worked together to provide a distinctive look that is reminiscent of the old sandy hills at Pinehurst. Native grasses, including wire grass, a wispy species that never needs to be cut, will present the golfer with shot opportunities like those present on many Australian courses.

Old Marsh will always have an extra-special meaning for me. Just behind the fifth green there is a bronze bell that is used to signal the players behind that the group in front has completed play.

On the post that mounts the bell is a plaque with an inscription paying tribute to the man who taught me all I really needed to know about the game of golf. It reads, "Ring the bell for my dad, Paul F. Dye, who loved his family and everything about the game of golf."

	Old Marsh Palm Beach Gardens, Florida Par 72	
	Men	Women
Yardage:	6914, 6387, 5884	5884, 4974
Rating/ Slope:	73.6/143, 71.3/137, 67.8/120, 63.8/110	73.1/128, 68.1/116

Blackwolf Run

The greatest compliment that can be paid to the architect is for players to think his artificial work is natural.

Dr. Alister Mackenzie
Golf Architecture
1920

As I approached the heavily bunkered second green at Blackwolf Run's River Course one mild summer day, I noticed a smartly dressed golfer playing the adjoining first hole, head into the shoetop-deep rough, with a scowl on his face.

Unable to find his golf ball, he turned angrily toward me and sternly growled, "Well, Mr. Dye, how are *you* doing today?" Recognizing the challenging tone, I cautiously replied, "Depends on how *you* are playing!"

Despite the fact that this gentleman was probably headed for seven or eight on "Burial Mounds," the opening par-five, he smiled back at me. With that kind of start, he'd be cussing Pete Dye all day long, but a man who can grin in the face of a triple bogey will come back for more.

The thirty-six holes at Blackwolf Run outside Kohler, Wisconsin, are the result of the efforts of Herb Kohler, a man's man if there ever was one.

Herb is an erratic player with a game full of surprises. He tells anyone who'll listen that whether he's playing good or bad, he'll end up with 97. A big man with a heavy beard, Herb will count every stroke, and his incredible enthusiasm for the game of golf is amazing.

Kohler, Wisconsin, is located west of Sheboygan, one hour northeast of Milwaukee. My reluctance to build a golf course in the remote wilds of southern Wisconsin brought back memories of Edmond, Oklahoma, but Kohler is a far different environment.

Entering the town, one immediately notices the well-planned Kohler community, designed by the renowned Olmsted firm. The Kohler name is everywhere, and Herb's grandfather John Michael, who founded the Kohler Company in 1873, is responsible.

The centerpiece in Kohler is the American Club, the only five-diamond hotel in the Midwest. The spacious hotel is located directly across the street from the Kohler Foundry. Originally a rooming house for the Kohler Company immigrant workers, the expansive, long, beautiful three-story Tudor-style building was transformed into a hotel in 1918.

Alice and I tell Herb we think of him often because the Kohler toilet at our Florida home has a high-pitched humming sound. Herb has promised to fix it, but we're not sure if he's going to do it for free!

Herb's idea to build a golf course along the Sheboygan River Valley on the outskirts of Kohler was met with local skepticism, but he realized that a championship golf course was essential to accommodate guests at his resort hotel. Herb chose the name Blackwolf Run in honor of the prominent chief of the Winnebago Indian tribe who defeated the Chippewa and Menominee Indians in the early 1800s.

Herb first contacted me in 1984. Alice wanted to know why I would even consider building a course in snow country, but Herb's enthusiasm and love for the game won me over.

After some discussion regarding my ability to blend the course into the natural terrain, we struck a handshake deal. I immediately began preparing the initial routing for eighteen holes, never considering the possibility that we would build a second course two years later.

My inspiration for the design at Kohler came from my enthusiasm for the land. In the old days, architects chose the land they desired instead of being told they had to build a course on a piece of property that had been selected by the owner.

The acreage outside Kohler had formerly been used as a hunting area and was distinguished by wooded, rolling hills, wetlands, and little streams and creeks that zigzagged around and through the property. There was a certain feel to the area that told me a great golf course could be built there.

At Blackwolf Run, I intended to design a course that would provide memorable shot opportunities. This was in line with my goal of challenging golfers with demanding shots.

Before my visit to the British Isles, it was a downright mystery to me why a twenty-five-handicap golfer would pay thousands of dollars to fly to Scotland and not break a hundred. The answer to that question came in 1963 when Alice and I visited the ancient country. We saw firsthand golfers' tremendous excitement when they achieve a brief moment of glory on one of the legendary Scottish holes. Regardless of their total score, players never forget one incredible shot played on a challenging hole.

Our construction crew began work on Blackwolf Run in June 1985. Construction of that first eighteen took place over two summers, and by August 1986, the course was nearly completed. Opening day was scheduled for June 1, 1987.

Unfortunately, Mother Nature dealt the course a knockout punch. In September 1986 an unrelenting, torrential rain hit the Kohler area. It was as if a firehose had been turned loose on the golf course: eight inches of rain fell in four hours, washing out greens, irrigation pipe, and drain tiles.

After two years of hard work our golf course was virtually destroyed. The crew was devastated, and I remember seeing construction superintendent Scott Poole in tears.

All of us were disheartened, and it was a sorry bunch who greeted Herb when he pulled up to the construction trailer. True to his character, Herb took one look at us and simply said, "When do you fellows plan to start back to work?" Herb's positive attitude was a badly needed boost, and the crew was back on the job the next day.

Working with Herb was fascinating, but we almost ended our

relationship before it went very far. Herb's love for trees is well known, but his reaction to a decision I made at the par-three seventeenth hole almost brought us to blows.

The center of the dispute was a group of cottonwood trees along the bank of the Sheboygan River between where I intended to place the tee and the green. For months Herb and I battled back and forth, since Herb wanted to place the tee back in a clearing that would have saved the trees but would have required a 170-yard walk from the sixteenth green to the seventeenth tee.

I actually built all of the other holes on the course before asking Herb to make up his mind about the tee location. Trees'-best-friend finally told me he would meet me on seventeen at high noon and a decision would be made so we could complete the golf course.

Noon came and went, and so did another proposed meeting Herb set up for five o'clock. He finally dragged himself out of one of those long corporate meetings by 7:30 p.m. and drove his Jaguar madly toward the seventeenth hole.

"When I came over the hill," Herb remembers, "I saw a silver bellow of smoke tarnishing the evening sunset. The closer I got the more smoke I saw, but there was no one around."

There was no one around because my construction crew and I had quickly left the premises. Except for a security guard, Herb was all by himself.

"When I got a bit closer I saw the blazing fire, but there was no danger because while I saw that a number of logs and brush were burning brightly, huge piles of earth surrounded the inferno," Herb recalls. "I asked the security guard where Pete Dye was, and if he knew he didn't tell me."

A clerk at the American Club informed Herb that I was gone, bag and baggage. I knew he'd be steaming since I cut down those trees and burned them, but it was three hours before he could blast me on the telephone.

I tried to explain what I'd done, and how I'd carved out a tee and green and so forth, but he wouldn't listen. He demanded that I return to Kohler for an "eye-to-eye" as he called it, and I did—two days later. Herb had a chance to vent his anger at me, and the incident ended up bringing us closer together.

Alice also had her moment with Herb. After playing her first round on the course, Alice's exact line was, "Herb, you have a great seventeen-hole golf course."

"Aghast" is the word Herb uses to describe his feelings. When he recovered enough to ask Alice what she meant, he discovered that her comment again involved his passion for trees.

The original tenth hole, a straight 385-yard par-four, had a grove of apple trees where the fairway should have been, and Alice did not consider it a golf hole. She pointed out to Herb that the trees had to be removed, but despite her plea and mine, Herb stubbornly refused.

The destructive rains of 1986 resulted in almost a year's delay in opening the course, but when it did open it was an instant success. To understand the reason why Blackwolf Run was a big hit, it's necessary to learn about the nature of Wisconsin golfers. The word *ardent* doesn't adequately describe their enthusiasm for the game, and like their golfing brethren in Scotland, they will play under any weather conditions.

That enthusiasm caused people to form lines outside the pro shop nearly every day the first summer the course was open, which triggered a call from Herb telling me: "We need another eighteen holes." I agreed to come back to Kohler, but the location of the land available restricted my ability to add another eighteen in the conventional manner.

Acreage to be used for the second eighteen did not exist in one continuous section but was located on either side of the original course. After walking the proposed site, I knew the only way to build a second eighteen was to integrate the old holes with the new, creating the River Course and Meadow Valleys Course.

Since the original Blackwolf Run golf course had been so well received, even to the point of being listed by *Golf Digest* as one of the United States' best new public courses, I knew I would be taking a risk in splitting its holes to build a new course. I had no choice, however, so I attempted to visualize the break-points where I could join holes in hopes of completing two championship courses worthy of the first one.

For the River Course, I built nine new holes and blended them in with nine from the original course. After finishing the old fourth hole, players take a gorgeous walk through beautiful, dense woods to a panoramic fifth hole that introduces rolling terrain. Golfers are ushered onto a new landscape, with a striking change in elevation. There they play nine new holes before returning through the woods to finish on five of the original ones.

For the Meadow Valleys Course, we bypassed Herb's former apple tree hole and incorporated ten new holes into the eight remaining original ones.

When I designed Blackwolf Run, I incorporated not only many of the physical aspects of the great rolling courses in the United States and Scotland but also several mental ones as well. I wanted golfers to leave the course proud as hell of that one great shot or the play of one hard hole, regardless of their total score.

Since I try to design golf courses with every level of player in mind by building different tees and angles of difficulty, I intentionally set up the course to create several opportunities for golf shots that would be memorable. Even the most stringent right-wing conservative may be a gambling maniac when it comes to golf, and I want to make sure risky shots are presented as often as possible.

Great opportunities for courageous golfers to strut their stuff are abundant at Blackwolf Run. Golfers can attempt to play holes that were designed to bring unparalleled excitement into the game.

Reminiscent of the tenth hole at the Belfry in Ireland, where the Americans retained the Ryder Cup in 1993, the 316-yard par-four "Cathedral Spires" tenth hole at the River Course invites the player to take the high road, the middle road, or the one filled with potential disaster.

Three choices await the player at the tee. Driving out to the left side of the narrow fairway is the least risky, but the second shot is a dangerous one to a narrow green, with the Sheboygan River lurking behind it ready to capture any overzealous attempt at birdie.

Hitting the tee shot toward the middle of the fairway seems attractive, but towering cottonwood trees and a small, deep pot bunker are strategically positioned to capture any weak shot from the player.

Most risky, of course, is the direct line drive by the coura-geous, veins-of-ice low-handicapper who decides to rifle a zinger off the tee straight at the green. The peaceful Sheboygan River full of trout and hundreds of high-compression balls awaits those whose efforts fail to match their hopes.

Herb Kohler is right when he says I stood soaking wet in a driving rain on the back of the tenth tee and told him, "I believe this is the greatest hole I've ever built." Somehow the three alter-native ways to play the hole distinguish it from any other, and even in that rainstorm it looked beautiful to me.

A second example of an exciting shot at Blackwolf Run appears at the par-three fifteenth hole on the Meadow Valleys Course. It can play anywhere between 160 and 227 yards for men, and the name "Mercy" is indicative of its demanding nature.

What differentiates this tee shot is the vastness of the hole from the golfer's perspective. The tee is slightly elevated, and the shot is played across a ravine to a large oblong green, set alone with no trees or other background to frame the hole.

One small sand bunker is positioned to the left side. From any of the multiple tees, it's a demanding shot to a green that is nearly 50 yards deep.

A third confounding shot is waiting at the sixteenth, a 540-yard-from-the-back-tee par-five at the River Course. After a left-to-right drive from the tee onto the sloping mounds of the fair-way, I tease accomplished players with the prospect of hitting the green in two and the higher-handicapped players with an ap-proach shot that generates real excitement.

Any shot to the green is a gamble, since the Sheboygan winds into the hole up by the left side of the green, catching a hook or pulled shot. The green is protected by a single linden tree, which grows just at the bend in the river and squarely in line with many of the approach shots to the green.

In all of these situations, golfers can choose their own fate. After the round, I hope, these are the shots, successful or not, that they will talk about and remember.

The River Course has four par-fives. Their design features are indicative of my approach to the intended three-shot hole, whose relationship with par has been altered significantly over the last decade.

Par is intended to be based on the number of strokes required by the player to hit the green plus two putts. In the past, on a par-five that meant three approach shots were anticipated, but equipment changes have made par-fives reachable in two.

Nothing excites spectators like a go-for-broke second shot from a Tour professional that results in an eagle attempt. John Daly's hitting the 630-yard par-five seventeenth at Baltusrol in two during the 1993 United States Open had never been done before. It caused quite a stir.

According to USGA recommendations, a men's par-five starts at 470 yards. For professionals that distance is easily reachable in two with an iron.

Most of the reachable par-fives are built with the professional or low-handicap amateur in mind. That doesn't mean they can't be just as exciting for the men and women member players.

Professionals or low-handicap amateurs playing a reachable par-five realize they can lay up and have a short wedge to the green. Logically that is probably the best play, but if the proper temptation is presented, they will abandon logic and try for the green in search of an eagle.

I often position a water hazard to the side on par-fives because I want to maximize the risk/reward factor. When bunkers were cared for with V-shaped rakes, the resulting furrowed sand demanded a precise shot, but these days smooth bunkers present little penalty.

Grassy knobs and side undulations help define the green but offer little distraction. Water has become the only real hazard, so many times I will nestle a winding creek or lake by the green to tantalize the golfers with an approach that provokes the proper anxiety.

From the tee on my par-fives, I wish the golfers could see the flagstick on the green so they know their intended target and are conscious of the entire hole. Whether I've designed a reachable par-five or one that is hopefully unreachable, I want the golfer to be lured toward the pin.

While the thought is to hit the safe shot away from any hazard, there is some inner voice that forces a player to take a chance and aim for the pin placement even though it is near the trouble. Perhaps it's simply a gambling instinct, but more times than not, the safe play is discarded.

The sixteenth at the River Course is a perfect example, since long hitters are confronted with angling their approach shot around a tree and away from the Sheboygan River on the left when they go for the green in two. This design does not prevent the players of less skill from hitting two shots to a position some 130 yards short of the green, where they are then tested with a very precise shot.

There is no need for a forced-carry shot here, since the river fulfills my desire to have a hazard beside the green. When the flagstick is placed on the left side, the mental anguish begins and players must decide whether to gamble and play close to the pin or bail out to the right.

On most every course I build, I try to provide the golfer with four par-fives that intermingle with the other holes according to the relative difficulties of those interceding holes.

If I've challenged the players with two rugged par-fours and a long and difficult par-three, I'll spot a short, straightforward par-five next as a bit of a breather. If the golfers played the previous three tough holes well, then the par-five is a chance for them to go under par. Players who are still reeling from a string of bogeys get a chance to recover a shot and gather their wits for the upcoming holes.

On the other hand, if I've just given the golfers two easy par-fours and a dainty little par-three, I'll probably beat them over the head with either a short, disaster-filled par-five or a longer hole with sufficient trouble to grab their attention.

Variety is vitally important to me, so I mix and match the par-fives according to degree of difficulty and playing strategy. At the River Course at Blackwolf Run, the par-fives are placed at one, eight, eleven, and sixteen.

The eighth (Hell's Gate) and the sixteenth (Unter Der Linden—Under the Linden Tree) are the most difficult of the par-fives, but the eighth is positioned after two medium length par-fours—Jackknife (361 yards) and Glencary (400 yards)—and the sixteenth follows two rather short par-fours—Blind Alley (346 yards) and the Sand Pit (354 yards).

Two of the par-fives, one and sixteen, have hazards on the left side, and two, eight and eleven, to the right. Only sixteen should be reached in two.

Both courses at Blackwolf Run are full every day they are open, and many of the medium- and high-handicap players tee the ball just as far back as possible in order to challenge every set of obstacles the course offers.

It must be self-persecution and a true love of the game, because try as I might, I don't know if I could ever design a golf course that would be hard enough to keep dedicated golfers off to the sidelines. Somehow they just love to dig in there and fight tooth and nail with me, and though they'll curse, yell, scream, and call me names, that *one* memorable shot will always bring them back for more.

At Blackwolf Run, I borrowed a bit from Old Tom Morris at St. Andrews by building a shared green. The eighteenth at the River Course joins hands with the eighteenth at the Meadow Valleys Course. Since there is always the possibility that a golf course I design may one day hold a major championship, I'm always cognizant of the spectator positions. By combining those two greens close to the hillside by the clubhouse, there is a large area for spectators.

We also added a second green on the Meadow Valleys Course finishing hole, aptly named "Salmon Trap." I felt some folks would have trouble hitting a long approach shot across the wide river to the shared green, so an alternate green was placed on the near side, allowing a choice.

In 1999 Blackwolf Run will host the United States Women's Open. The tournament will be played on eighteen holes, which will include ones from both the River Course and Meadow Valleys.

This idea of combining the holes into a "composite course" is similar to Royal Melbourne in Black Rock, Victoria, Australia, where they combine twelve holes from Alister Mackenzie's old West course with six from the new East course when a championship is played. At Kohler, the eighteen the women play will be the original course, including the tenth hole Alice and Herb wrangled over, which has been redesigned without Herb's apple trees.

In spite of my unfounded reservations, Herb constructed a huge clubhouse built from Canadian lodge-pole pine logs and wooden shingles. The beautiful wooden antlers that serve as light fixtures are reminiscent of those at the Old Course Hotel at St. Andrews. Talented artist Ann Timberman sketched a portrait of Herb and me, along with a collage of the holes at Blackwolf Run, that hangs proudly on a prominent wall.

Golfers who have played Blackwolf Run are amazed at the different mixture of grasses and plants. Over the years, Herb Kohler has traveled not only around our country but overseas to play golf. While he loves the look of the Scottish courses, Herb was also highly impressed with the different mix and height of the wild grasses at The Honors course in Chattanooga.

When he returned from a visit there, he told me he wanted that look for Blackwolf Run. Since The Honors has a small membership and daily play is limited, I cautioned him about doing this on a public course, where golfers would spend time looking for balls that would disappear in the tall grass.

My words did nothing to change Herb's mind, and soon John Green, the good-natured director of landscape for the Kohler Company, was working with me to carry out Herb's directive. John is an absolute magician, and soon Blackwolf Run was overflowing with long, wild grasses and prairie plantings that gave the course the same look as the whin and heather do on the Scottish courses.

My skepticism that public golfers would dread playing a course that featured such conditions was, as Herb continues to remind me, dead wrong. Playing in and around long grasses on the mounds and dunes provides a unique challenge, and regardless of their score, these dedicated golfers keep coming back for more.

At Blackwolf Run, the manicured fairways, long grasses, and prairie plantings side by side provide a perfect contrast. Those prairie plants, which undergo seasonal changes in color and texture, combine with native flowers such as white shooting stars, yellow tickseed, black-eyed Susans, purple cone-flowers and orange-flowered butterfly weed to present what John calls "a painter's palette" for the course.

John Green likes to tell people he's seen the intense side of both Herb and me. The story has varied over the years, but according to John: "Pete and Herb drove out to the par-three fifteenth hole in Herb's battered Jaguar to decide once and for all where the green would be positioned. As they walked and muttered to one another, I noticed the right back tire of the car was flat. Seeing this, I went up to them and told Herb I would have someone fix it, but there was no response.

"Just as I was about to call for help, I saw that the left back tire was also flat, so I joined the twosome and announced that since both tires were flat I would call for another vehicle. Once again, there was dead silence.

"I finally walked away, but just as I began speaking into my walkie-talkie, Herb and Pete bounded over toward the car, got in, and sped away, *ca-thump, ca-thump,* completely oblivious of my words and the two flat tires."

As this book is being written, I anticipate building another thirty-six-hole complex for Herb Kohler along the shores of Lake Michigan. The thirty-foot drop along the coastline should provide enough excitement for those public golfers who will be able to experience seaside shots similar to those on coasts around the world.

Working with a man like Herb Kohler, whose love for golf matches mine, has been quite an experience. I always know where I stand with him, except when his unusual sense of humor takes over.

Herb has been down to visit Alice and me several times in the Dominican Republic, but the last time there he may have worn out his welcome. Making fun of me when I'm out at 5:30 a.m. with my net bag and flippers searching for golf balls in the Caribbean is bad enough, but my unusual birthday presents may very well have banned him from ever visiting us again.

Ever the curious one, Herb heard that I had once provided a "special irrigation" service to a house of ill repute located in the town of La Romana.

Intent on having residents of that house thank me for my twenty-year-old effort, Herb invited three of the colorful ladies of the evening to my birthday luncheon. After presenting me with a god-awful red-and-white-bellied parrot that never quit squawking, Herb paraded the three singing señoritas over to me, where they plastered my forehead with kisses.

Somehow I think Herb was just getting even with Alice for her remark about his seventeen-hole golf course!

Blackwolf Run—River Course Kohler, Wisconsin Par 72		
	Men	Women
Yardage:	6991, 6607, 6110	5115
Rating/ Slope:	74.9/151, 73.2/146, 70.9/137	70.7/128

Blackwolf Run—Meadow Valleys Course Kohler, Wisconsin Par 72		
	Men	Women
Yardage:	7142, 6735, 6169	5065
Rating/ Slope:	74.1/143, 73.0/138, 70.4/132	69.5/125

The Pete Dye Club

An ideal or classical golf course demands variety, personality, and above all, the charm of romance.

Charles Blair Macdonald
1928

The toughest, most tenacious, never-give-up son-of-a-gun I've ever worked for is James D. LaRosa.

At our first meeting in 1976, the West Virginia coal company entrepreneur told me, "Pete, there are three ways to do things. The right way, the wrong way, and the *Italian* way." Little did I know that the golf course he had me design for him "the Italian way" would take *sixteen* years to build.

Despite that long stretch of time, without Jim LaRosa's unflinching perseverance, and that of his son Jimmy Joe, this country would not have a very special golf course dedicated to the millions of coal miners who have given their lives to that time-honored industry since the late 1800s. Anybody who toughs it out for sixteen years gains my respect, and I think so much of Mr. LaRosa's efforts that I agreed to allow the course to take my name.

To understand the significance of Jim LaRosa's epic commitment to building a golf course in the hills of Clarksburg, West Virginia, it's important to understand the significance of its setting. There was mystical aura to the land when Jim first guided me around it, and he was quick to educate me as to its history.

According to Jim, West Virginia sets right in the middle of some of the richest coal country in the United States. More than one hundred seams of coal lie underground in that state, the most important one being the Pittsburgh seam. More than two billion short ton of the Pittsburgh coal were mined in and around the area finally chosen for the Pete Dye Club.

Clarksburg sets on the banks of the West Fork River and Elk Creek in northwest West Virginia. It was incorporated in 1785. Stonewall Jackson was born, raised, and buried there—and would be Clarksburg's most famous native if it weren't for Jim LaRosa.

James Dominick LaRosa is the son of Italian-immigrant parents who faced tremendous hardship in the early years of this century. Originally from Calabria, a rural section in southern Italy, Jim's dad came to the Clarksburg area in search of a job in the coal mines.

Jim's work ethic was established through his childhood jobs: shining shoes at the bus station, collecting and selling junk, and carrying luggage for train passengers at the station in nearby Glen Elk. When not working, Jim played softball, basketball, and baseball, and years later he would realize a dream by becoming friends with his childhood idol, Joe DiMaggio.

While Jim was growing up, his father worked as a laborer, hod carrier, and cement finisher for a local construction company. After service in World War I, James Sr. began to pursue real-estate ventures, including ownership of restaurants and hotels in the Glen Elk area.

In 1951, Jim's father entered the coal business by purchasing 1,600 acres at a coal sale. LaRosa Fuel Company was formed, but profits were few. Jim remembers that the only way they made money was to buy coal, tipple it into railroad cars, and try to resell it at a profit.

The status quo continued until 1955, when Jim went into business for himself and, using borrowed money, began to eke out a living for his family. Keeping the company afloat was a difficult task, but in 1966 Jim risked every cent he had to purchase almost fifty thousand acres of coal. Shortly thereafter, when the coal market took an upturn, Jim was well on his way to achieving business success.

It's logical to believe that anyone who stuck with building a golf course for sixteen years would be an avid golfer. The exception would be Jim LaRosa, who barely acknowledged the existence of the game prior to his son Jimmy Joe's interest.

Even though Jim professed little tolerance for golf, Jimmy Joe's enthusiasm rubbed off on his father. Soon Jim was taking the young golfer over to Wee Burn Country Club in Connecticut to see professional Mike Krak.

Jim LaRosa's interest in building a golf course also stemmed from his love for earth-moving. With massive machines available at the strip-mining operation, Jim thought that he could keep construction costs to a minimum.

After Mike Krak first recommended me to Jim, I hopped a plane to Clarksburg. The first property Jim showed me was called Columbia Hollow, and since strip mining had just been completed, he thought the land could be reclaimed as a golf course.

I walked to the top of a snow-covered hill and gazed across the horizon. My first thought was to build a course in which one hole followed another around the stripped mountain like links of sausage, but the snow made it impossible for me to see whether the land had any real possibilities.

I returned to the property in the spring, but I could see that it was not suitable for a golf course. When Jim asked for my opinion of its potential, he recalls my telling him that he should call it "Miracle Mountain Golf Course, since it would be a miracle if anyone played it!"

I thought I'd seen the last of James D. LaRosa, but I should have known better. I was busy with other work, but one day he called to tell me he had located another site that "he just knew had more promise."

Weeks later I flew to Clarksburg, and there stood smiling Jim. Apparently he'd studied U.S. Geological Quadrangle maps and spotted 450 acres in an out-of-the-way spot three miles from Clarksburg.

Out I went to this godforsaken property through brush, high

weeds, unreclaimed spoil piles, and coal-gob mounds, which are as disgusting as they sound. Jim acted as a guide through countryside he didn't even own, and three hours later I had seen most of the land.

Jim waited patiently for my opinion, as anxious as a real-estate agent trying to make his first sale. Finally, I turned toward him. "If you can acquire the property, I'll build you a golf course under two conditions," I told him. "First, give me the keys, and second, stay out of my way!"

Little did I know that I'd be one for two, since Jim did not stay out of my way. I did get him to agree to a 235-acre buffer zone around the golf course where no houses could be built, but from day one Jim wanted to build the course the right (Italian) way.

Since there were to be no homesites to finance the course and most private membership clubs never make it into the black, Jim certainly did not shake my hand and agree to hire me to build his golf course for monetary gain. It would take me a while to figure that all out, but over the years I understood as I got to know Jim a bit better.

In addition to working hand in hand at the Pete Dye Club with Jim and his son, I was ably assisted by my golf course construction superintendent, Lee Schmidt. Lee was one in a long line of apprentices who deserve as much or more credit than I for my success.

My relationship with the designated construction supervisor is critical. If I don't have someone who will carry out my vision and work with me to improve the initial design in every way, I'm in big trouble.

Communication is the key, since the character of the golf course is only as good as the person who built it. Famed writer Herbert Warren Wind once said that I am the only person who is incoherent in three languages, so anyone who works with me has to learn "Urbanaese" and somehow translate my instructions into meaningful golf holes.

Assisting an established designer as course construction supervisor can be a stepping-stone for the would-be architect who aspires to make a name for himself in the profession.

Such fine architects as Donald Ross, Seth Raynor, Robert

Trent Jones, and Tom Fazio all got their start when Old Tom Morris, Charles Blair Macdonald, Stanley Thompson, and George Fazio, respectively, allowed them to learn while building their great courses.

When I choose a construction supervisor, I look for two vital characteristics: youth and someone with golf ability who loves the game. Experience has shown me these two traits make a huge difference when I need to trust someone to build my courses.

I select young men to assist me because I want individuals not set in their ways who are willing to experiment. Whenever possible, I want a good player who loves the game, since from the earliest days of design it's been recognized that one who knows *how* to play the game well has greater ability to produce courses of merit.

That doesn't mean the individual has to be a scratch handicap. For instance, Lee Schmidt can't break 80, but he can play three or four holes at a time as good as anybody and he absolutely loves the game.

Jack Nicklaus says he's not sure a high-handicapper can recognize design features that make up a great golf course, while a good player is able to not only do that but pinpoint poor features to avoid.

Ever since I worked with Cliff Compton way back at El Dorado in 1959, I've been blessed with outstanding young men. At times, I'm not sure where they come from, and some have questioned my methods, but my working relationship with many of these young men has resulted in lifetime friendships.

Lee Schmidt, an Indiana native, probably worked with me longer than anyone. Beginning with Wabeek, a course in Detroit codesigned with Nicklaus in 1971, Lee has assisted me through the Links Course at Casa de Campo, Kingsmill, La Quinta, the Stadium Course at PGA West, and the Pete Dye Club. Lee is a member of the American Society of Golf Course Architects and now works for Jack Nicklaus, overseeing courses in the Far East. Jack recently told me he's so pleased with his work that he'd like to have "two dozen Lee Schmidts around."

Bobby Weed, who was the construction superintendent at Long Cove, is another associate who is a member of the American Society of Golf Course Architects. He is now chief designer for the PGA Tour and a talented architect in his own right.

Tom Doak, who worked with Bobby and me at Long Cove, worked at Plum Creek, Riverdale Dunes, and Piping Rock. Tom has built some fine courses on his own and authored a recent book, *The Anatomy of a Golf Course,* which details the essential elements of golf course architecture from start to finish.

Michael O'Conner started with me at the Citrus course in La Quinta. Mike built the Eagle Pines course at Disney World and La Romana Country Club in the Dominican Republic, and is currently working with me at Mystic Rock at Nemacolin Resort in Farmington, Pennsylvania.

Jason McCoy masterminded Kiawah for me, and has continued to be my point guard for Brickyard Crossing and the new Medalist Club in Hobe Sound, Florida.

I've had some other outstanding men as construction superintendents, including David Postlethwait, who worked at Oak Tree; Scott Poole; Rod Whitman; and Tim Liddy, who recently modified Coffin Golf Course, a great Bill Diddel layout in Indianapolis.

Working with these gentlemen may be the best part of what I do, even though my relationship with each of these aspiring golf course architects is as different as their personalities. Most began with me by picking up sticks and handling other assorted menial tasks, but if they have a willingness to learn and can work according to the "Dye clock," which means long hours, then I'll show them everything I know about the profession.

I very rarely use formal drawings, so my assistants must learn to interpret my hand gestures and sentence fragments and then take a crack at what they think I have in mind.

When I initially scribble out a sketch of a hole, it contains only a rough outline of the tee, fairway, and green locations. I provide circled numbers to indicate elevation levels for various points on the hole and use broader strokes with my pen to designate fairway, bunkers, and greensite locations that I want to be seen from the tee.

I always want my assistants and the construction crew to accentuate design features and not be shy in building a mound larger than I suggested or a more severe contour on the green than marked on the rough sketch. It's harder to push dirt up than to push it away, so I would rather be softening a mound or contour than having to constantly build it higher.

My directions serve merely as a starting point, with the only constant being the angle of the hole. Since my courses feature alternating left-to-right and right-to-left shot sequences, I insist we stay true to that pattern.

Operators of large machinery are seldom golfers, so I never throw golf terms at them. If I want a hole for a bunker, I say dig me a basement there, or make me a housepad, and presto I get a deep hole or a flat grade that I can easily shape to suitable golf course contours.

Many times I really don't plan what I end up doing anyway, and David Postlethwait, who worked with me almost ten years, used to tell his workers not to pay any attention to me. After one of my mixed-metaphor-laced speeches trying to explain a directive, he interpreted my ideas to the crew. "Now, men, Mr. Dye doesn't like what we've done, but he doesn't know what he wants, so we'll just play around awhile and see what happens."

Interestingly enough, nearly every man who's ever assisted me spent time in Clarksburg working on the Pete Dye Club. I suppose it's been a training ground, but when a course takes sixteen years to build, everyone has a chance.

Since there was to be no real-estate development within close proximity of the Pete Dye Club, I could afford to choose as much land as necessary. I would conceptualize eighteen very different holes, but I paid a great deal of attention to the par-threes that would be the star of the course.

The par-threes can be the cornerstone of a golf course, as the player can always see the putting surface. Regardless of which tee the golfer chooses, each presents the opportunity to hit the green. More memorable shots are hit on the par-threes than on any other holes.

To create the opportunity for a once-in-a-lifetime shot, I consider every factor in the design for a par-three. They include setting for the hole, direction, variety of length, position in the eighteen-hole sequence, difficulty factor, green size, contour, and the type and placement of hazards.

The setting for the par-three hole is crucial, and I search out unusual locations trying to provide a unique look for the hole so that each of the four par-threes will excite the golfers when they stand ready at the tee. If possible, a par-three hole will be along a river, lake, or creek, beside a marshland, in a sand dune, or framed by a clump of trees.

Varying directions for the par-threes are desirable as well. Wind conditions provide the stiffest test for a golfer. I want the players to execute alternate with-the-wind, cross-wind, and against-the-wind shots. At the Pete Dye Club, the four par-threes all run in opposite directions.

Length of the holes should vary as well. From their multiple tee locations, I intend the golfer to play wood shots as well as short, medium, and long irons in alternating sequence.

Positioning par-threes in the order of holes takes considerable thought. Many times it's dictated by the setting I have located, but I also take into account the hole's degree of difficulty in relation to its neighbors.

The four par-threes at the Pete Dye Club are positioned at numbers four, seven, thirteen, and sixteen. In order, they are a long par-three at number four, a short, easier par-three at number seven, a Redan-type, devilish par-three at number thirteen, and an extremely long, downhill, straight par-three at number sixteen.

The difficulty levels are dictated by green size, slope, and the type and placement of hazards. An attempt is made on par-threes to alternate the position of bunkers or water to the left or right of the greens. I do design forced-carry shots on par-threes, as I know where the play is starting. If they are playing the right tee, golfers should be able to manage the carry.

On long par-threes, I normally position a hazard at greenside but provide a bail-out area for the fainthearted. Medium-length par-threes will feature at least two hazards, and I'll toughen up the shot from any bail-out area by sloping the green away from it. Short par-threes permit me to be a bit meaner, since I believe in surrounding the green with all kinds of vicious hazards.

Some of the first to play at the Pete Dye Club compared its look to Ballybunion's, the time-honored course on the west coast of Ireland, whose densely forested hills resemble those of Clarksburg.

But more than anything, it is the connection with coal that makes the Pete Dye Club so special. All around the course, there are reminders of mining days, including a mind-boggling forty-step walk through a damp underground mine shaft between the sixth and seventh holes.

At the eighth hole, the valley near the green is framed by a wall flecked with sparkling black coal. Black-cinder sand fills the bunkers on four holes of the course.

At the tenth, the golfer will see a rotary car-dump coal tipple. Twenty-two coal-laden mine cars are positioned on a track that "turns the hole" as it plays off the tee.

While Jim LaRosa and I laugh about it now, he and I have had our differences during construction of the course, especially when he tried to play architect. Even though he hardly plays the game, and his dirt-moving experience is limited to strip mining, Jim had a tendency to fiddle with the course when I wasn't around.

Jim's problem was that he would hear about some design feature at a faraway course and believe we should try it at the Pete Dye Club. On several occasions I returned to find that something I spent months building had been eliminated.

After spending a great deal of time with Jim, I realized that his fascination with building a golf course had to do with the realization that his earth-moving machinery could help create something beautiful. Strip mining is not the most popular business, and I felt that Jim saw the evolution of the Pete Dye Club as a very positive experience for him and his workers.

On one occasion, even though the course wasn't even finished, he started to worry about a problem that might occur if the United States Open was ever played there.

I had dug a hole for a huge lake near the clubhouse and the eighteenth green had been roughed in. Apparently Jim was told that if he ever hosted the Open, there wouldn't be enough room for *parking*, so he began to look for additional space. I left Clarksburg believing the lake and green area were safe, but when I returned Jim had filled in the lake and the greensite was no more. I was mad as hell, and didn't return until that lake reappeared.

There was also an old railroad tipple that wound around the location for the tenth hole, built on a "gob pile," containing slate paintings, sulfur balls, shale, and rock from roof falls. I felt that the tipple, which traversed Simpson Creek, personified the coal theme for the course and asked that it be left in place.

Once again I left Clarksburg, but when I returned, the tipple was gone. I threatened to disappear again, so Jim rebuilt the tipple and restored it as well.

Jim says that tipple inspired him to broaden his plans to feature the coal theme throughout the course. Shortly thereafter, Jim constructed a twenty-five-foot cascading waterfall that begins in the mine. The high iron content in the water turned the rock around it orange, providing a striking background for hole ten.

Despite delays caused by weather, construction problems, Jim's changes, and financing difficulties, Jim LaRosa's sixteen-year dream came true when he opened the first nine holes at the Pete Dye Club. The second nine opened in the fall of 1994, and while the course may have my name on it, it was Jim's vision and unconditional devotion that made such a spectacular course possible.

For all of those sixteen years, Jim says I listened to and then rejected every single one of his ideas. He never gave up though, and finally caught my attention by urging me to build "the smallest green in the world" on the seventeenth hole.

When the course opened this fall, I'm sure Jim pointed to that green with pride. "I actually inspired Pete Dye to build this green," he will tell anyone who'll listen—even though at seventeen thousand square feet, it is one of the *largest* in the world.

The Pete Dye Club Clarksburg, West Virginia Par 72		
	Men	Women
Yardage:	7170, 6750, 6218	5759, 5127
Rating/ Slope:	74.0/134, 72.0/130	N/A

The Ocean Course at Kiawah

A good player prays for wind every day, but he must not pray too earnestly.

John L. Low
1928

When seventy-seven-year-old, British-born Sam Ryder died in 1936, his only request was that his favorite mashie club be buried alongside him. The founder of the fabled Ryder Cup matches may have taken that sacred club to his grave, but he left a lasting symbol of what the great game of golf is all about.

In a day and age when professional golfers can win a million dollars during a weekend, the Ryder Cup competition between touring professionals from the United States and Europe stands alone as a monument to playing for pride and country. Except during the Olympics, at no other sporting event is the American flag waved as proudly amid the resounding cries of "USA, USA."

Until recently, winning the Ryder Cup was taken for granted in the United States. The turning point elevating the competition to international prominence came when the Europeans defeated the Americans in 1987 at Jack Nicklaus's Muirfield.

Because the American team had dominated the competition for so long, that European victory deeply punctured the pride of our touring professionals. When a tie in 1989 at the Belfry resulted in the Europeans retaining the cup, the anticipated matches in 1991 became not only a patriotic quest but a dedicated effort to save the pride of the American touring professional.

Joe Walser called me in August 1988 with the news that the 1991 Ryder Cup matches had been moved from the Stadium Course at PGA West to the proposed course at Kiawah because playing in the Eastern Time Zone would allow television viewers in Europe to watch more during prime time. For the first time in history, the heralded event had been awarded to a course that did not exist, and there was less than two years to build one worthy of the event.

While building a golf course for the Ryder Cup would be of paramount importance, once the competition was over, the course would be played by resort golfers. It therefore needed to not only severely test Ryder Cup competitors, but be ready for the onslaught of public golfers who wanted to experience the thrill of competing on the same golf course where the Ryder Cup was decided.

When I first walked the seaside land at Kiawah, I immediately fell in love with the site. The combination of the beautiful ocean views on one side and the vast saltwater marshes on the other captivated me. While tough work lay ahead, I told Joe Walser I would have bent down on my knees and begged (perhaps even traded in Alice) for the opportunity to build a course on such magnificent property.

The Ocean Course would be built on a fragile two-and-a-half-mile stretch of beachfront along the Atlantic at the extreme eastern end of Kiawah Island, South Carolina. Located twenty-one miles south of historic Charleston, where southern traditions hold fast, Kiawah Island gets its name from the Kiawah Indians, peaceful hunters and fishermen who had lived in the area.

Based on the narrow perimeter of the land proposed for the course, I envisioned a routing where the front nine holes would loop clockwise to the east and the back nine would loop counterclockwise to the west.

No land could be used for homesites because of environmental restrictions. "I'm like a kid with a lollipop," I told writer Dick

Taylor regarding my opportunity to work with one of the greatest pieces of seaside property in the United States.

To spearhead the work at Kiawah, Lake City Community College graduate Jason McCoy came in as the construction superintendent. Jason, Alice, and I walked the property many times, especially since we were confronted by a challenge we had never faced before: no prevailing wind. It was strong and gusty but would blow from different directions throughout the day.

When the proposed routing for a course is laid out, I know that 90 percent of the time the prevailing wind will come from one direction. I can then decide what holes will play with the wind, against it, or across. The distances of the various holes will be determined by the direction of the wind.

At Kiawah Island, which lies east to west off the Carolina coast, I was surprised to discover that there was no prevailing wind because it blows alternately from the east and then the west. The holes would also run to the east or to the west, requiring a design that would one day play into the wind and the next with it. Since wind significantly affects the length of the holes, many tee positions would be needed.

When I design a long par-four or a par-five, the three tee positions for men can have a variance of more than one hundred yards. On shorter holes, that variance declines, since the tee positions are closer together.

This permits more design flexibility on longer holes than short ones. Depending on the wind direction, the tee markers can be set forward or back.

The size of the greens we build is also affected by wind conditions. At Kiawah two golf courses in one were being built, since the direction of the wind could require a long approach shot one day and a short one the next.

The depth of the greens at Kiawah was designed to be receptive to all shots. Front-to-back distances measured between forty and fifty yards, so that both a highly lofted shot or a lower-trajectory one could hold the green.

The par-four ninth at Kiawah is a good example of how a hole can adapt to either wind direction. Designed to play at 465 yards, an additional tee was strategically placed so that the yardage could be reduced if the wind was roaring into the golfer's face. On days when the wind was favorable, the hole would play to its maximum length.

When PGA officials first visited the site for the course, they almost threw up. There before them was a vast expanse of *nothing* where their beloved Ryder Cup was to be played, and they left shaking their heads in bewilderment.

After a lengthy permitting process, we received permission to begin clearing the land in July 1989. Jason began cutting out the corridors for each hole, and we were making good progress when in late October, Hurricane Hugo put a stop to everything when it blasted the coastline. In the aftermath, access roads were closed, so we had to take a boat to the island. Marking stakes were also blown away, and many of the oaks on the property were windburned so badly that they never recovered.

Where there had been one continuous sand dune along a two-mile stretch before Hugo, there were now several smaller ones six to eight feet apart.

Hugo put us behind schedule, but just as the American team was caught up early on in the spirit of international competition, so were Jason and the construction crew. This spirit intensified as the days went by, especially when nearly every single person who visited the site told us that the course would never be ready for the Ryder Cup.

All of the early publicity regarding the potential readiness of the Ocean Course for the Ryder Cup had been negative. PGA officials, the prospective players, and other interested parties were all unanimous in their conviction that the course would never be in top condition by October 1991 for the matches.

Even though Hugo's devastation had ripped apart our construction schedule, the challenge to prove all of the naysayers wrong brought the construction crew closer together in an emotional, determined effort. Alice and I were caught up in the groundswell too. We joined the team effort to clean up after the hurricane, which meant eighteen-hour workdays that included many evening hours under the lights.

Hugo obliterated all the vegetation and left the split dunes barren. In the process of trying new methods to replace the grasses, Jason McCoy came up with something quite innovative.

Before this time, no one had figured out a way to transplant sea oats and beach grass from existing dunes to new ones. Jason researched every piece of literature he could find and talked to several experts, but no one had been successful with transplanting.

Persistence paid off when Jason came up with a process called fertigation. Liquid fertilizer was introduced into the irrigation system and injected directly into the sandy dunes. Within months, Jason and his Guatemalan crew successfully transplanted more than a million plants. In fact, they ended up with more than they needed, and we used the excess on the back nine.

The stabilized dunes looked ageless, but there were those who were concerned that the sea oats we had planted would be killed when Ryder Cup galleries trampled them. Just the opposite occurred when the footsteps pounded the seeds into the ground: the sea oats flourished.

Jason's contributions overshadowed his attempts to frighten me to death during the first few months of construction. It was bad enough that he almost gave me a heart attack by shooting his gun at a snake not two feet from me, but he also led me so close to an alligator's nest that the hissing sound made me jump six feet backwards!

If any course influenced the design of the holes at Kiawah, it would be Ireland's jewel, Portmarnock, located on a long narrow piece of links land between the Irish Sea and an inland tidal bay. Tournaments at Portmarnock, where at least four holes border the bay, have been played in the wildest extremes of weather. Like Kiawah, the wind roars around the course, changing direction hourly, and the golfer must be prepared to adapt on the spot.

Features of that seaside links are very similar to the Ocean Course, but a great deal of earth-moving was required at Kiawah to emulate the ageless rolling hills and dunes of the Irish links.

Courses like St. Andrews, Ballybunion, and Portmarnock were all created on sandy silt, with undulations formed by wind, the receding tides, the grazing habits of sheep, and patterns left by burrowing animals. At Kiawah, we used bulldozers to construct the old "links" look that is reminiscent of those seaside links courses.

On most courses in the British Isles, the grasses are bent and fescue. They need little water to grow in those misty climates and produce the close tight lie that is the essential ingredient for bump-and-run golf.

At those courses, the temperature seldom gets above 70 degrees, while at Kiawah hot summers can run the thermometer well up into the 90s. Bent and fescue grasses were unsuitable for the Ocean Course, so we stolonized the broader-leaf Bermuda, which requires constant watering.

In order to try to feature some of the bump-and-run flavor of the Scottish links, a smaller-leafed Bermuda was used for the approaches to the greens and the putting surfaces. Hitting the ball in the air may be more prevalent at the Ocean Course, but we kept the green entrances open for the opportunity of bump and run.

The successful experiments at Old Marsh regarding drainage and irrigation were continued at Kiawah. In compliance with the environmental regulations in the area, we developed a unique internal drainage system that not only recycled water but protected the adjacent marshlands from any chemicals used in course maintenance. We drained the fairways into catch basins. They were connected to an intricate series of underground pipes, and all of the rainwater and the water used for irrigating the course flowed back into the irrigation pond and was pumped back onto the golf course.

This allowed more than 50 percent of the water required to irrigate the course to be reclaimed, cutting the cost of providing water in half.

By using pumps, we were able to keep the freshwater in the irrigation pond always at two feet above the sea-water level. Since the fairways and greens were constructed at a minimal elevation of five feet above sea level, there was three feet of dry sand to filter water that does not reach one of the fairway catch-basin drains.

In addition to these innovations, we planted native grasses in the lagoons. They serve as natural filters for the water before it is pumped back onto the course.

Since logging operations left dikes in the area, the amount of the saltwater in the Willets and Ibis ponds had been greatly reduced. By opening the dikes and replanting them with saltwater grasses, we were able to restore the natural saltwater marsh.

"I don't know what you are thinking of," Alice said to us one day after completing a walk along the sand dunes. "You're building a course right next to the ocean but not letting the golfers see it!"

Alice's perception was correct, since vision of the beach was blocked by a high ridge of dunes. I could have dug out sections of the ridge to allow peeks at the surf, but Alice kept insisting on unobstructed views.

Using sand dug from lakes and pockets around the course, the fairways were elevated six feet on eight inland holes and all of the holes bordering the ocean. Thanks to Alice, golfers can enjoy watching the tide roll in and out and experience the beautiful Kiawah Island coastline.

While Alice improved the view, her idea inadvertently made the course more demanding. Elevated fairways made the course even more windswept than it would have been if the fairways were tucked down.

The crew's hard work paid off and the Ocean Course was ready to be planted in July 1990, almost a year to the day after we broke ground. Even then, skepticism persisted as to whether the course would be playable for the Ryder Cup.

Six weeks before the October due date, American captain Dave Stockton paid a visit with several prospective Ryder Cup players. Modifications were still being made, but the condition of the fairways and greens prompted Lanny Wadkins to tell reporters, "No way will this course be ready for the Ryder Cup."

Lanny's comments were mild in comparison to those of other Ryder Cup hopefuls, including Tom Kite, who abandoned his car when it got stuck in the sand near the clubhouse site. No practice putting green existed at that time, and the proposed players, while pleased with the layout, were very critical of the condition of the course.

I disregarded their pessimism and was still confident of our eventual success, since I knew our strongest growing period for

Bermuda grass was yet to come. However, comments by Dave Stockton and Bernard Gallacher, captain of the European team, did catch my attention.

Dave was quoted as saying, "If I didn't have to worry about the Ryder Cup, this would be the greatest golf course in the world." Dave also told writer Ron Whitten prior to the tournament, "The course reminds me of Shinnecock Hills, Cypress Point, and even the inland Augusta National."

During a pretournament visit, European counterpart Gallacher called Kiawah "an American course with wind" and praised Alice's suggestion that I elevate the inland ground so that players could see the Atlantic on each hole as a "brilliant idea!"

While the playing field was readied for the competition, speculation arose as to what side the course favored. Experts battled back and forth, but I had my opinions about why foreign players were as dominant then as they seem to be now.

The United States Professional Golf Tour has force-fed its players a steady diet of courses that are perfectly manicured, with tight fairway grass, uniform sand bunkers, and greens that are quick but most times unvaried in speed. While this allows the professionals the opportunity to shoot subpar scores, I don't believe it is a test of their mental skills.

The foreign players like Greg Norman, Nick Faldo, Nick Price, Ernie Els, Colin Montgomery, and Bernhard Langer, who have played a variety of courses all over the world, seem stronger mentally because they don't expect a pristine layout every time they tee it up.

While PGA touring professionals have been brought up on manicured courses since junior golf, the foreign contingent have been raised on bad lies and rough weather requiring mental toughness. Most American professionals are disturbed when they have a difficult lie, but the foreign player will take one look and think, "Let me at it."

Recently crowned 1994 Masters Champion Jose Maria Olazabal put it best to reporters after his victory: "I think you'll see more Europeans winning here [in the United States] . . . The big advantage we have is that . . . we can use our imagination. We're used to making up shots . . . ."

Besides Spain's Olazabal, there are players from Fiji, New Zealand, Austria, South Africa, and Sweden who have played on every cow pasture imaginable. They learn to hit the ball out of divots, nasty lies, bare ground and thick rough, and steep-sided bunkers.

Perhaps more than any other game, golf requires mental preparedness. Whether players have a perfect textbook swing or not, their success in competition depends on their ability to think clearly before making each shot.

To be sure, the lone golfer matches wits against the architect, the golf course, and the elements. There are no backups here, no substitutes, just a one-on-one with the course.

Three of the greatest to ever play the game had mental toughness as their trademark. People may squabble about who is really the best there ever was, but Bobby Jones, Ben Hogan, and Jack Nicklaus were thinkers extraordinaire, and all produced great victories overseas in spite of adverse conditions.

Like many of the foreign players these days who have risen to prominence, these legendary performers were able to mount a mental outlook on the game that provided them with confidence regarding their physical ability to play every shot. This permitted a mental restraining order sufficient to control their emotions and anxieties. Golf course architects should prey on those potential moments of anxiety and pressure; the great golf professional's response is to beat them at that game.

That's why the cream rises to the top in major championships played on great golf courses that are not reduced in difficulty. Unfortunately, misplaced loyalty by stubborn governing bodies for the "feelings" of the touring professionals many times prevents a great course from being played at full strength.

I felt we had designed a course at Kiawah that would challenge both sides with demanding shots, especially since every player had to deal with the wind factor. Good judgment was required, for the wind subjects the golfer to a mental matchup on every tee.

As the Scots say, "No wind, no golf," and my positioning of the holes at Kiawah brought the wind element into the game on every shot. Dave Stockton predicted that this factor would give the Europeans an advantage over the American team, but I felt his comments were intended to stir up his squad and urge them to prove him wrong.

At Kiawah, the art of long-iron play is reinstituted. All of the holes demand accuracy, and with the wind variance, golfers may show expertise with long-iron play.

Since the course would be played by resort guests, several sets of tees were built at the Ocean Course, enabling players to approach the course on their own terms. For amateurs, the championship tees are ridiculous, but the various tees on the Ocean Course allow golfers of any ability to enjoy the ride.

I feel so strongly about golfers playing from the correct tees that I often attempt to "hide" the championship markers. Most golfers should not even see where the professional or the scratch player's tee is tucked, because if they play the hole from that tee they never get the same look or feel the professional does. This defeats the purpose of the design.

The need for shot-making at Kiawah is especially evident at the fourteenth, seventeenth, and eighteenth holes.

The Ocean Course makes a turn back east to begin its finishing stretch along the beach. The long par-three fourteenth hole is designed in the tradition of the great Redan holes.

The elevated green slopes from front to back, and only the back left portion is visible from the tee. The green demands a high shot when the pin is located on the front, but when the pin is located on the back, it demands a low-trajectory shot that will land on the front of the green and roll down to the back. A golfer who attempts the carry to the back of the green and lands on the slope will find trouble—a big sand bunker is hidden at the back left of the green.

There wasn't going to be a lake on the par-three, 197-yard from the back tees seventeenth, but Alice felt we needed a dramatic element to confront golfers at this point. Since players of Ryder Cup caliber can handle bunker shots with ease, to make a realistic challenge we dug an eight-acre lake that stretches from the tee to the offset green.

That green, which runs away from the player diagonally to the right and is nearly a double-one at 10,000 square feet, has sea oats and big dunes behind it. Sand extends all the way up to the back edge of the green. The front is hidden with aquatic grasses.

Quite by accident, I felt that this less-abrupt feature made it more difficult for the golfer to estimate the distance of the hole. Somehow the heavy growth of aquatic plants presented an optical illusion for the player and made club selection a bit tougher.

Following the seventeenth comes the 438-yard, par-four eighteenth, which plays from a tee located on sand dunes next to the beach. Driving the ball straight down the pipeline is the key since there are dunes graced with sea oats and wild grasses on both the right and the left.

Fourteen, seventeen, and eighteen stood poised and ready for that dramatic Sunday when the Ryder Cup would be decided. On the surface, none of the three holes seemed overly difficult, but when the tension of close matches built up, these holes became monsters.

When the Ryder Cup teams began competition on the Ocean Course on Friday September 27, 1991, they didn't recognize the golf course they had practiced on all week. All during the practice rounds, a mild wind had come from the southeast, but overnight it had not only gained intensity but switched to the opposite direction.

A westerly wind now greeted the players. All of the finishing holes, which had been downwind the day before, now suddenly would be played against a stiff breeze.

This switch in conditions provided an absolute neutral playing field for the competitors, since they all were required to plan their strategy from square one. Nobody had an advantage, since no one had practiced shots they would now need in the three days of competition.

For instance, at the par-three fourteenth the competitors were forced to hit two and three irons where the day before they had used a seven or eight. At eighteen, what had been a five- or six-iron approach shot downwind to the green now became a long iron or wood shot.

Nowhere was the change more dramatic than at the par-three seventeenth. I had hoped the hole would be pivotal, and thanks to Alice's lake, the wind change, and the pressure, it more than proved its mettle.

The Americans and their British opponents battled to a virtual standstill as the matches headed into the last few holes on Sunday. John Daly had sent a fax that was pinned to the wall in the U.S. team's dressing room: "Good luck and kick butt." The Americans had responded with superior play to match that of the Europeans.

Just as the eighteenth at the Belfry in 1989 had proven to be the deciding hole in the European tie, the drama would culminate at the seventeenth at the Ocean Course for the 1991 matches. Germany's Bernhard Langer's famous six-footer at eighteen might have decided the competition, but long before that never-to-be-forgotten moment, the seventeenth created anxiety for both captains, team members, twenty-five thousand spectators, and millions of television viewers around the world.

All during the practice rounds, the wind at seventeen was blowing downwind. Players from both teams hit seven and even eight irons on the 190-yard hole, and no player had trouble with the carry over the lake.

When the flags went up, the wind shift made the hole treacherous. The Europeans adapted much better to the all-carry 190-yard shot, but the American team's shots seemed to be sucked toward the lake. Payne Stewart, Mark Calcavecchia, Paul Azinger, and Chip Beck doused their shots not once but *twice* each.

That excruciating drama at seventeen, and the subsequent miss by Bernhard Langer on eighteen, capped off an incredible weekend for the construction crew, Alice, and me. We jumped up and down and celebrated with the rest of the Americans when victory was assured on a course whose excellent condition made the crew victorious too.

When I return to the Ocean Course, which is enjoyed by thousands of resort golfers every year, I can still feel the excitement of that magical Sunday when Dave Stockton, Lanny Wadkins, Payne Stewart, and the rest of the team stood in the pounding surf of the Atlantic and held the Ryder Cup high.

I will never forget Arnold Palmer's win at the Heritage, Jerry Pate's triumph at the Tournament Players Championship, or John

Daly's storybook win in the PGA, but for sheer emotion, nothing compares with that spectacular United States Ryder Cup victory at Kiawah Island in 1991.

The Ocean Course
Kiawah Island, South Carolina
Par 72

	Men	Women
Yardage:	7371, 6824, 6244	5327
Rating/ Slope:	76.9/149, 74.9/141, 72.1/134	72.9

Brickyard Crossing

A controlled shot to a closely guarded green is the surest test of
any man's golf.

A. W. Tillinghast

WANTED

Designer to build new eighteen-hole golf course. Location of land: city industrial area. Characteristics of
property: High-tension power lines and railroad tracks
border flat terrain. Gigantic water tower visible from
the site. Rusted link fence separates land from single-
family housing. Quadrant borders cement wall, par-
tially concealing oval racetrack and towering spectator
stands.

Sounds great to me!

That's because I was first interested in that unusual setting for
a golf course adjacent to the Indianapolis Motor Speedway 500
racetrack more than thirty-five years earlier!

Speedway Golf Course was three decades old at the time and
an integral part of the Motor Speedway complex located on West

16th Street in Indianapolis. In 1960 it hosted the 500 Festival Invitational Tournament for PGA professionals, and even though I was just a novice designer, I saw the tremendous potential for the golf course. When Tony George, grandson of the legendary Tony Hulman, whose family owns the Speedway, hired me in 1991 to design a new course to be known as Brickyard Crossing, it meant I had come full circle with my involvement at the home of Indy-car racing.

Host to seventy-eight international 500-mile automobile races since 1911, the Indianapolis Motor Speedway was first built in 1909 by four prominent Indianapolis businessmen.

The Speedway was built seven miles northwest of downtown Indianapolis to "create a great outdoor laboratory" for the young automotive industry. Originally a combination of two long straightaways measuring five-eighths of a mile each and two short ones of one-eighth of a mile in length, the Speedway was later expanded to the current two-and-one-half-mile oval.

Barney Oldfield claimed the Speedway racing speed record of the day when he toured the track at 82 miles per hour. Several events were scheduled each month at the Speedway, but maintenance was a problem until more than three million paving bricks were grouted in cement to pave the racetrack.

The first 500-mile race was held on May 30, 1911, and forty drivers participated as members of automobile-factory teams in search of the $25,000 first prize. Ray Harroun, whose crew included our great golfing friend Peggy Kirk Bell's father, won the race in a six-cylinder Marmon Wasp by averaging 74 miles an hour.

Over the years, such renowned 500-mile race drivers as Wilbur Shaw, Bill Vukovich, Parnelli Jones, Rodger Ward, A. J. Foyt, Jr., Mario Andretti, and Rick Mears have won the coveted Borg Warner Trophy. In the late 1940s, I was so smitten by the sport that I joined with several others in sponsoring a car for the 1950 race. Spider Webb was the driver, but unfortunately he did not complete a lap!

Terre Haute, Indiana, native Tony Hulman, who purchased the Speedway in 1945, brought the racetrack to international prominence, but it was Eddie Rickenbacker, the famous World War I

aviation ace, who first expanded the facilities around the Speedway to include a golf course. In 1928, Indianapolis native Bill
Diddel was hired to create an eighteen-hole layout.

The course featured nine holes inside the track and nine holes
adjacent, with the players making their way to the "500 Nine" by
way of "Brickyard Crossing," a wooden bridge that hung precari-
ously over the backstretch of the track. Even though the nine
holes inside were quite lengthy, they took up less than a third of
the 224 acres inside the oval.

Alice and I always respected Mr. Diddel's work at such fine
Indianapolis courses as Hillcrest, Meridian Hills, Country Club
of Indianapolis, Coffin Municipal, Woodland, and Fort Harrison,
so we went to him to discuss our entering the design profession.
While he discouraged us with his comments about our capability
to make a living, Mr. Diddel, who was tapering off his career at
the time, actually predicted the future when he told us that golf
course design was changing rapidly because the need to irrigate
would increase construction costs substantially.

Mr. Diddel also told us about a recent development at the
Kenwood Country Club, a notable thirty-six-hole complex in Cincinnati that he designed in 1930. They contacted him about in-
stalling a watering system, but he refused.

Mr. Diddel said he was a traditionalist and thought golf should
be played on fairways that were wet when it rained and dry when
it did not. He thought that was golf and that it should be played
under more natural conditions where there was no attempt to
artificially alter the course.

I emphatically told Mr. Diddel I agreed with him and thought
his standards were wonderful and admirable, and that I was going to do the same thing. I went on to say that I would hold the
line on all the new fancy stuff and be a purist and traditionalist
as well.

Bill looked me right in the eye and said, "Pete, if you do, you'll
starve."

Soon after the memorable meeting with Bill Diddel, I was
appointed general chairman of the 500 Festival Invitational Tournament, in 1960. At that time, Alice and I were building our first
course at El Dorado as well as trying to improve the Country

Club of Indianapolis by planting trees, adding bunkers and bettering turf conditions.

All of the great names of the day came to play the PGA Tour event at Speedway. The first three rounds were played on Wednesday, Thursday, and Friday, with the race being staged on Saturday. After extensive cleanup of all of the chicken bones and other debris, the final round was held on Sunday.

Such great professionals as Mason Rudolph, Mike Souchak, Bill Casper, Doug Ford, and Arnold Palmer all made their way to the Speedway. They were enticed perhaps as much by seeing the 500-mile track as by playing the "World's Most Unique Golf Course," as it was known in those days.

Housing for the players was a major problem because of the thousands of race fans who flocked to Indianapolis, so we finally ended up using an unoccupied wing of the hospital at the Indiana University Medical Center in Indianapolis. The accommodations weren't all that bad, but I do recall Chick Harbert telling me, "I've stayed just about everywhere in my life at golf tournaments, but never in a damn hospital."

When ticket sales for the tournament lagged behind expectations, I peddled them around Indianapolis myself, visiting every drugstore and grocery outlet within fifty miles of the city. We came up with the great marketing idea of $7 for seven days, which included practice rounds, the pro-am, and the four-day tournament, but even that bargain didn't sell.

We needed $100,000 in revenue to break even. The expenses were $50,000 and the remaining $50,000 was prize money for the professionals. Mike Souchak was asked whether $50,000, which was second only to what the George May Tournament in Chicago offered, was enough to play for with all the race hoopla involved. Without hesitation, Mike told me, "We pros would play down Main Street for $50,000."

Clarence Cagle, head of operations for the racetrack, had so many demanding concerns, including the cleanup of trash after the race, that conditioning the golf course was left to me. As the date for the tournament fast approached, I realized I needed help.

The day before the first round, I telephoned all of my golf superintendent friends. Just hours before the first professional teed off, lawn mowers descended on the Speedway from every direction. With the superintendents' cooperation and about twenty mowers operating up and down every fairway and on the greens, the Speedway was in prime shape when the first tee shot was hit on the opening hole.

In the initial tournament in 1961, all of the race drivers participated in the pro-am, and Arnold Palmer livened up the tournament by eagling the eighteenth to force a playoff, which he later lost to Doug Ford. In 1962, Jack Nicklaus came to the tournament, but he finished twelve strokes behind Billy Casper, who birdied the "Wilbur Shaw" eighteenth hole to win the championship.

My appreciation for how talented the PGA professionals were was reinforced when I saw the way they played at Speedway. Unfortunately the golf course did not measure up to PGA Tour standards, since it was an unwatered layout that had length, but little rough and minimal greenside bunkering.

This led to my consideration of several improvements for the course. One hole I considered modifying was eighteen, a long par-five where Little Eagle Creek crossed in front of the green.

The idea might have sounded crazy at the time, but I envisioned flooding the area from the creek to the green so that professionals would have to carry a small pond on their approach shot. After the tournament, the cork would be taken out of the drain so the daily fee player at Speedway would not have to deal with the water.

A brief conversation after the tournament with owner Tony Hulman never resulted in any changes. Later Mr. Hulman, who apparently thought little of me and my suggestions, hired Mr. Diddel to add nine holes to his original nine located outside the oval track. The new eighteen was built on limited acreage and lost its unique identity, as players no longer crossed inside the track.

I learned that Tony George was considering renovation of the Speedway course in 1991, but even though I was interested, deciding whether I could in good conscience tear apart a course designed by Bill Diddel did cause me concern.

As with a work of art, I have always been careful not to alter another designer's work. I hope I will be paid the same courtesy when I've gone to the great beyond.

Early in my career, when I could have used the work and the fee, I was offered two opportunities to revise golf courses designed by two of the great architects in the history of the profession.

When Oak Hill, the wonderful Rochester, New York, course designed by Donald Ross in 1923 was to host the United States Open, officials of the USGA thought the par-threes were too short. The Oak Hill greens committee decided to lengthen them. Later, when the Open was to be held at Inverness, designed by Bernard Nicholls and modified by Donald Ross, USGA officials believed that the course was too tight for galleries to roam and requested that I alter the position of three or four holes.

Not only was I aware of the great tradition of those courses, but I had great respect for them since I competed in the 1949 United States Amateur at Oak Hill and the 1957 United States Open at Inverness, where I played well enough to finish ahead of Palmer and Nicklaus.

In both situations, I thought long and hard before turning officials down. Alice and I discussed the matter thoroughly, and finally told the local committees we would make the revisions if they would promise to return the holes to their original character after the championship. They refused to consider that request.

What made the situation at Speedway different was that Tony George was going to completely revamp the original course in accordance with renovation plans for the race track. Knowledge that Mr. Diddel's design would be severely altered whether I pursued the design assignment or not convinced me to contact Tony. I also felt Mr. Diddel would like to see the crossing of the brickyard resumed after an absence of many years.

When he was fifteen years old Tony George worked for club professional Rollie Schroeder at Speedway in the cart bin. Tony is a remarkable, energetic man who first assumed the presidency of the Speedway while still in his twenties.

Rollie Schroeder, who has been the head professional for almost thirty years, says, "If Tony George were any more laid back, he would be in an easy chair," but his relaxed manner and his tendency to utter few words hide a fierce intensity, especially when it comes to business.

When Tony and I discussed his ideas to enhance the Speedway Golf Course during a friendly round at Crooked Stick, I had a hunch he was not considering major renovation.

Jeff Stuart, the golf course superintendent, explained that Tony did want to improve the condition of the course by replacing bluegrass fairways with bent grass. In addition, the inside nine holes had been gradually reduced in size to make room for the Speedway Museum and the loading of the bus tours that drive around the track. Tony wanted to incorporate some of these holes into a new, more spacious eighteen.

At my suggestion Tony also became interested in building spectator mounding along the backstretch of the racetrack and creating a lake that would beautify the corporate tent area.

My vision for the course was more expansive, since I saw the tremendous access the site had for accommodations, parking, vendors, restrooms, and security. My enthusiasm for building a championship course that could test Tour professionals caught Tony's imagination and he became very receptive to my ideas.

Tony was accustomed to contracts that nail down every possible scenario in a business agreement. He was surprised when I offered to take the job on a handshake agreement—"fire me if you don't like the work I'm doing; pay me when the work is done."

This casual contract worked perfectly. The day after the course was completed, I received payment in full and a nice note from Tony.

The terrain inside and adjacent to the Speedway was basically flat. Little Eagle Creek cuts through the property, and there was an abundance of large trees but no other unique landscape features.

In preparing the initial routing, it was necessary to take into account the amount of acreage that was available for the course. Tony wanted a driving range built near the motel on the south boundary. The backstretch of the racetrack was on the west, the housing development on the north, and the railroad tracks and power lines to the east of the property.

Based on these restrictions, four holes were designated inside the track, and fourteen wound around Little Eagle Creek.

Professional players are hitting the golf ball farther than ever. That was a prime consideration in determining the length for the eighteen holes at Brickyard Crossing. However, because golf is a thinking sport more than a power sport—unlike boxing, where the fighter is looking for the knockout punch—golf rewards patient players, who realize that they must conquer all eighteen holes to be successful.

From the gold tees Brickyard Crossing measures just under 7,000 yards, and proportionally less from the forward ones. While these distances are minimal in a time when long courses are the norm, players will find that the length is arranged so that the course is as demanding as any 7,500-yard test.

The fact that the course measures exactly 6,997 yards was intentional. Rollie Schroeder and I discussed this point, since I believe golfers encounter a psychological hangup when they hear that a course measures more than 7,000 yards.

At Brickyard Crossing there are five extremely long par-fours. To balance out the length of these holes, the remaining five par-fours are very short but contain menacing hazards that require precision shot-making.

In my view, this type of balancing of short and long holes is the wave of the future. The golf course architect can never anticipate how technology will continue to enhance the golfer's ability to hit the ball farther, but by careful planning, each course can combat the length factor by minimizing its effect on the game.

At Speedway, the pattern of providing wide fairways for the golfer to hit from the tee was continued. The drive is one of the most thrilling shots in golf and I never want to take the driver out of the player's hand.

While it would seem to be just the opposite, golfers sometimes get in more trouble when there is a wide fairway. If they realize there is plenty of room, they are inclined to get overzealous.

At Brickyard Crossing, my primary mission in building wide fairways and growing rough only an inch and a half high is that it gives the ardent golfer a better chance to advance the ball toward the green. Brute strength is not a factor, since all golfers have the chance to gamble with the shot to the green.

The slight exception to this rule at Brickyard Crossing comes at the fourteenth, a tantalizingly short 311-yard par-four that also features a wide fairway but a small, severe, "crater from Mars" pot bunker that was constructed right in the middle of the prime landing area. The pot bunker appears much larger than its actual size, and it can be skirted, as there is more than 40 yards of fairway on each side.

The long hitter can carry the bunker, but all others must skirt it to be rewarded with a short pitch and a good chance for a birdie. If the drive is really launched, the green is reachable from the tee, leaving the golfer a putt for a possible eagle.

While the short par-four fourteenth may garner much of the publicity in years to come, the par-three seventh Redan-type hole is likely to be the one many golfers will discuss. When Rollie Schroeder first saw the seventh hole, he thought it looked out of place. Rollie could not immediately figure out what my intent was in building such an elevated tee and green just after golfers cross the track and play the first hole inside the oval.

Golfers standing on that elevated tee have a great view of the entire backstretch. There is no way to compare the view with that of the Pacific from the eighteenth tee at Pebble Beach, but there is an undeniable electricity that comes from looking out over the historic backstretch and imagining four hundred thousand race fans in the spectator stands on race day. The golfer who has experienced and heard the roar of the thirty-three race cars is overwhelmed by the peaceful silence.

"The more I played the seventh hole the more I appreciated both its design and its purpose," Rollie says. "Seven's simplicity is its best asset, and a friend of mine told me it's a true Scottish Redan-type hole that takes time to understand."

Construction obstacles are always present when any golf course is built. While we encountered buried cars and other junk at Harbour Town and Long Cove, we were surprised at the variety of trash and treasure buried underground at the Speedway. There were discarded gas tanks, broken cement abutments, mangled race car parts, and even treasured old paving bricks.

All had to be removed, but we did a costly, environmentally sound job. Jason McCoy, the construction superintendent, and Jeff Stuart made certain that we complied with every rule.

The design at Brickyard Crossing included multiple spectator mounds, which gave great views of the course. People who visited the once-flat land during construction were amazed to see the giant piles of earth that had sprouted in strategic spots.

Former Indiana State Amateur and Indianapolis City Champion Cookie English toured the layout when the bulldozers were piling the dirt to heights of thirty feet or more. Cookie took one look at those huge mounds and said, "Pete, where did all that dirt come from? There must be a huge hole out here somewhere!"

The mounds inside the track serve a dual purpose. Not only do they provide excellent spectator positions for golf fans but they also are very popular as designated "Family-No-Alcohol" spectator areas during the 500 Mile Race.

Midway through construction, Tony found me sitting on one of the newly built spectator mounds. After we exchanged the normal pleasantries, he said, "We are going to replace the old crash wall that encompasses the two-and-a-half-mile track. Would you have any use for it?"

I had no idea of the size, weight, or form of the wall, so we went to take a look. The engineers had just started cutting it so I asked about the time frame for the removal and the size and weight of each section.

I learned that the sections would be approximately twenty feet long, eight to twelve inches thick, four feet wide, and weigh approximately two tons. I told Tony I could use the whole two and a half miles of wall. He drove me back to the mound without ever asking me what I was going to do with the sections—but his silence meant go ahead.

The golfer will find the wall as bulkhead on the banks of Little Eagle Creek. Later I found that keeping this old historic wall at Speedway and making it part of the course was dear to Tony's heart.

I told Rollie Schroeder that a hundred years from now golfers will be talking about those sections of the wall. Ghosts of treacherous, death-defying crashes creep into the players' minds, as the history of the wall adds a special aura to the course.

At last count, there were more than twenty-five million golfers in this country, and the number rises every day. Those millions of golf addicts play their zillions of rounds on more than fourteen thousand golf courses, of which more than two-thirds are public.

From the outset, there was never any question that Brickyard Crossing would continue to be a public golf course. That was in keeping with Tony's commitment to keep the course open to those players who are the backbone of the game.

"My grandfather always wanted to cater to the public, and it would not be in keeping with our philosophy if we made the course private," Tony says. He intends not only to keep the course public but also to charge a daily fee that will not price it out of the range of the ardent golfer.

This philosophy gives everyone a chance to play a championship golf course like the ones they see the professionals play on television. Building such courses is very important to me, for I know how much the public golfer loves the game and the opportunity to play notable courses. Most are higher-handicap players, and while no one knows for sure what brings them back every day, Alice and I do have our own theory.

There is a basic fascination with golf that is unlike other games. No ordinary person could go one round with the heavyweight boxing champion, expect to hit a Nolan Ryan fastball, throw a football like Joe Montana, or leap from the free-throw line for a reverse overhead slam dunk like Michael Jordan. But a golfer may at any time hit that one spectacular shot just as well as Ben Hogan, Arnold Palmer, or Greg Norman. Just the chance to do that is what keeps bringing them back.

While the inclusion of railroad tracks, power lines, old chain-link fence, and the gigantic water tower might have scared away other golf course architects, I believe these traditional landmarks actually add to the essence of Brickyard Crossing. When one stands on the fifteenth tee, the panoramic view includes all of these, as well as the famed 500-mile race course and the spectator stands. Somehow they all blend together.

When a nationally known golf writer came for a look-see at the course in late 1993 before it opened to the public, he told me, "Pete, you've got a great course here. Too bad you've got eyesores," referring to the power lines and railroad tracks. Straight-faced, I told him that I'd had them brought to the course to copy the first hole at Prestwick in Scotland, where railroad tracks and high-tension wires border the right side!

While Prestwick is heralded as a great "Scottish" course; perhaps one day Brickyard Crossing will be labeled a great "American" course. Not only is it surrounded by essential pieces of Americana, but the 16th Street industrial area adjacent to the famous Speedway exemplifies the strong work ethic that has made the United States of America a great country.

While the Ocean Course at Kiawah Island may have its beautiful marshes, the Teeth of the Dog breathtaking views of the Caribbean, and La Quinta that majestic mountain view, Brickyard Crossing has a special setting and atmosphere that distinguishes it from any other golf course in the world.

Standing in the fairway on one of the four holes inside the track and visualizing four hundred thousand people in the stands is incredible. Recalling memories of Parnelli, A.J., and Mario only adds to the excitement of playing golf in the shadow of the "Greatest Spectacle in Racing."

Tony George's vision of the championship layout at Brickyard Crossing provides golfers with an exceptional experience. There may be some exciting shots in golf, but just imagine trying to concentrate on hitting a tee shot on the par-three seventh hole as a race car roars by at 220 miles per hour!

Numerous amateur and professional tournaments were played at Speedway in the thirty years following the first 500 Festival Invitational Tournament. Respected amateurs such as Fred Wampler, the Purdue graduate and Big Ten champion who went on to win on the Los Angeles Open on the PGA Tour, and Sandy Spuzich, the 1966 United States Women's Open champion, also both regularly played there.

In 1968 the "500" Ladies Classic was held at Speedway. LPGA Hall of Famer Mickey Wright won the championship and the $2,250 first prize, but Alice turned in a remarkable performance for an amateur when she finished third behind Mickey and Kathy Whitworth.

Championship golf returned to the Speedway in 1994 when the course hosted the Brickyard Crossing Championship, a PGA Senior Tour event. That followed a spectacular $50,000, eighteen-hole opening-day tournament in May that featured PGA professionals Greg Norman, Craig Stadler, John Cook, Bob Lohr, and Indiana native Jim Gallagher, Jr., who represents Brickyard Crossing on the PGA Tour.

Indy-car drivers Rick Mears, a four-time "500" champion, 1985 winner Danny Sullivan, and Formula One champion Nigel Mansell competed, along with NASCAR drivers Dale Jarrett and Jeff Gordon. Comedian Tommy Smothers, former vice president Dan Quayle, and Boston Celtics basketball star Larry Bird also played, to make it a most memorable day.

My teammates in the modified Florida scramble were Jeff Gordon, Nigel Mansell, and our captain Greg Norman, who won the individual event with a course record four-under-par 68. Our group won the team championship, prompting Nigel to tell the crowd that the achievement ranked right up there with other awards he had received recently. I got a laugh from the fans when I told them that while I was happy for him, our win might mean a bit more to me since it was the first thing I had won since the nearby Clermont, Indiana, Blind-Bogey championship forty years ago!

More important to me was six-time PGA Tour winner John Cook's comment to reporters that Brickyard Crossing was a great course "because it's very playable for both the touring professionals and the public, who don't want golf courses that beat their brains out." Somehow, I think Bill Diddel would have liked those words.

	Brickyard Crossing Indianapolis, Indiana Par 72	
	Men	Women
Yardage:	6994, 6621, 6028	5028
Rating/ Slope:	74.5/137, 71.7/130, 68.4/122	68.3/116

Epilogue

When I dug that first shovel of dirt at El Dorado Country Club in 1960, I never had any idea that one day I would be in a position to publish my views on golf course architecture. Doing so has brought back many wonderful memories, and permitted me to recall significant events that changed the course of my life.

Throughout all those years of hard work, I was blessed to be inspired by the accomplishments of my gifted predecessors. Their simple approach to the design of golf courses became mine, but it was the words of a man who designed just one course in his life that reminded me of why I have dedicated myself to the profession for more than thirty years.

In June 1988, George Peper and *Golf Magazine* sponsored a gala celebration in New York City to commemorate the centennial of golf in America. One hundred heroes of American golf were invited, and I was honored to be included in that select group.

Byron Nelson, Kathy Whitworth, Jack Nicklaus, Mickey Wright, Arnold Palmer, Nancy Lopez, Ben Hogan, Patty Berg,

Sam Snead, Tom Watson, Pat Bradley, and my friend and fellow golf course architect Robert Trent Jones, among others, were all in attendance. The ceremony honoring Jack Nicklaus as the player of the century was a moving one, but it was an inspirational speech by the immortal Ben Hogan that stole the show.

Besides captivating the spellbound audience with his astute analysis of the swing of the golfer whose picture graced the cover of the program, Mr. Hogan talked about what golf meant to him. In an emotional ending to his speech, the Wee Ice Man simply said in a hushed tone, "I love this game. I *really, really* love this game!"

Mr. Hogan's words brought tears to my eyes, for it is that same love for golf and its great tradition that has sustained me through the years. From the early trial-and-error days at El Dorado in the late 1950s through my recent work at courses such as Brickyard Crossing and the Medalist Club, that emotion has made me never forget that whatever my contribution to the game, it needed to be made in accord with the highest standards of professionalism.

While time and space have permitted me to discuss fewer than twenty of the courses Alice and I have designed, every golf course I have ever worked on is special to me. My opportunity to mold God's earth into a test that golfers can enjoy has given me great satisfaction, and I am extremely indebted to those who have given me the chance to build golf courses all over our country.

Donald Ross once wrote, "My work will tell my story," and that is how I hope to be remembered. My designs reflect a traditionalist philosophy about the game, and we must never forget that golf is played best when done so in the purest of forms.

I look forward to building new golf courses for a long time to come. Every potential site I see brings new challenges, and I continue to learn more every day.

My inspiration comes from the golfers themselves, who in spite of kicking and cursing, find that a trip around a Pete Dye golf course is always memorable. Golf has given me a life that is rich in experience, personal achievement, and friendship, but I find the greatest satisfaction in believing that I have somehow contributed to making the game I love a more exciting one to play.

Golf Courses by Pete Dye

Arizona

Karsten Golf Course at Arizona State University, with Perry Dye
Red Mountain Ranch, with Perry Dye

California

Carmel Valley Ranch Golf Club
La Quinta Hotel Golf Club—Mountain Course
La Quinta Hotel Golf Club—Dunes Course
La Quinta Hotel Golf Club—Citrus Course, with Alice Dye
Mission Hills Resort Golf Club
Mission Hills Golf—Dinah Shore Course, with Alice Dye
Moreno Valley Ranch Golf Club (27 holes)
PGA West Golf Club—Stadium Course, with Alice Dye
Rancho Santa Fe Farms Golf Club, with Perry Dye

Colorado

Country Club of Colorado, with Roy Dye
Glenmoor Country Club, with Perry Dye
Plum Creek Golf and Country Club, with Perry Dye

Florida

Amelia Island Plantation Golf Club (27 holes)
Bonnet Creek Golf Club—Eagle Pines Course
Delray Dunes Golf and Country Club
Disney World—Cypress Course
Harbour Ridge Yacht and Country Club—River Ridge Course,
    with P. B. Dye
John's Island Club—North Course and South Course
The Medalist Club, with Greg Norman
The Moorings Golf Club, with Alice Dye
Old Marsh Golf Club
Palm Beach Polo and Country Club—Cypress Course, with P. B. Dye
The River Club at Grand Harbor
TPC at Sawgrass—Stadium Course, with Alice Dye
TPC at Sawgrass—Valley Course, with Jerry Pate and Bobby Weed

Georgia
Atlanta National Golf Club, with P. B. Dye
Sterling Bluff Golf Club, with P. B. Dye

Illinois
Oakwood Country Club
Ruffled Feathers Golf Club, with P. B. Dye
Yorktown Golf Club (Par 3)

Indiana
Brickyard Crossing, with Alice Dye
Crooked Stick Golf Club, with Alice Dye
Eagle Creek Municipal (27 holes)
Forest Park Golf Club (Brazil)
Harbour Trees Golf Club
Heather Hills Country Club, with Alice Dye
Monticello Country Club
Plainfield Elks Golf Club (9 holes)
Royal Oak Country Club (formerly El Dorado Country Club)
    (9 holes), with Alice Dye
William S. Sahm Municipal (formerly North Eastway), with Alice Dye

Iowa
Des Moines Golf and Country Club—Blue Course and Red Course

Kentucky
Kearney Hill Golf Links, with P. B. Dye

Maryland
Martingham Golf and Tennis Club, with Roy Dye

Michigan
Radrick Farms Golf Club, with Alice Dye
Wabeek Country Club, with Roy Dye and Jack Nicklaus

Mississippi
Pine Island Golf Club

Nebraska
Firethorn Golf Club, with Alice Dye

North Carolina
Cardinal Golf Club
Landfall Club—Dye Course, with P. B. Dye and Bobby Weed

Oak Hollow Golf Club

Ohio
Avalon Lakes Golf Club
Fowler's Mill Golf Club (formerly TRW Golf Club) (27 holes),
    with Roy Dye
The Golf Club
Little Turtle Club, with Roy Dye

Oklahoma
Oak Tree Country Club—East Course and West Course,
    with Alice Dye
Oak Tree Golf Club

Pennsylvania
Montour Heights Country Club, with P. B. Dye
Mystic Rock at Nemacolin

South Carolina
DeBordieu Golf Club, with P. B. Dye
Harbour Town Golf Links, with Alice Dye and Jack Nicklaus
Long Cove Club, with Alice Dye
The Ocean Course at Kiawah, with Alice Dye
Prestwick Golf Club, with P. B. Dye

Tennessee
The Honors Course

Texas
Austin Country Club, with Alice Dye
Stonebridge Country Club, with Alice Dye

Virginia
Kingsmill Golf Club—River Course

West Virginia
Pete Dye Golf Club

Wisconsin
Americana Lake Geneva Golf Club—Briarpatch Course (formerly
    Playboy Club Hotel), with Jack Nicklaus
Blackwolf Run Golf Club—River Course and Lake Course

Dominican Republic
Casa de Campo—Teeth of the Dog, La Romana Country Club, and
    Links Course, with Alice Dye